THE
SHIGA
HERO

THE SHIGA HERO

William F. Sibley

The University of Chicago Press
CHICAGO AND LONDON

WILLIAM F. SIBLEY is associate professor in the Department of Far Eastern Languages and Civilizations, University of Chicago.

THE UNIVERSITY OF CHICAGO PRESS, CHICAGO 60637
THE UNIVERSITY OF CHICAGO PRESS, LTD., LONDON
©1979 by The University of Chicago
All rights reserved. Published 1979
Printed in the United States of America
83 82 81 80 79   5 4 3 2 1

The translations included in this volume are based on the fourteen-volume edition of Shiga's works, *Shiga Naoya zenshū,* published in Tokyo by Iwanami shoten. ©1973 Shiga Naokichi.

Library of Congress Cataloging in Publication Data

Sibley, William F
  The Shiga hero.

  Bibliography: p.
  Includes index.
  1. Shiga, Naoya, 1883–1971—Criticism and interpretation.   I. Title.
PL816.HZ846   895.6′3′4   79-14120
ISBN 0-226-75620-3

CONTENTS

PREFACE

THE MAIN BURDEN OF THIS STUDY of Shiga Naoya's works is carried
by the four-part essay on the Shiga hero. The introduction is designed
to set forth, and to amplify somewhat, the terms of the partial reconstruction of Shiga's works contained in the essay. A deliberately cur-
tailed biographical sketch of Shiga has been relegated to the latter part
of the introduction in an effort to keep it in the background—no easy
matter when one relies a good deal, as all of us must, upon the
Japanese secondary literature with its heavily biographical bias.

Of the ten stories that follow the essay, four have previously been
translated into English: *Kinosaki nite,* by Edward Seidensticker; *Seibei
to hyōtan* and *Han no hanzai,* by Ivan Morris; and *Kamisori,* by
Francis Mathy.[1] I have given my own versions here in order to provide
the general reader with ready access to several of Shiga's best stories in
one place; also because I feel these particular stories deserve to be
translated several times over; but certainly not because I imagine in all
cases to have improved on the earlier translations.

The use of my own versions in the extensive excerpts from the novel
An'ya kōro which appear throughout the essay is likewise dictated by
expediency. It would have been preferable from the point of view of
the general reader, and no doubt for the sake of stylistic felicity as well,
to cite the relevant passages from Edwin McClellan's fine translation,

A Dark Night's Passing (Tokyo, New York, San Francisco, 1976). But I did not want to deny myself the latitude, which the gap between the languages certainly permits, for seeing individual passages in a somewhat different light, with slightly different emphases, from what is to be found in a careful and creative translation of the whole novel.

I would like to thank Edwin McClellan, my teacher and friend, for much moral support in this project, most especially for aiding and abetting views and interests of mine which he has not necessarily shared himself. And I warmly acknowledge all the help I have received from the former curators of the Japanese collections at the University of Chicago and the University of Michigan, James Morita and Naomi Fukuda.

1. "At Kinosaki," translated by Edward Seidensticker, and "Han's Crime," translated by Ivan Morris, in *Modern Japanese Literature*, edited by Donald Keane (New York, 1956); "Seibei's Gourds," in *Modern Japanese Stories*, edited by Ivan Morris (London, 1961); "The Razor," translated by Francis Mathy, in *Monumenta Nipponica* 13, nos. 3–4 (1968).

INTRODUCTION

SHIGA NAOYA (1883–1971) wrote a fairly large number of short stories, many pieces that are still shorter and essentially nonfiction, a few narratives of intermediate length (so-called *chūhen shōsetsu*), and only a single full-length novel, entitled *An'ya kōro,* which has been translated by Edwin McClellan as *A Dark Night's Passing.*[1] In spite of the modest quantity of his works that would be considered by conventional Anglo-American standards belles-lettres or "serious literature," in his own country Shiga has at various times over the past sixty years been exalted as a master craftsman of the modern literature and a special spokesman for the genius of the nation (*bungaku no kamisama,* "the lord of literature," is the journalistic tag he was given late in his career), and has alternately been excoriated, particularly in the years after the Second World War, as one of those most responsible for the stunting of modern Japanese fiction.

In an often cited sweeping comment on much of modern Japanese fiction, Kobayashi Hideo stated, "Since Tayama Katai learned from Maupassant the literary value of daily life itself, no writer has succeeded as well as Shiga has in boldly, even violently, wresting from his own life a work of art; no one has adhered so scrupulously as he has to the approach of the personal novel [*shishōsetsu*], in which the logic of everyday life becomes the logic of literary creation."[2]

1

Less grandiosely, Akutagawa Ryūnosuke, a contemporary, greatly admired Shiga for his ability to write what Akutagawa called "stories without stories" *(hanashi no nai hanshi)*. But he too takes on an almost reverential tone when he further observes, "Shiga Naoya is the purest writer among us. His works are first and foremost those of a man who lives a fine life . . . by which I mean a morally spotless life."[3]

As if in reply to Akutagawa's homage, Dazai Osamu wrote of Shiga some twenty-five years later, "What everyone says is so 'fine' in his works amounts to nothing more than the man's conceit, the courage of a bully. . . . If he writes that he has farted it will be published in large print, and we are supposed to read this with the utmost solemnity. What nonsense!"[4]

Looking at Shiga's works themselves, one finds the most prominent, recurring themes to be obsessive memories of childhood; fantasies of murder and parricide, sometimes acted out on the stage of the narrative, elsewhere imagined by the narrator or the central character through evident substitutions; a deeply ambivalent attraction to alternately protective and destructive older women; and ultimately, the incest wish and the death wish, which appear in various partially displaced or sublimated forms. The evidence of his relatively slender œuvre, the only evidence of interest, leads one to the conclusion that, whatever Shiga was as a man, as a writer he has been neither so banal and literal-minded as Kobayashi's remarks (contrary to his intention) would suggest, nor so "pure" as Akutagawa would have us believe, nor finally so consumed with self-importance, relentlessly self-involved though his writing surely is, as Dazai's diatribe makes him out to be.

Shiga is an author who (to paraphrase William Gass on D. H. Lawrence) wrote of nothing, in story, tract or letter, ever, but himself.[5] "Anything can be made into fiction," Shiga himself once commented. "Whether a particular subject turns into a story or novel, an essay, biography, or diary depends entirely on the author's attitude as he writes rather than on the material itself" (7:35).[6] The interchangeability of such different genres in Shiga's mind, not excluding even biography, is a clear expression of the subjectivism bordering on solipsism that characterizes all of his writing. He has indeed been both canonized and castigated as the most successful (in Kobayashi's view) and most intransigent (in the eyes of his detractors) practitioner of those curious subgenres that so dominate Japanese literary-historical treatments of the first half of the twentieth century: the *shishōsetsu* ("I novel" or, better, in Henri Peyre's more broadly based terminology, "personal fiction")[7] and the *shinkyō shōsetsu* ("the novel of mental states").

Much has been made of these subgenres in the secondary literature on modern Japanese fiction, both in Japan and in the West. In Japan, this preoccupation can be seen as determined in large measure by the radical departure from various traditional and early-modern modes of prose fiction that subjective and "psychological" narratives represented when they first emerged in the early decades of this century. Secondarily, the emphasis on this critical perspective became a compelling self-justification on the part of well-entrenched literary scholars for their inexhaustible, sometimes prurient curiosity about authors' lives, down to the most minute and tedious details. In a vicious circle or, for many of them, it would seem, in a happy little round dance, these scholars turn quickly from the works to the lives, again to the works for more documentary "data," and finally back to the biographies of bona fide real lives, laid out on the most cumbersome scale, that are their ultimate objects.

The distinctly disapproving attention given in the slim secondary writings by Westerners, chiefly Americans, to the predominance of personal fiction in modern Japanese literature clearly owes a good deal to prevailing currents in Anglo-American criticism during the period when this literature was being "discovered" and introduced. The excesses of the New Critics—rather, of such epigones as the Jamesian purists—are well known and need not be discussed, except to suggest that their indifference to, and in not a few cases their ignorance of, the realities of much of modern Western fiction has no doubt conditioned our collective response to Japanese personal fiction. The seminal French writers to whom Kobayashi alludes in the remarks cited above—Flaubert, Maupassant, and others—did establish an utterly detached and dispassionate practice of their craft as one pole of modern fiction in the West. But we must also recognize the strong countertrends toward inwardness which culminate in so-called psychological fiction. Leon Edel has maintained that when the interior focus of the narrative reaches a certain degree of intensiveness, we have to contend with an altogether different kind of fiction, not merely with a new emphasis on one among many means of telling stories. In reading psychological fiction, he suggests, we should adopt a different set of responses from those we apply to more traditional narratives.[8] Similarly, Ian Watt has considered the novel "proper" to be an ambiguous and transitional form: a reflection of the shift "from the objective, social and public orientation of the classical world to the subjective, individualist and private orientation" of modern life and literature.[9]

If Shiga did indeed start from the doubtful premise that, in Kobayashi's words, the "logic of everyday life" may serve as "the logic of literary creation," he has carried this formula to its often illogical conclusion. It hardly requires a trained psychologist to recognize that on a deeper level of reality our days are filled at least as much with irrational impulses and inchoate emotions as with orderly social intercourse and articulate thoughts. It is this sort of reality, bound up with and triggered by the external trivia of "everyday life" but having a separate life of its own, that Shiga has taken as his prime subject. Like various other writers both in Japan and the West, he has arrived independently at a wholly intuitive kind of psychoanalytical consciousness. And yet the "anything" that, in his above-quoted remark, Shiga asserted could serve as what Henry James called the "germ" of a story or novel, suggests a randomness that, as we shall see, does not obtain in the subject matter of his fiction.

Whatever the subject, when his "attitude" has determined that his work is to be fiction (that is, a *shōsetsu*), the focus is most often inward and backward, introspective and retrospective. As is the case with all deeply subjective fiction, much of Shiga's raw material is unmistakably rooted in his own inner experience, we may conclude; for he could scarcely know another's mind so thoroughly. But one may not find very interesting or particularly germane the dubious game of correlating closely the outward events of his life with the representation of psychological effects supposedly produced by them, the game so vigorously played by the biographical critics. His own words on several occasions invite a good deal of skepticism on this score: "It is hard to capture one's own psychology with some measure of accuracy. No matter how much one may grasp of the psychological states that arise in one's mind, there is always something that slips away. Then there are other things which one naturally does not want to touch.... Dreams, at least, are completely honest. But they are also sometimes treacherous" (7:13).

Dreams and elusive "psychological states"—moods, feelings, impulses, are finally what is most real in Shiga's fiction, together with concrete impressions, the sights and sounds that are fused with these things. Attempts to tie this intangible stuff directly to what we "know" about his life and times are not entirely convincing. And one need not make some facile identification between Shiga and his hero Kensaku to

see in the latter's misgivings about psychological self-expression toward the end of *An'ya kōro* some of Shiga's own thoughts on the
subject: "At first Kensaku proposed to write down in detail the mental
states he had experienced since coming to this mountain retreat. But
his preliminary deliberations left him unsatisfied. The thoughts that
had ruled him until recently were purely chimerical. And if he tried to
write truthfully about the change he had since undergone, it would no
doubt sound equally vague and illusory. He concluded that he did not
know how to write about such things" (5:571–72).

The problem, then, is how to convey in an at least partially objectified form "purely chimerical thoughts," "vague and illusory"
mental states. Unlike his hero in this instance, Shiga does of course
eventually succeed in giving some outward form to his inner experience. He does this through vivid concrete images ("objective correlatives," in Eliot's much overquoted phrase, later repudiated by himself),
detailed descriptions of dreams (nature's contribution to the process of
visual objectification), and in general through the elaboration of a
restricted symbolic vocabulary that includes elements borrowed from
various established lexicons, fixed idioms that are frequently invoked
in a sense peculiar to Shiga, even occasional neologisms.

That Shiga was in a general way a writer of personal fiction is borne
out by a common-sense reading of the works and need not be
confirmed by protracted exercises in biographical criticism of the most
literal-minded kind. As the following essay will show, the recurring
events that form the narrative kernel of most of his major works are in
any case most often non-events, rooted in "chimerical thoughts"
whose actual occurrence in Shiga's mind are unknowable. That he also
wished to become a "psychological" novelist is attested to by such
passages as those quoted above, though the works themselves do not
always fit obviously into this category and show ample traces of
Shiga's self-doubts about this approach to writing fiction. What dis-
tinguishes Shiga from several other Japanese writers who, in the first
decades of the century, set about writing various kinds of both personal and psychological fiction is his motive for undertaking the
project in the first place, and the transparency with which, both in the
works and outside, the motive is revealed. In a story entitled *Wakai*
(Reconciliation, 1917), Shiga's hero, who is himself a writer, describes a kind of autotherapy which he has practiced in his works
behind a thin veil of fiction: "I would write about [my own
problems] from the point of view of the impersonal author. . . .
Through putting down on paper various unpleasant events which

might well occur in my own life . . . I hoped to prevent them from actually happening to me. As I set down each episode I would imagine that I had escaped acting out an identical situation myself" (2:367). And after he had completed a large portion of his major works, Shiga reminisced: "It strikes me that in those years there was something pathological in me [as well as in my writing]. Lately, my interest in sick states has diminished. But I still cannot deny that one derives a certain élan from such sickness—an excitement which permits one to experience and to express things not accessible under normal conditions of sanity" (7:6). These words cast considerable light both on Shiga's idiosyncratic practice of the craft of fiction and on what might be called his ulterior motives for writing in the first place. For further elucidation of the project which he undertook in much of his writing we may profitably look, not to those biographical critics who will tell us only of his pure life and his sincere art, but to a seemingly unlikely source: Jean-Paul Sartre's observations on the method of Jean Genet—clearly not a writer who resembles Shiga Naoya very closely. In *Saint Genet,* Sartre characterizes Genet's approach as follows: "En nous infectant de son mal, Genet s'en délivre. Chacun de ses livres est une crise de possession cathartique, un psychodrame."[10]

Something of the sort may be said of Shiga's personal, subjective, and autotherapeutic method, if only with certain modifications—his purpose is far from being so openly diabolical; and only of some works: several early short stories and the long novel *An'ya kōro,* most notably its first part. Although the purely formal qualities of Shiga's prose are not inconsiderable in these works, they cannot disguise the apparently private fantasies, the "egotistical daydreams," as Freud once described modern fiction,[11] which emerge on the surface from time to time and in some cases shape—or misshape—the work as a whole.

On reading the first part of *An'ya kōro* Masamune Hakuchō complained, "This is not a book to be read for pleasure."[12] Indeed, contrary to Freud's generalization about the "fore-pleasure" which the writer must provide in order to entice us to deeper levels of consciousness, Shiga seems often to begin by inflicting pain instead of pleasure upon his readers, in the form of recurring obsessions, "regressive" fantasies, and evocations of nameless fears. To be sure, many of these fears and fantasies are universal, and we may recognize them from our own childhood, our dreams or even our waking thoughts. But we have had to repress them and therefore resist their open manifestation. Yet if this were in fact wholly the case, and if it is pleasure alone that we seek, Shiga's works could never have won the relatively wide audience which they continue to find among successive generations of readers.

It is above all, and in some cases nothing but, style which, as "incitement pleasure," draws the reader into Shiga's works. Shiga's indifference to the larger formal features of narrative craft is often striking. Apart from the special vocabulary and the terse, rhythmical style which he has painstakingly created, there are few formally satisfying elements in his works, a minimum of well-constructed plot, dramatic incident, "big scenes," and sustained dialogue. If one's perspective stresses such larger formal attributes of the genre, as does that of Edward Seidensticker in his discussion of Shiga, one would no doubt agree with him that Shiga's only successful works have been a handful of short stories.[13] But, as Seidensticker himself has pointed out, the modern Japanese temperament has not yielded many sturdily built novels laid out on a grand scale in the classic nineteenth century European manner.[14]

Early in his career (1911), Shiga wrote in his diary, "I always manage to grasp the details of things but have little capacity for understanding the whole. I suppose it is enough if a writer captures life's details, but it bothers me a bit to think that I haven't got the whole. And yet, it sometimes seems to me that the whole is not to be understood in any case. . . . And I also wonder if, should I ever come to grasp the whole, or allow myself to apply to it some facile conceptualization, I would not in the process be stopped dead in my tracks" (10:463). In addition to being personal, subjective, and often intuitively psychoanalytical (with an eye to autotherapy), Shiga's approach to fiction is, then, also highly fragmentary. In an effort to grasp some of the "whole" which eluded Shiga, or which, as the foregoing diary entry would imply, he deliberately eschewed, one would want to emphasize those elements in his individual works that contribute to some unity linking all of them. Chief among these, beyond the consistent surface of his well-honed style, is surely the single central character who, in one guise or another, appears in nearly all of Shiga's stories and novels, and whose viewpoint, with occasional interventions by the omniscient author, predominates in the great majority of his narratives.

This character is given a number of different names in the various works where he appears, and often speaks to us directly in the first person. We encounter him at several different stages in his life and in a variety of social roles. But in his inner life he is recognizably the same figure throughout Shiga's works. Although one need not be concerned

with exact correlations and literal identifications, this created character and the microcosm he inhabits can no doubt be closely associated with the creating author and his world. By analogy with the
"method" described in the above-quoted passage from *Wakai*, we may
choose to imagine that Shiga projects what enters his consciousness
onto this single character, sometimes in an unusually direct fashion.
But to escape from the ironclad assumptions about these matters that
prevail in the Japanese critical climate, it is necessary to belabor the
point, as one would not feel obliged to do when speaking of such
Western personal novelists as the Lawrence of *Sons and Lovers,* say,
or Proust. And so it will be useful to refer to Shiga's recurring protagonist in all cases (except for two early, openly confessional stories)
as the Shiga hero, to distinguish this persona, alter ego, surrogate, etc.,
from Shiga's "real self," who is unknowable.

We recognize the Shiga hero precisely because his inner identity is
always shifting. He is most often portrayed in the act of transforming
his view of himself, of others close to him and of his immediate
surroundings, social and natural. But the reader comes to discern
certain patterns in these subjective transformations and, in large outline, a kind of cycle that recurs with inexorable regularity.

There are of course numerous subordinate characters, who are
revealed to us from the hero's point of view and who take on a
provisional reality through him. Also vivid images and wonderfully
spare settings, often drawn from the realms of dreams and nature,
which sometimes fulfill roles as important as the characters'. But it is
first and foremost the single figure of the Shiga hero, both constant and
protean, that gives some unity to the individual works and the entire
œuvre. We come to depend on him for our bearings in the often
amorphous world of Shiga's fiction.

The following discussion is ordered according to the inner
development—the truncated "life cycle"—of the Shiga hero rather
than the chronology of their publication. The terms of discussion are,
in the loosest sense, psychoanalytical rather than, in the strictest sense,
literary-critical. Henry James, writing in an age, and for an audience,
which shared a remarkably broad set of assumptions, still found it
necessary to warn: "It is so embarrassing to speak of the writers of one
country to the readers of another that I sometimes wonder at the
complacency with which the delicate task is entered upon. These are
cases . . . which compel the critic to forfeit what I may call his natural
advantages. The first of these is that those who read him . . . shall allow
him his general point of view and his terms. Here he has in a manner to

define his terms."[15] Living in an age when, concerning things literary in any case, a great many different sets of assumptions, some of them remarkably narrow, are each shared only by a relative few, one is not likely to lapse into the complacency that James warned against. Without attempting anything like a true definition of terms, I may at least give here some idea of my "general point of view" on the use of certain psychoanalytical notions with specific reference to Shiga's works.

Unlike certain critics of a psychoanalytical persuasion, Freud himself disavowed any intention of "explaining" by his method whole works of art, much less the creative process itself.[16] On several occasions he acknowledged his debt to imaginative literature, for example, in the following passage from "The Relation of the Poet to Daydreaming": "A writer is to avoid all contact with psychiatry, we are told, and leave to physicians the portrayal of morbid psychic conditions. In reality no true creative writer has ever heeded this commandment. The portrayal of the psychic life of human beings is actually his very special domain; he has always been the precursor of science and scientific psychology."[17]

Contrary to Freud's profession of respect for the integrity of literature, some of his followers have tended to psychoanalyze writers as though they were patients, giving short shrift to the works in the process. Against this tendency Jung has written, "We shall do well, I think, to make fully explicit all the implications of that way of accounting for artistic creation which consists in reducing it to personal factors. The truth is that it takes us away from the psychological study of the work of art, and confronts us with the psychic disposition of the poet himself."[18]

In the same context Jung speaks of "the psychological novel," as does Freud in the work cited above. Both of them clearly use the term quite broadly to designate all modern fiction in which the thoughts of the characters are recorded by the narrative—in contrast to the restricted, technical sense that Edel and other literary critics have given to it. Like Freud, Jung credits the more able "psychological" novelists with a job well done; there is little, he says, that professional psychoanalysts would care to add to what such novelists have already made fully explicit in their own terms. (Shiga, as we shall see, seldom makes things explicit in an analytical manner.)

To the "psychological novel" Jung counterposes what he calls "visionary" fiction: works which derive their existence "from the hinterland of man's mind." Far from the everyday experiences which the conventionally psychological narratives articulate for us, the world revealed in "visionary" works is "foreign and cold, many-sided, demonic and grotesque."[19] Many readers and critics are disturbed by this sort of fiction, and the writers themselves are often embarrassed when confronted with their visions in cold print. Some authors even seek to explain their works away. (Shiga tried to do this at various points toward the end of his career.) Jung suggests that if we find something of value in these outcroppings of unconscious and primordial experience, we shall at times have to "protect" them from the writer's own excuses.

One need not accept all of Jung's "spiritualist" and primitivist leanings to recognize that his general orientation is appropriate to one significant aspect of Shiga's works, as well as a useful antidote to the factual-mindedness that prevails in much of Japanese criticism. One would want to emphasize, then, the "visionary" side of Shiga's fiction. But he has of course also written long stretches of conventional "psychological" narration (in Jung's terms) which cannot be overlooked. Here we shall have to contend with Shiga's sometimes confusing attempts to describe his hero's moods and feelings in a direct, discursive fashion and by means of a vocabulary that is finally inadequate to the task.

The terms of the two most interesting Japanese discussions of Shiga I have read, those of Nakamura Mitsuo and Yasuoka Shōtaro,[20] are both biographical and historical. But Yasuoka's approach, certainly the more idiosyncratic and provocative of the two, is not at all conventionally literary-historical, for he starts from the premise that "Shiga's most conspicuous trait is that he has been influenced by no one and has created his works exclusively within himself."[21] He then proceeds to amplify his summary of major figures and events in Shiga's life—and in his works, which he sees as mirror images of the life, with engrossing observations on a variety of episodes in the subjective history of twentieth-century Japan, drawing upon his own life, of course, and on the kinds of collective experience shared by large segments of an entire society which few of its members, not to mention outsiders, would be able to articulate. Yasuoka's book is, then, partially historical writing about literature, not literary history proper, nor the sort of quick raid on literary "data" often staged by social and intellectual historians.

Shiga himself always appeared indifferent toward history, to a perhaps unusual degree for an educated man of his generation, and in the later stages of his life became openly antihistoricist. Concerning the rapid acceleration of historical change in modern Japan, he once wrote, "Our generation has experienced more in our lifetime than all the generations of the past millennium put together. I am not sure whether we ought to rejoice in this fact or greatly lament it. In any case, it has been interesting" (7:15). Despite this avowal of a vague curiosity about the astonishing phenomena of modern Japanese history, he betrayed scarcely any interest in specific events or large historical trends in his works. He expressed a certain contempt for writers who concern themselves closely with social issues and contemporary affairs—the type of mentality which, in Hamlet's scornful words, "has only got the tune of the times . . . a kind of yeasty collection." In Shiga's own words: "All those who in their work take advantage of the prevailing currents of their times must rise and fall with the times. Without these strong currents, we suspect, such men could accomplish nothing" (7:12).

To be sure, turning one's back on one's times is not the same as escaping from history altogether. In his works Shiga has instinctively ignored the "prevailing currents" of his times. And at the end of his career he explicitly rejected the whole notion of history as a progressive force. "If only so-called civilized man were to vanish from the earth," he said, in a black mood of postwar pessimism, "surely the world would be a more peaceful and a more beautiful place" (7:422). Yet, in ways which I hope to suggest, although I will nowhere focus on the historical dimension, Shiga could not have written what he has written until after Japan had made its precipitous entry into the modern world and "the mainstream of history." And he could only have found a receptive audience for his partly primitive and archetypal vision following the traumatic separation from the womblike matrix of traditional life which, to one extent or another, all educated Japanese were forced to undergo.

At the risk of ignoring Jung's caveat against reducing an artist's work to "personal factors" and ending up with no more than "the psychic disposition of the poet," it seems advisable, since Shiga is an intensely personal novelist, to begin with a brief account of his life. But only to begin this way. One would want to reverse the customary practice, then, and, on the basis of a prior reading of the works, to emphasize in a biographical sketch only those elements that seem germane to the original myth which Shiga has created around his protean hero. In such a frame of reference, the years of his childhood and early adolescence would assume a central importance. But since the Japanese biographical critics proceed from a quite different bias, as does Francis Mathy in his short and very readable study of Shiga in

English, these are precisely the years that are most neglected.[22] For even though several of the principal writers on Shiga agree that his best fiction is clearly rooted in his experience of childhood and adolescence, with respect not only to its subject matter but also to what might be called its perceptual style, so strong, still, is the traditional Confucian image of the first twenty-odd years of life as a fixed training ground, with a given set of gates and obstacles, that they do not allow the evidence of the works to deter them from their headlong rush into lengthy discussions of his formal education, various literary cliques he is said to have belonged to, and the like.

Fortunately, Shiga has written a few short pieces about these periods in his life that are frankly autobiographical in nature, without even the thin veil of fiction he assumes in his early attempts at the personal novel, not to mention the considerably distanced authorial stance in *An'ya kōro*. There are also a few telling entries in the early portions of his otherwise often laconic and pedestrian diary. In addition to these, we may consult rather speculative views of Shiga's youth that have been set forth by two of his more astute biographer-critics.

Shiga was born in 1883 at a small port near Sendai, Ishinomaki, where his father was employed by a branch of the Dai Ichi Bank. Before the Meiji Restoration, his father's family had been high-ranking retainers of the small Sōma clan in the region of present-day Fukushima-ken. His mother's family had likewise been in the service of a minor daimyo, the lord of Kameyama castle near Ise.

When Shiga was three, his parents moved back to Tokyo and took up residence with his paternal grandparents. Soon afterward his father went alone to the then distant province of Kanazawa, where he worked for three years as an accountant at the Fourth Higher School. This rather humble position marked the beginning of a highly successful career in various financial enterprises, in the course of which he acquired a fortune sufficient to provide his son with an independent income for life.

The father's prolonged absence corresponded to the formative years between four and seven in the young Shiga's life. During this time, he and his mother continued to live at the house of his paternal grandparents in Tokyo. As an only child and the future head of the family's main branch, Shiga was clearly the center of the adults' devoted attention. He himself has told us that, perhaps because of the death of an older brother shortly before his own birth, his early upbringing was taken over by his strong-willed and protective grandmother. As was often the case in traditional Japanese families, the young mother occupied a rather ambiguous place in the household of her in-laws. Her position was perhaps made all the more difficult by the absence of her husband, and by the special care which her mother-in-law lavished on her only son. Contrary to the well-established Japanese custom, Shiga's mother rarely had her child by her side even at night. He slept in his grandmother's room instead, as, for the most part, he continued to do well into the years of adolescence.

Shiga has written several fragmentary but striking reminiscences about his mother, who died when he was only thirteen. In part they are remarkable precisely because Shiga's attitude toward his subject seems so ambivalent: predictably sentimental in places but at the same time extremely detached.

The best-known of these recollections is a short sketch entitled *Haha no shi to atarashii haha* (Mother's Death and a New Mother, 1912). Written when Shiga was twenty-nine, it describes the death of his mother and his earliest encounter with his stepmother, whom his father married not long afterward. Together with a curious little piece which is appended to it, *Haha no shi to tabi no kioku* (Mother's Death and a Painful Memory, 1912), this evocation of his parting with his mother concludes the first volume of his collected works (i.e., the 1956 *Zenshū*). Suggestively, if no doubt coincidentally, the last volume devoted to short fiction in the *zenshū* ends similarly with another recollection of his mother. Entitled *Shiroi sen* (The White Line, 1956), it was written when Shiga was seventy-two. All three of these slight works center on his mother's death and on earlier glimpses of her which the memory of the sad event calls up. Finally, there is a relatively long entry in his diary, dating from the time when the first two works were written (1912), which also dwells on the details of his mother's death, though here within the context of a dream he has just had about it.

As one might expect, Shiga's four accounts of this single episode in his life are repetitious. I shall summarize them briefly with an emphasis on whatever differences are to be found among them, and in chronological order—although it is obvious from Shiga's abiding preoccupation with the subject that it is not simply another cluster of facts to be dated and put in their proper place.

Shiga begins *Haha no shi to atarashii haha* by clearly identifying himself as the narrator. He tells us that while on a holiday at the seashore (he had just graduated from elementary school), he received a letter from his grandfather informing him that his mother was pregnant. As she had not conceived in the thirteen years since he himself was born, this was cause for rejoicing. At once he set about finding a suitable gift with which to congratulate his mother. On his return to Tokyo he learned that she had recently begun to suffer from severe complications in her pregnancy. In her feverish state she seemed hardly able to recognize him.

His mother's condition grows steadily worse. At one point his grandmother calls him to the sickroom and asks his mother if she knows him. The narrator describes her reaction: "My mother focused her eyes on my face and stared for a while in silence. Then she looked as though she were about to cry, and I felt the same look come over my face. Slowly and indistinctly she murmured, 'I don't care if he's dark, if his nose is crooked.... So long as he's strong, it doesn't matter'" (1:343).

The narrator of *Haha no shi* (hereafter abbreviated in this way) does not comment on the above passage. But some forty-five years later, in *Shiroi sen,* Shiga observed:

> When I wrote these words I thought that they were little more than delirious gibberish. Only recently have I come to realize that such was not the case. It is true that I have a dark complexion and my nose is in fact crooked. Of course I had some idea of what my mother was getting at then, too, but I took it as a vague and half-teasing remark at most, with no other meaning attached. Now it is clear to me that she was not in any way trying to make fun of me. Years ago, when I was an infant at her breast, she no doubt used to look down at me very intently and lament to herself that my skin was not a bit lighter, that my nose bent slightly to the left. (4:608–9)

The most striking scene in *Haha no shi* takes place after the mother has died, when the young Shiga enters alone into the room where her body lies:

> I went in to offer some incense and found the room empty. Quietly I removed the white cloth that covered her face. A kind of froth, such as crabs spit out on the beach, had gathered around my mother's mouth. "She's still alive!" I thought, bounding out of the room in my haste to tell my grandmother what I had seen.
>
> My grandmother came back to the room with me and looked for herself. "It's only the breath that was left in her—it comes out that way," she said. Then she took out a tissue and carefully wiped the foam away. (1:346)

The part of *Haha no shi* that concerns us here ends with a brief
description of the mother's burial:

> The blows of the hammer as they nailed the coffin shut
> penetrated deep inside me. It was excruciating. When they put
> the coffin in the grave I thought to myself, "It's all over now."
> Then they began to shovel clods of red earth into the trench,
> and again a metallic clinking sound echoed within me.
> "Will that be all, sir?"
> Scarcely waiting for an answer, the diggers unceremoni-
> ously finished their job. I watched the grave fill up with a
> shower of dirt. Even if she came back to life, she wouldn't be
> able to get out. (1:346)

The fragmentary piece *Haha no shi to tabi no kioku* begins with an
abbreviated account of the mother's death in which some passages
from the previous story are repeated almost verbatim. After the words
"my mother was dead," the narrator abruptly and enigmatically tells
us: "It was the season when I was supposed to be wearing my socks, so
it must have been six months or a year and a half before my mother's
death." He proceeds to relate a seemingly trivial incident in which his
mother tried to persuade him to put on his socks when she discovered
him playing barefoot one winter afternoon. As he continued to ignore
her, she playfully set a pair of socks on his head and returned to the
kitchen.

"I was enraged," Shiga recalls. "I ran after her shouting, 'That's
very rude.' I kept it up, and then I began to shove her with my *whole
body*" (italics are Shiga's). The recollection concludes: "My mother,
who was a timid soul, did not know what to do with me. She simply
gave me a sad look. And still I would not leave her alone" (1:356).

Shiga comments that, as far as he can remember, this was the only
time that he ever gave his mother cause for sorrow, and that after her
death he had come to regret it very much. He adds pointedly that,
while his father often accused him of having been a trial to his mother,
such was not the case. And he has since apologized many times at her
grave for this single tantrum in which he had indulged.

In the diary entry for 13 January 1912, shortly after he had written
the first draft of *Haha no shi to atarashii haha* Shiga recorded a dream
in which several of the story's details occur, though with certain
alterations. The entry is naturally not intended as a work of literature
(unlike the wonderfully contrived diaries of Gide and Kafū, Shiga's
diary is mostly a businesslike list of the day's doings). Yet it is in-

teresting to note how much of the dream's "manifest content" is reflected in the story, or vice versa.

The dream begins with a scene at his mother's deathbed which is more or less identical to a portion of *Haha no shi*. His mother asks to have brought to her an old cushion that the children use for play: she does not want the clean bedding to be soiled after her death. Here Shiga's dream becomes confused as to whether or not his mother has in fact spoken these words; and subsequently, when he returns from his errand, he finds his grandmother lying under the mosquito net in place of his mother. (Shiga's grandmother was still alive at this time, though she had recently been seriously ill.)

In the dream, there is a new emphasis on the father's role in these events. When Shiga tells him of the mother's harrowing request, he replies, "If that's what she wants, you should give it to her." Shiga comments in the diary that his father's response has implied not so much a resigned acceptance of the mother's dying wish as a thorough approval of "the motivation behind it." He adds: "At the moment I thought to myself, 'My mother may be *his* wife—but I seem to be the only one who is moved by what is happening.'" At the end of the dream he returns to find his grandmother in the room instead of his mother. He does not question the sudden change of events (one seldom does in dreams) and goes on with his ministrations as though nothing has happened, massaging her feet and explaining a commotion that has arisen outside the room. He tells her that it is a group of workers "on their way to raise a ridgepole in the neighborhood," though in fact the noise comes from some visitors who have arrived to be on hand at her death (10:533–34).

In the final reminiscence, *Shiroi sen,* Shiga looks back to the distant time when he wrote *Haha no shi*, etc., and expresses surprise that he did not then show more sympathy for his mother—virtually deprived of her only child by her mother-in-law and struck down by death at an early age. He tells us again of his father's assertions concerning his "willful" conduct toward his mother when he was a child. Shiga (now at the age of seventy-two, it will be recalled) confesses that, while he has always resented his father's "spiteful" accusations, there might have been some truth to them after all. But at present he can remember very little about his mother.

Shiroi sen concludes, however, with a recollection that appears nowhere else: "But I can still recall quite vividly the thick white line on my mother's *calf*. She would often tuck up her skirts like a maid and get down on her hands and knees to polish the veranda floor—and that was when the line showed on her *calf,* just below her white koshimaki. In my youth, the sight of a woman's legs always reminded me of my mother. And now it is only by recalling the white line on her *calf* that I can at last conjure up a clear picture of her" (4:609–10; italics are Shiga's).

Early in this strange and almost random soliloquy (it has nevertheless been designated a *shōsetsu*), Shiga quotes an art historian acquaintance to the effect that painters who die young may leave behind many "skillful" works; but their paintings generally show only the surface of things and fail to reveal "what lies behind" (4:603). He then suggests that this statement might well be applied, mutatis mutandis, to many of his own works. (Here he adds with a somewhat senile irascibility that, aside from writers themselves and a few scholarly friends of his, critics in general are of course "utterly useless . . . parasites.")

Shiga no doubt has a point. Or at least the general drift of his vague remarks implies an apt self-criticism: that he has sometimes shown us only the surface of things, with little effort to explore "what lies behind." What are we to make of these four descriptions of his mother's death and the recollections associated with it? Yasuoka comments: "We become acutely aware of the deep-seated feelings that Shiga has preserved for the mother whom he lost when he was only thirteen. The words strike us with such force that they convey no mere longing but something close to sexual desire. We can sense this strongly even in ostensibly simple declarative sentences such as: 'My mother would be reduced to tears whenever she told my father how willful and naughty I was—or so *he* says.' Here it all but gushes out at us. In the conclusion of *Shiroi sen* these persistent feelings are expressed still more blatantly."[23]

These remarks would be considered decidedly rash in the cautious scholarly circles of the post-Freudian West. But Yasuoka is a writer himself, not a scholar, and nowhere does he exhibit any interest in psychoanalytical thought itself. And so, when he makes this and similar observations about Shiga's inner relationship to his mother in the course of his study, he does so from the point of view of common sense—Japanese common sense, of course, which would seem to be more naturally attuned to these "persistent feelings" than is Western conventional wisdom on the whole.

If Shiga has for a long time failed to grasp "the truth of the matter," as he later commented, what sense will his readers make of these narratives and of the dream recorded in his diary? *Haha no shi* is the most polished work among them. In detail it is for the most part clear enough in its own terms. There is, however, something slightly disconcerting about the contrast between moments of unabashed and moving sentiment on the one hand, starkly concrete description on the other, for example, the froth around his mother's mouth "such as crabs spit out on the beach." And Shiga tells us that until recently he himself has been puzzled by the delirious words his mother spoke on her deathbed. "I don't care if he's dark and his nose is crooked. . . . So long as he's strong, it doesn't matter." It sounds quite remarkable out of context. But what extraordinary words for a boy of thirteen to hear from his dying mother!

Even if we cannot "understand" these words, any more than could Shiga when he wrote them, we do not wonder that he has remembered them and repeated them in three separate works. His explanation of them in *Shiroi sen* is no doubt plausible; and yet he admits that, in a general way, he has always understood their superficial meaning. It is, we conclude, the underlying force that they had for him then which he has failed to discern. And so we may question the implication in *Shiroi sen* that he now understands "the truth of the matter." It is more likely that he has forgotten the intense feelings which he experienced then, on the threshold of adolescence, even though he manages here to recapture a few moments from his early childhood.

Then there is the curious episode of the socks, which so enraged the young Shiga that he repeatedly shoved his mother with his *"whole body."* It will be recalled that Shiga has appended this brief narrative to *Haha no shi* in order to refute his father's contention that he was a great trial to his mother. We notice both here and in *Shiroi sen* how deeply his father's seemingly harmless remarks on the subject have rankled in him. And in his dream, as we have seen, Shiga comments to himself: My mother may be *his* wife, but I seem to be the only one who is moved." Similarly, he recalls in an essay which he wrote much later that his father did not cry when his mother died. "This made a lasting impression on me," he states, "and because of it I came to feel a strong antipathy toward my father" (7:18). Again, his self-analysis is plausible but somehow incomplete.

A few more details stand out in the stories and in his dream but may seem to us less than clear: the sudden displacement of Shiga's mother by his grandmother that occurs within the dream; the raising of the ridgepole, which he invents to explain to her the commotion outside the room; and, in *Shiroi sen*, both the single physical image that conjures up his mother for him and the remarkably repetitious, childlike style in which it is described. ("I remember" and "the white line on her *calf*" are each repeated three times in the short concluding paragraph.)

In the discussion of less "confessional" and less fragmentary narratives which follows, there will be occasion to examine more closely many such feelings, images, and dreams. But for the moment we are concerned with Shiga's life. I would suggest that if someone were to write a biography of Shiga with the aim of truly elucidating his works, these fragments would have to be emphasized. For they belong to the realm that Shiga has consistently stressed in his fiction—the realm of feeling, dreams, and almost obsessively sharp visual details.

Besides Yasuoka, Seki Ryōichi appears to be the only critic who has pointed to Shiga's preoccupation with the few recurring figures and themes that will be the focus of the discussion of the Shiga hero and his world. In a recent essay Seki expresses some dissatisfaction with what has been written so far on Shiga Naoya, and in particular with the existing critiques of his lifework, *An'ya kōro*. He observes that there have been numerous treatments of Shiga's life, the external development of his career, the circumstances surrounding the composition of various works, etc. "Yet there seem to be few substantive discussions of *An'ya kōro* as a whole," he remarks, adding that it is of course "a work which is difficult to understand in itself and far from easy to write about."[24]

This is a mild statement of a very curious fact: the principal novel of an author about whom a very great deal has been written—neither the way in which it is thought to have been composed nor the manner in which it was published, but the novel as we have it now—has been little discussed! Seki tells us that he would therefore like to contribute a thorough critical analysis of *An'ya kōro* and other works; but, as this is not possible (owing to the usual exigencies of space), he will rather hastily proceed to his conclusions about Shiga's "initial conception" of his major novels and "their essence."

He does indeed move swiftly to a few large, general observations, which are nonetheless provocative and very much to the point. Concerning Shiga's loss of his mother when he was thirteen and the strong "antipathy" toward his father associated with the event in her reminiscences, Seki comments in a rather offhand fashion, "Of course he had already experienced the so-called Oedipus complex, and this event served only to solidify strong feelings which were there to begin with." Seki then states that the image of himself which Shiga projects in his works—as distinct from his private self or his own self-image, we may interpret—clearly stems from the deepest roots in his past. By comparison to "his special position within his family" when he was a child, such things as his class origins, his schooling, his literary coterie have had only a small influence upon his development as a writer.

Although Seki is obviously well acquainted with his subject, some of his observations may seem simplistic. (For example, "Oedipus complex" here appears to mean little more than a deep distrust of the father—cf. his subsequent statement: "Such rifts between father and son, which have been the rule rather than the exception in modern Japan, naturally begin with the Oedipus complex.") Yet it is clear from his whole essay that Seki is not tied to any narrow point of view. On the contrary, he has done something quite unusual. He has taken a hard look at Shiga's works and has then attempted to discuss only those aspects of his life which appear significant in the context of what Shiga has actually written. While Seki's approach is still largely biographical, he ruthlessly excludes all the facts of dubious relevance—the sociological composition of the Peers' School in late Meiji, Mushakōji's pronouncements on art and life, etc.—which abound in the literature on Shiga.

Seki's emphasis might be called genealogical rather than psychoanalytical. He gives us a detailed account of complex relationships within several generations of Shiga's family and deduces from them a general pattern in which grandparents and uncles and aunts assume a larger role in the upbringing of male children than do their parents. The point of his argument in this section is not entirely clear. It does, however, convey the impression of an extended but closely knit family in which the lines of generation and the locus of paternal authority are ambiguous. From a contemporary Western point of view, the Shiga family situation may even be somewhat reminiscent of the confusing relations within Heian court families, which led to the social fact and the psychological dilemma of uncertain paternity (typified by the figure of Kaoru in *The Tale of Genji*). Seki speculates that these "involuted" family relationships must have had a strong effect on Shiga during his childhood; and that, as presumptive heir to the headship of the whole family, Shiga was no doubt made aware at an early age of his central position in this tangle of flesh and blood.

The analysis is interesting, if highly conjectural. I do not mean to suggest that Seki's findings are at all "trumped up," but he seems at pains here to lay the ground for a rather abrupt conclusion which he reaches concerning "the central motif" of Shiga's magnum opus. We are suddenly confronted with the statement: "*An'ya kōro* may be described as a classic tale of incest, for this is perhaps the most conspicuous feature of the work." Having allowed that this salient trait may be "quite unrelated to Shiga's own past," Seki adds: "Yet we cannot rule out the possibility that the incest wish [literally, 'an incestuous compulsion'] has been the prime motive behind his creation." And he ends by redefining An'ya kōro "from another point of view" as "in a real sense, a long tale of motherlove" (hahakoi: apparently a neologism of Seki's devising).[25]

Whether Seki's "genealogical" interpretation of Shiga's family background is valid or not, his general emphasis is borne out by the works themselves. Apart from all conjectures as to what kind of childhood Shiga himself had, the world which he has created for us often revolves around a child's complete entanglement in the biological and emotional bonds of the family; the hero whom he has portrayed frequently dwells on the uncertainty and untrustworthiness of fathers (in his mind there is more than one, as we shall see); and several works are partially informed by what Seki has called "motherlove," or by the persistent memory of it.

The sudden transformation of the dying mother into Shiga's grandmother in the dream recorded above makes clear in a way no biographical speculation could how thoroughly his grandmother fulfilled various aspects of the maternal role in his life. A further indication of the close interweaving of his childhood memories of the two women can be found in Shiga's flat assertion, which we need not accept too literally, that his grandmother was the "model" for the callous-compassionate mother summoned up in the first pages of An'ya kōro (7:20). The nature of this most central relationship in his childhood and early adolescence, its ambivalence, its great emotional intensity, is weakly adumbrated in his first published story, Aru asa (One Morning, 1908) and revealed with discomforting clarity in another early story, entitled Sōba no tame (For Grandmother, 1912; translated below). What is revealed in the much fuller treatment of the relationship contained in the second story is not by any means unequivocal love but a volatile mixture of desperate dependency, fear, contempt, admiration, and, underneath it all, an inextricable, warm blood-bond that appears both to fuse the two of them together and to cut them off from the rest of the family and the world.

The events of Sōba no tame are simple to the point of starkness, as we shall see is still the case with Shiga's more successful, and more truly fictive, mature writings. It begins with the death of Shiga's grandfather, a figure whom elsewhere Shiga credits with having been one of the three strongest influences in his life, but who is here so overshadowed by the grandmother as to suggest that, whatever dimensions he took on in Shiga's retrospective view, in this formative period he was something of a remote abstraction. The death of this apparently benevolent and gentle patriarch brings on fears of the not so gentle matriarch's impending death, more or less reasonable grounds for which the narrator finds in her advanced age and increasingly poor health. But the emphasis is very much on the irrational side of his foreboding, which is incarnated in the person of an albino mortician who arrives on the scene after his grandfather's death with uncanny speed, and which is further "objectified"—in a narrative device characteristic of the most deeply probing passages of Shiga's fiction—through a vivid dream.

Between the albino's first appearance and his reappearance in the dream that forms the core of the story, the narrator sketches for us a couple of incidents in his mercurial relations with his grandmother, interspersing brief glimpses of the albino "loping" down a nearby street, with his "pinkish, translucent skin" and his "gleaming gray eyes." The grandmother is depicted in one episode from before the decline of her health as emotionally and physically strong enough to have administered a caning to the sullen young Shiga as he lay naked in the bath, though not so strong as to succeed in inflicting any real pain.

The crystallizing dream occurs between the grandmother's two bouts with illness that are related in the story, the second of which is the more severe and far more dramatized in the telling (in a manner that foreshadows the virtual "set piece" scenes of critical illness in several later works). In the dream, the grandmother, having been reduced to a sadly emaciated state in reality, momentarily recovers her fierce and threatening aspect, which formerly complemented her usual adulatory indulgence of Shiga, as she first tears off the hands of the narrator's baby sister and then uproots a large piece of his scalp. With the swift passage of dream time, however, it is almost immediately perceived that in these acts she has been merely the unwitting instrument of the malevolent albino, whom Shiga heroically chases from the house, even lunging at him by the front gate just before— ostensibly—waking up, as we are told. Then, in a curiously convoluted detail that prefigures what is perhaps the crucial epiphany in the Shiga hero's later journey toward self-knowledge, the "real" Shiga in fact continues here to dream for a spell, during which he imagines his grandmother telling him that she herself has just had a dream identical to the one he describes to her.

Sōba no tame moves rapidly through the almost melodramatic scene of the grandmother's second illness, in the course of which Shiga engages in ferocious staring matches with the "gleaming gray eyes" that he conjures up in the corner, to its astonishing conclusion with her full recovery and the apparent death of the albino. The death of this shadowy adversary is never ascertained in any incontrovertible fashion; rather, it is deduced from a brief glimpse of somehow unusual-looking funeral preparations at the mortician's office and then accepted as established fact with a surge of triumphant euphoria. The narrator adds a brief coda of smug comments on the essential rightness of his conduct throughout this murderous battle of wills, with a belabored comparison to various kinds of criminal and institutional murders, of which he does not approve.

Shiga observed of this story, several decades later, "It may seem pathological and quite fantastic now, but for me at the time it was a purely factual, unvarnished account" (8:6). At the very least, we may grant that he has given us a remarkably sharp insight into the underside of his developing sensibility between the ages of roughly fifteen (when his grandfather died) and eighteen or so; and into the sometimes warm and doting, sometimes devouring, but always indispensable figure that his grandmother represented for him throughout his formative years. In spite of the story's devastating testimony to the deep and ambivalent bond between Shiga and his grandmother, and to its alternately self-inflating and paralyzing effects upon him (as an adolescent, we may suppose, he must in some way have colluded in preserving such qualities in the relationship), the biographers nevertheless extract from this work only the blandly sexist view that she was a strong presence in his early life and (as Mathy conveys the consensus) responsible "in great part for Naoya's willfulness and egoism."[26] Shiga's retrospective portrayal of the relationship in *Sōba no tame,* reflecting as it does, without condoning, the conventional Japanese moral outlook on such matters, elucidates the paradoxical ways in which a supremely self-confident patriarchal society, or in any case its upper middle class, tends to entrust its young male heirs to the almost exclusive care of women in the home while reserving the right to condemn the women for any serious moral failings that appear in early maturity.

Be that as it may, the salient contours of Shiga's first twenty-odd years as they emerge in the most memorable parts of his very fragmentary self-portrait may be summed up by saying that, whatever his various experiences of the outside world through school, play, and, indirectly, occasional contact with his rather distant male relatives, at home he was most intensely influenced by the absence of his mother and the overwhelming omnipresence of his grandmother. This strong-willed, temperamental woman made of him, as of her husband, we are told in *Sōba no tame,* a demigod. More often than not, we surmise, Shiga shared this view. And here, surely, are the beginnings of the myth of the Shiga hero.

Superficially, the most obvious legacy of Shiga's adolescent family life to the literature that he later wrote comes from his protracted conflict with his father. The theme of fathers and sons—properly speaking, several distinct fathers and one more or less constant son—does indeed bulk large in Shiga's fiction, contributing a good deal to the tenuous unity linking many of his works together. Naturally then, a very great deal has been made of this conflict in the biographical criticism. Nakamura, Yasuoka, and the rest treat in copious detail the more explosive incidents in the running feud between Shiga's alter ego and his father: a dispute over a contemporary cause célèbre (sparked by the widespread pollution from the Ashio copper mines early in the century, an issue with special ramifications for Shiga's family, which had once held a large interest in the mines); the confrontation over the son's sad, farcical affair with a family maid; the father's refusal to allow the son to bury his firstborn child in the family plot; etc. But far beyond this tedious litany of wrongs, actual and supposed, inflicted upon the "real" Shiga by his flesh-and-blood father, one finds on reading the works much interest in the shifting reactions to them by the Shiga hero: the tortuous undercurrents of this other side of the "family romance," with their ultimate, though in no true sense final, outpouring in the first part of *An'ya kōro.*

In Shiga's life, such as it can be deduced from his more confessional works and the more reliable biographical studies of him, we may be less struck by the force of what Mathy calls his "bold confrontation" with his father than with the little contradictions and hypocrisies in which it abounds, of a sort altogether familiar to most of us in the West from the private annals of middle-class families during the two centuries or so of the development and rapid change of capitalist society. Despite the apparently very bad relations between Shiga and his father, he continued to live at home in Tokyo until the eve of his thirtieth birthday. There he enjoyed what Honda Shūgo, Yasuoka, and others have designated, in a happy phrase, *heyazumi:* roughly, "life with a room of one's own" (in Shiga's case, it was in fact a separate annex to the main house, which he shared much of the time with his grandmother.)[27] For many middle-class Japanese of the pre-war generations, Honda and others suggest, the phrase summons up a life of enviable luxury with, above all, the privilege of retreating at will from the typically large extended family and the crowded world outside, to be alone with one's books, pictures, and records (the latter appear to have arrived only toward the end of Shiga's idyll), and with one's own thoughts and fantasies. With the recent publication of the first portion of Shiga's diary, not available during his lifetime, covering the years 1904–5, we can see that, for all the tensions in the relationship with his father, Shiga thrived in his solitary *heyazumi,* appearing to meet with the troublesome father only on rare occasions and leading both inside and outside the house very active social, cultural (broadly speaking), and (especially from 1910 on) sexual lives.

Shiga's "cultural" and extracurricular educational activities, which in his case were clearly more formative than his formal education (both at the Peers' School and at Tokyo University he cut classes regularly and compiled a very mediocre record, eventually dropping out of the university), consisted of a good deal of reading that belies his later disclaimer on this subject, and an astonishingly frequent attendance at traditional popular entertainments: kabuki, *yose,* and—a particular favorite, it would seem—women's *gidayu.* In the diary entry for 31 July 1904, he records that since 24 December of the previous year he has been to the theater (apparently *gidayu* for the most part) fifty-eight times, and to the storyteller's *(yose)* "slightly under seventy times" (10:129)! Intermittently he engages in lengthy critiques of the performances he has attended in which the emphasis is very much on the skill, and the sheer physical attractions, of the reciters and actors, most especially those of the women *gidayu.* The tone is identical to the one adopted by young men of later generations in star-struck discussions of movie actresses; only rarely is there any mention of the quality of the plays or narrative ballads themselves. And unlike Sōseki or Kafū, who also spent much time in the *yose,* Shiga does not appear to have subsequently drawn upon the rapid-fire idiom and the irreverently satirical style of the comic monologues in his own writing. It is possible even that his indulgence in these popular pastimes was one reason for his suppression of the first part of the diary when the rest of it was published during his lifetime (there are certainly no scandals nor any potentially libelous statements to account for it).

Another possible reason for the deletions would be the not uncommon vanity of the established writer and his desire to cover his tracks from the harsh gaze of overzealous scholars. For, in contrast to the peremptory statement when he was almost seventy that he had read "scarcely any" Japanese literature, and not many Western works either,[28] we find that in fact Shiga did read quite widely in his early twenties. How well he read remains an unanswerable question, since he very seldom engaged in any but the briefest comments on books, often simply noting that he had bought or finished reading them on such and such a day. In the light of the "influence" of certain authors widely ascribed to Shiga and other members of his so-called school in the secondary literature, it is interesting to observe, for example, that he did read some Tolstoy in this period, but almost exclusively the late Tolstoy of the neo-Christian and quietist tracts, and does not appear to have read *War and Peace* (or any other full-length novel) until well after the time he himself stopped writing. Conversely, it is surprising to see how much of Edo-period fiction he *did* read in these years, as well as that of certain Meiji authors who hark back to the *gesaku* tradition, and on the whole with evident relish. In addition to Saikaku, for whose works he later acknowledged a deep, though sometimes grudging, admiration, he read Kyōden, Samba, Tanehiko, Higuchi Ichiyō, and in considerable quantity, the prolific Izumi Kyōka. He observed of the leading *gesakusha* Kyōden and Samba, "They are a lot of fun to read, but Meiji fiction has certainly made great advances over what was written in their epoch: their basic approach was to launch into a large number of plots and subplots, all connected with 'and then there was this, then there was that' and tied up neatly at the end in a grand finale" (10:118). Five or six years later, when Shiga was in the throes of making himself into a writer full of modern high purpose, it is very unlikely that he would have admitted even to himself that he found late Edo fiction "fun."

He made interesting comments, quite favorable, on Ozaki Kōyō, whose great popularity in the Meiji period surely had to do with his having retained many of the traditional tricks of the Edo story-teller's trade (10:131); and in a brief, impressionistic paragraph or two on *iki*, that central esthetic-emotional-social value in Edo merchant-class life which is so difficult to define, Shiga's views prefigure in a very skeletal form some of Kuki Shūzō's perceptions in his famous extended essay on the topic (10:132). One regrets in particular Shiga's bare notations of his readings in Izumi Kyōka, perhaps the greatest of the neo-Edo writers in the modern period, whose excursions in a few of his more densely wrought works (*Kōya hijiri* and *Uta andon*, for instance) into a timeless, archetypal world peopled with quasi-mythical figures present a common ground with some of Shiga's best fiction.

It would appear, however, that after these few years of extensive immersion in various aspects of Edo culture, high, medium, and "low," Shiga resolutely turned his back on the real attractions they held for him in his youth. And with the exception, noted earlier, of Natsume Sōseki, the principal architect of modern psychological fiction in Japan (and a valuable patron of Shiga in the early stages of his career), he lived up to his later disclaimer from his mid-twenties or so onward, referring in his diary chiefly to Western works, and not very many of them. To specify some of his readings in Euro-American literature, history, and religion—Dante, Shakespeare, Goethe, Rousseau, and Hoffmann; Emerson, Maupassant, Tolstoy, Gorky, and Ibsen—is to say very little about his developing sensibility, since he usually comments, if at all, in the blandest terms on their works, which by and large form a quite standard list of "readings in Western civilization" that had been preselected and partially translated by a slightly earlier generation of Japanese scholars and writers. Occasionally one encounters a suggestive entry, such as the following quotation from Anatole France (a writer who has had perhaps a more enduring appeal in Japan than in any Western nation): "One cannot acknowledge people's ideas as their own unless they are an outgrowth of their own feelings; or, if their ideas result from intellectual speculation on their own part, until they have clearly become felt as well" (10:566). Shades of the remarkably undissociated sensibility, not to say anti-intellectualism, that Shiga was to show in his own work. But on the evidence of the diary it seems as doubtful that he ever read carefully through an entire novel by France as that he took the time in these years to read any of Tolstoy's major works, rather finding in the gloomy late humanism of their extraliterary pronouncements some confirmation of his own outlook on the world.

Concerning the reading habits of one of his friends, Shiga remarked in his diary, not without some projecting of his own habits, one assumes, "People like Koyamauchi seem to read an awful lot of books but they read in a very slipshod way. They don't really take it seriously, I suspect. But perhaps this is precisely the way that people who are themselves writers should read" (10:91). Here is certainly a not very indirect statement on Shiga's part of the kind of convoluted misgivings about reading the works of others that Proust expressed so entertainingly in *Sur la lecture*, when poised on the brink of his long-delayed debut.

Some of Shiga's activities and aspirations during his prolonged "adolescent moratorium" came to focus around Uchimura Kanzō and his original strain of nondenominational Protestantism and, a few years later, around the journal *Shirakaba* and several fellow members of its editorial staff. A great deal more has been made of these two affiliations in the secondary literature than appears to be warranted by what Shiga went on to write. The reasons for the gross overemphasis are easy to imagine: for biographies drawn up on traditional lines, the lives of authors, like those of medieval Confucian and *kokugaku* scholars, require a mentor *(sensei)* and a school or faction. Uchimura and the so-called Shirakaba-ha ("School") have fulfilled these requirements for Shiga's biographers. To the extent that as a young man Shiga did conform to such residual traditional norms of his society, the lengthy discussions of these matters tell us something about his life; but they tell us very little about his works, which in any case speak for themselves.

Though never baptized a Christian, Shiga did for several years attend regular meetings of Uchimura's group. He later maintained that he had not been especially attracted to Christian doctrine, nor even to Uchimura's highly individual interpretation of it, but rather to the charismatic character of the man himself. "I was not particularly impressed with the doctrine," he reminisced (many years after renouncing the religion), "although this was naturally what was most important from Sensei's point of view" (7:294). We shall note that the few direct references to Christianity in Shiga's works are either querulous or openly disparaging. Of greater significance, perhaps, is a more diffuse and only implicit kind of "Christian" influence which we may discern in the background of his entire œuvre.

The tacit reaction to the foreign religion that may be inferred from various works is, with one tentative exception, at the end of *An'ya kōro,* negative and largely constricting in its effect upon the author, as Shiga himself has suggested. In a journalistic postwar piece entitled *Waga seikatsu shinjō,* Shiga confessed: "Had I not come in contact with the religion of Jesus [*Yasokyō*] I could have led a more carefree life and would no doubt have written in a broader vein. Although I have regretted this experience in the past, I think now that it has been in my best interest. Without it I would perhaps have become a more slovenly sort of man" (7:420).

As is generally true of the more than superficial kinds of influence, the effect which Uchimura's uncompromising version of Christianity had upon Shiga's development as a writer can only be deduced from his works in a speculative manner. Shiga's own pronouncement on the subject would indicate a lifelong ambivalence toward the stern precepts of Uchimura's puritanical faith—in which, contrary to Shiga's

designation of it as "Yasokyō," a merciful saviour appears less important than a strict Old Testament God. (One imagines that, in the
eyes of Shiga and other adolescent disciples, God was represented by
the figure of Uchimura himself.)

Within the world of the Shiga hero we will find a good deal of
"religious" interest in the broadest sense, but the more positive kinds
of religious experience in which the hero participates are purely infor-
mal and intuitive. If there is any salutary influence of established
religions to be found, it is that of the archaic Shinto cult and, especially, of the late Mahayana—Zen and Amidism—which are invoked
intermittently throughout the latter part of An'ya kōro.

Finally, some brief mention of the much-discussed "Shirakaba-ha"
is unavoidable. This is the so-called school to which Shiga is assigned
by all the literary historians. But on reading the works of his fellow
"members," one concludes that there is little resemblance among these
authors. They were simply a group of good friends (Shiga was particularly close to Satomi Ton, Arishima, and Mushakōji), who, having
earlier belonged to the same literary circle at the Peers' School, in 1910
founded a monthly magazine entitled Shirakaba ("White Birch"). It
was devoted to fiction, poetry, and essays, and also to the reproduction and introduction of modern European painting and sculpture.
The magazine continued publication until 1923, the year of the Great
Earthquake.

Shirakaba itself does not seem to have produced much fiction of
lasting value, though there are several important exceptions (the first
version of Arishima's Aru onna appeared in its pages, as did a number
of Shiga's early short stories). Mushakōji Saneatsu was the prime force
behind the venture, and is perhaps the flimsiest "major figure" that the
Japanese literary histories have established for us so far. "Musha," as
he was often called, was clearly Shiga's most intimate, lifelong friend;
in 1924 Shiga married his cousin, a wellborn Kyoto woman née
Kadenokōji; and it is to Musha that Shiga dedicated An'ya kōro. But
beyond these close personal ties, it is hard to see any literary connection between the two.

As an example of the sort of connections that have been set forth in
the secondary literature, let us cite from Nakamura's study of Shiga.
"It may be said of the whole body of Shiga's literature," he begins
rather grandiosely, "that it materialized through a process of fleshing
out the patterns of Mushakōji's thought."[29] This does not mean very
much. For Mushakōji's "thought," a manic effusion of platitudes
about humanity, art, and genius, means very little.[30] One doubts that

Nakamura, who has written many stimulating works on the literature, would care to pursue this statement (indeed, he quickly adds to it that of course "Shiga did not acquire from his old friend any thoughts at which he could not have arrived spontaneously on his own").

Tsurumi Shunsuke, who is not a literary scholar but an intellectual historian, has suggested that the real contribution of the Shirakaba movement was simply the undemanding comradeship which it afforded to the individual "members" as they went their separate ways.[31] This opinion seems quite sensible. Shiga once recommended to aspiring young writers that they follow his example and seek the moral support of a group of friends. But, with the observation that he and his companions had kept apart from each other in their approach to writing itself, he cautioned: "Literary associations as such don't do much good" (7:427).

Midway in the period when Shiga was educating himself and beginning his career as a writer, more or less corresponding to his twenties, there is an abrupt shift in the tone and style of his diary, from the almost exuberant and chatty entries of 1904–5 to the spare, laconic entries (1906 and 1909 are entirely missing) up to 1910–12, where one encounters frequent outbursts of soul-searching, leading to strong self-affirmation on the one hand, painful self-doubts and recrimination on the other. In his early twenties, he lamented that he seemed incapable of "as they say, 'falling in love'" (10:213), elaborating at one point: "It has become cruelly apparent in any number of actual situations that I am lacking in love—I merely tolerate others" (10:129). The verb rendered here as "tolerate" *(yurusu)* could suggest a sexual frame of reference, but the phrasing is vague.

The first mention of a visit to one of the quarters of licensed prostitution (Susaki), at the age of twenty-two, is likewise ambiguous; although it indicates only a brief sight-seeing tour, the next day's diary entry contains a diatribe against "the existence of vast pleasure quarters that, night after night, lead men into sin—clear proof of our animal nature." The entry concludes with a perfervid meditation on the fate of the illegitimate issue that frequently results from this promiscuity, despite all precautions. In a tone of intensely personal moral outrage which would seem to portend that of the Shiga hero upon learning of his "true" origins in *An'ya kōro,* the young Shiga wrote here: "And suppose I were to come upon the abandoned child of one of these couples, the unwanted by-product of a sequence of every imaginable sin—stealing, killing, raping, all for the sake of satisfying the most potent of animal desires . . . that child would be, in spite of it all, the most unsullied, beautiful, lovable creature in the world. What a paradox!" (10:198).

Not until his twenty-sixth year did he acknowledge, retrospectively, his first visit to what he calls "that sort of woman" and, a year later, his first case of venereal disease (10:418). Subsequently, there is increasingly frequent mention of encounters with whores and with geisha of various grades, notations made in part, it would appear, as groundwork for a projected work designated "my 'Tales of Yoshiwara'" which one gathers he never began (10:474, 643).

But the first unequivocal declaration of love is for himself. Early in the year 1912, a watershed in Shiga's life and career, he observed of Rousseau, whose *Confessions* he had been reading, "I do not know whether Rousseau is 'great' or not, but I *feel* that he is not. Reading his work, I felt that I have within me—myself as I am now—at least as much as he did.... Mankind need only—or in any case, I need only devote my life to mining what is in me.... That is all" (10:556). And the next day he proclaimed:

> I have come truly to love myself. I now find my face truly beautiful. And I believe there are few men who have possessed the greatness that I have within me.
>
> I must devote my life to extracting from myself all that is worthy of love, all that is beautiful and great.
>
> I take it as a big step forward that I am now able to affirm and to rely upon myself so strongly. It has nothing to do with what is commonly called "feeling secure." (10:557)

Jaded as we are after four or so centuries of the various cults of self-reliance and self-glorification that have permeated Euro-American civilization, some of us will find these words either amusingly callow or offensively trite. To most Japanese of Shiga's, not to mention an earlier, generation, they might well have sounded blasphemous, obscene, or simply mad.

Predictably, but a few weeks passed before another little twist in the angle of his adolescent self-scrutiny elicited from Shiga: "Lately I seem to be anxious and irritable, and *sabishi* [one of the few truly untranslatable words in the language, perhaps approachable only through such circumlocutionary oxymorons as "sweet sadness," "pleasant loneliness," and the like]. But I am pleased to sense that underneath there is now a certain kind of strength in abundance.... I must maintain this *sabishi* frame of mind and not fall into facile compromises" (10:567). And a few days later the self-involved pathos gives way to unwitting self-parody: "There is apparently a word *Weltschmerz. That* is what I feel" (10:569).

Quite soon after, however, Shiga's *Weltschmerz* seems to have abated, and we find him palpably overjoyed at his father's divulgence (though Shiga grumbles about not having been told much earlier) of the full extent of the patrimony he holds in reserve for him: 600,000 yen. It is not clear from this entry how much access Shiga is to be allowed during his father's lifetime to this considerable fortune; but it does appear that he has been released from the sort of cash nexus with his family, revealed clearly in the diary up to this point, which has restricted him to small doles of ten and twenty yen at a time from his father and his grandmother, thus reinforcing the protracted psychological dependency. And so he records with relief, and with implicit faith in the durability of capitalism, that he will "never have to be tied down by trivial considerations," and vows that he will prove to be a "blessing" to his family (10:571).

Despite the evident financial settlement, Shiga was not freed of the burden that a large family placed upon an eldest son in his society. He was at this time briefly alarmed by what proved to be a passing illness for his father, and remarked while it still appeared serious, "It would be very hard on me if my father's condition were to get worse—I want the family situation to stay just as it is" (10:564). Later that year, after publishing his first attempt at longer fiction, *Ōtsu Jun'kichi* (1912), he set out on a long journey that took him to Onomichi on the Inland Sea coast and various other provincial towns. He spent the next two years traveling and writing. During this period he undertook a long novel, partly at the request of Natsume Sōseki, then the literary editor of the *Asahi shimbun*. Shiga never finished the work, despite Sōseki's gentle proddings and encouragement. But the preliminary draft, entitled "Tokitō Kensaku," provided the foundation for *An'ya kōro*. After a short "preview" of the work that appeared as a short story in *Shirakaba*, Shiga's only full-length novel was published in two large sections, the first in 1921 and the second, after a long interval that suggests what a large place in his maturing life the work occupied, in 1937.

This long gestation of *An'ya kōro* and its eventual publication were without question the most significant "events" in his career. By comparison, the petty details of his semipublic life, occasional meetings with various writers, lectures and speaking tours, etc., and the merely external data on his private life seem no more interesting than those in the lives of other authors who, like Shiga, put much of their substance into their works. The glimpses of Shiga at work which may be gleaned from a few descriptions he has given us of his alter ego at work (fortunately he seldom dwells on his hero's very intermittant preoccupation with *his* writing) give us a very different picture from the highly colored portrait of the gregarious literary entrepreneur winning fame and fortune that we often get in the biographies. This glimpse, for example, from *Ko o nusumu hanashi:* "I worked between midnight and dawn. In the still hours of the night a faint ringing sensation would grow to a low roar as I became more and more engrossed in my work. I felt as though everything in my mind was out there, before my eyes" (2:102).

Two telling incidents from the period when Shiga was most intensely engaged in making himself into a writer attest to an enormous concentration of emotional-intellectual energy, and to his abiding belief in such phenomena as extrasensory perception and "precognition" that we have seen at work in *Sōba no tame.* The morning after finishing *Kamisori* (The Razor, 1910; translated below), his chilling tale of impulsive murder in a barbershop, he read in the newspaper that his next-door neighbor had committed suicide with a razor on the previous night. Shiga concluded that at the very time he had been mulling over how to describe the barber's slashing of his victim's throat with a razor, his neighbor was "no doubt deliberating over how to cut his own throat" (1:625). And on the evening of the day he finished writing *Dekigoto* (An Accident, 1913; translated below), a story about a streetcar accident that nearly proved fatal to a small child, Shiga himself was struck by a train on the Yamate Line, in the accident that serves as the point of departure for *Kinosaki nite* (At Kinosaki, 1917; translated below). Although Shiga's persona in the latter story accepts in a remarkably mature, clear-headed fashion the large role of blind chance in men's lives and deaths, we infer from these two incidents in his own life, and his reaction to them, that in this most creative period of his career he still saw himself as both subject to and, at times, the active agent of some hidden, all-determining Fate, a vision of which was (in his earlier quoted words) "not accessible under normal conditions of sanity" (8:6).

Despite these occasional glimpses of Shiga that do remind us of the now lucid, now shadowy interior landscape inhabited by the Shiga hero, the older Shiga gets the further the created life of his single central character appears to diverge from the image of Shiga's "real" life which, no doubt faithfully reflecting a certain surface reality, the biographer-critics have carefully drawn for us. Concerning the whole vexing question of Shiga's shifting relations to the Shiga hero, he himself summed up, with specific reference to the hero's chief manifestation in *An'ya kōro,* "Kensaku is more or less the author himself. That is, in similar situations I would most likely do as he does, or I would want to do so—or, in some cases, I have already done so" (10:20). Shiga is, to be sure, begging the question here. But underlying the charming evasiveness, there is some important truth.

The Shiga hero, then, not Shiga, is the subject of the following discussion of the works. The treatment of this subject will often seem repetitious, obsessive, and reductive. All of these traits are to be found, among many others, in Shiga's principal works, where they seem as necessary to his purpose as they are to mine. They are likewise common features of orthodox psychoanalytical constructs, which indeed appear close to Shiga's intuitive grasp of his hero's "psychology" in certain respects. The inevitable violence done to individual works by isolating this one particular aspect will only prove defensible if the partial reconstruction of each of them, in a perspective considerably altered from Shiga's more ambiguous point of view, throws some light on the "whole" which he considered both unattainable and not (at least for himself) worth pursuing.

THE SHIGA HERO'S
CHILDHOOD

Could it not be easily demonstrated, by a philosophical
comparison between the works of the mature artist
and the state of his soul as a young child, that genius
is no more than the ability to recapture childhood in a
precise and potent manner?
—Baudelaire

Baudelaire never ceased to regret the *verts paradis
des amours enfantines*. But . . . it was for the absolute
security of childhood that Baudelaire yearned.
—Sartre, *Baudelaire*

THERE IS, I HAVE SUGGESTED, only one fully developed character in
Shiga Naoya's works, who may be associated to widely varying degrees with the author himself. This character appears in dozens of
short stories, the so-called trilogy beginning with *Ōtsu Jun'kichi,* and
the single long novel, *An'ya kōro.* Ranging in years from early childhood to the threshold of middle age, he is called by many names:
Shintaro, Seibei, Ōtsu Jun'kichi, Older Brother, Tokitō Kensaku, and,
quite often, "I." But though his name and outward guise may change
from story to story, in important respects he is recognizably the same
throughout.

I propose here to trace his development through some of the stages
and situations in which we encounter him. For the most part I shall
refer to him as the Shiga hero, or simply as "the hero." Yet among all
of Shiga's protagonists, Tokitō Kensaku in *An'ya kōro* represents an
unusually sustained, semifictional characterization. And so I shall
refer to him by name toward the end of this discussion of the Shiga
hero's "dark night's journey."

In an interesting essay, Kamei Katsu'ichiro has objected to interpretations of *An'ya kōro* that treat it as an account of the hero's
search for identity (*jiko keisei*—literally, "self-formation"—is the
Japanese phrase). "There is nothing which he must become to be

35

himself," Kamei comments. "In essence this self has always existed; he needs only to test in the real world the strength that he already has in him."[1]

Such remarks are both a testimony to the compelling power of the Shiga hero's portrayal and an indication of how different a view of human development this distinguished Japanese critic has from those held by many in the contemporary West. (It should be added that Kamei's outlook is not necessarily typical of postwar Japanese intellectuals, whose approach to these large questions may often be closer to some of ours than to those of their older fellow countrymen.) While Kamei appears to see "essential" fullness and innate selfhood even in the young child whom the hero recalls for us in the opening pages of *An'ya kōro,* those of us who share to some extent the psychoanalytic and existential images of man will see only ripening instincts—mere "drive fragments to be assembled,"[2] Erikson calls them; and the tenuous beginnings of being. "There is no such thing as character," Sartre has said, "there is only a project of oneself."[3]

It is no doubt true that, as Kamei's remarks would suggest, the mature author-hero Shiga always has in mind the end result of the slow growth, the gradual coming into consciousness, of his alter ego's adult self, even when he portrays him as a forlorn child or a troubled adolescent. But the constant recurrence in Shiga's prose of symbolic ("poetic") language and imagery which Akutagawa and others have stressed, and the underlying rhythm which, as Shiga himself has implied, reverberates from below the cluttered surface of the mind, also suggest that as he writes he is able to project his mind back into much earlier states of mind and "down" to subconscious levels of experience. In other words, he does at times what inspired poets and the relatively rare writers of Jung's "visionary" kind of prose are generally supposed to do. But he does so rather more systematically than most writers, as I have suggested earlier, and with ulterior motives of a sort which do not, perhaps, inspire many poets.

Shiga's purpose as a "personal novelist" or, more precisely, a writer of "subjective stories" *(shin'kyō shōsetsu)* according to the Japanese critical scheme, has been to psychoanalyze himself through his alter ego, though in a highly intuitive, nonanalytical manner. As indicated by the above-cited remarks of *Wakai*'s hero about his attempt at autotherapy through fiction, the method is to transfer his innermost problems onto the ego of a single central character and let the story run its course. A kind of free association, then. The instrument by which the random process is given therapeutic rigor—also, not incidentally, an esthetically pleasing surface—is his spare, incisive style, with its inexorable rhythms that do not permit the hero to hide behind his defenses along the way. He may regress into disturbing fantasies and memories of the past, or go forward toward some strenuous effort to resolve his inner conflicts in the "real" world. But as in conventional therapy the patient is constantly prompted by the stern gaze of the analyst to carry on with the business at hand, the Shiga hero is only rarely allowed to indulge in idle sublimations—to get out of himself and into the objectified, abstract realms of society at large, "pure art," and nature as mere scenery to be contemplated.

Whether we first encounter him as an adolescent in Shiga's earliest work, *Aru asa* (1908), or as a young child in the first-person reminiscence with which *An'ya kōro* begins, he is enmeshed, and will remain so for most of his journey, in what Jung once called "the boring emotional tangles of the family situation."[4] Even with our own, more limited notions of art and life, some of us may wish that the Shiga hero were not so closely and invariably tied to these rudimentary relationships, both real and imagined. But in the sparsely populated world of Shiga's novels and stories, this is, after the inexorable rhythm of the style, the most basic premise. One either accepts it or chooses not to read on.

It has been noted that *An'ya kōro* recapitulates in a new light much of the subject material treated in earlier novels, and that it transforms several of the characters who appear in previous stories and autobiographical sketches—although, with one exception, they are not beyond recognition for those who have read these other works. In the opening pages of the long novel, the hero, now in his twenties, reminisces about a few incidents in his early childhood. Here he introduces the characters who will figure centrally in his inner life for much of the narrative, even though they may not appear as live people on the stage of the novel.

First, there is his grandfather, whom he recalls having met at the age of six, shortly after his mother died. (In *An'ya kōro*, the mother dies while he is still a small child; in other, more closely autobiographical stories, her death is placed at a later stage in the hero's life. In Shiga's own life his mother had died when he was thirteen.) The hero is not initially aware that the "shabby" old man with the "sunken eyes" and a "stooped back" is his own grandfather. But by an "uncanny instinct" the child "feels" that this is a close relative.

Here we are given our earliest example of how the Shiga hero feels and intuits the "truth," or whatever is subjectively important to him, in the most various situations that arise throughout his life. We may not question that a child could intuit the facts of the matter in this special case. But we shall see him relying almost exclusively upon such impulses and instincts at a much later age, and in far more complex situations. Indeed, the crises in his life, and the dramatic highpoints in the many narratives that create (or recreate) this life, usually occur when the adolescent or adult hero allows himself to be ruled by his strong instincts.

The grandfather, who is depicted as a man of unmitigated ugliness and venality, will disappear after the brief but chilling evocation at the beginning of *An'ya kōro*. He is also the one exception mentioned above: the only figure introduced here who cannot be found in any other Shiga stories, even in some altered form. There is, of course, a grandfather who plays an important role in several semiconfessional novels. But he is always a very positive figure ("one of the three or four most admirable men I have ever known," said Shiga of his own grandfather), and is in fact the only major, more or less constant character in Shiga's works whose portrayal is wholly sympathetic. The grandfather in *An'ya kōro* is by contrast not a real character at all but a vivid childhood memory which will be evoked only once more at a crucial turning point in the adolescent hero's life.

Shortly after this first encounter, the child is sent to live with the unpleasant grandfather and his young mistress, "a woman of twenty-four or so named Oei." (The house where the old man and Oei live is in a place called Ogyōnomatsu, which, as Yasuoka has pointed out, was where the family of Shiga's own mother lived after coming to Tokyo.)[5] The boy is disgruntled that he alone of the several children has been sent to live with his grandfather. But he accepts it with a precocious stoicism: "I had often been subjected to such unfairness since I was an infant. There was nothing new about it. I did not even think to ask anyone why I had been singled out. And yet the vague presentiment that in later life the same kinds of things would go on happening to me, and in the same way, made me somehow sad. Then I thought of my mother, dead these two months, and grew all the sadder" (5:6–7).

Then the hero recalls his father, who is "always, always cold." The boy has also been "subjected" to this coldness from as far back as he can remember; "there has never been anything else" in their relationship. And so it does not make him particularly sad. Yet on occasion he has been both frightened and enraged by his father. The hero recalls (or, as I have suggested, relives) the time when his father, in an unusually good mood, challenged him to a wrestling match.

The boy is delighted and throws himself eagerly into the game. "I did not care so much about winning," he tells us, "but I wanted to make my father acknowledge my strength. The more he repulsed my attacks, the more recklessly I ran at him." But the father refuses to yield an inch. Then, suddenly, he is "a different man." He tells the boy that the game is over. When the boy continues to rush at him, he pins him down and ties his hands behind him with a sash:

> His face was pale from exertion and had a mean, predatory look. Leaving me as I was, he turned away toward the desk behind him. At that moment I began to hate him.
> The sight of my father, his broad shoulders heaving as he tried to catch his breath, was hateful to me. I kept my eyes trained on him until my vision blurred over. Then I lost control and burst into tears. (5:14)

Finally, two more figures are introduced through two further memories from the hero's childhood. We are given a glimpse of the grandfather's mistress: "Ordinarily, Oei was no beauty. But with the thick makeup she applied after her bath, she seemed very beautiful to me. When she had finished dressing she would drink some sake with my grandfather. The warm wine made her slightly giddy. Humming a popular tune, she would take me on her knees and hug me tight in her strong, thick arms. I felt stifled, but at the same time I had an exhilarating sensation of being carried off somewhere far away" (5:11). Then, thinking back to the time when his mother was still alive, he begins his recollection of her with the statement that her treatment of him was "on the whole quite callous." He recalls the time when his mother discovered him sitting precariously on the rooftop.

"In an unnaturally sweet tone" she coaxes him to stay still while she sends a servant to bring him down. Afterward she gives him a sound thrashing.

And he remembers begging her once for some candy that his father had just brought home.

When she refuses, he continues to pester her, and at length takes hold of her wide sash as she starts to leave the room: "This time she became truly angry. She grabbed me by the wrist and dragged me over to the cupboard. Holding my head locked in one arm, she began to stuff thick slices of yōkan into my mouth. I tried to resist by clenching my jaws together, but I could feel little strands of the sticky candy oozing into my mouth through the gaps in my baby teeth. I was too frightened to cry" (5:10). And still, ever since she died, he has repeated to himself: "But no matter what happened, Mother really loved me. She was the only one."

Here, in the remarkable prologue to *An'ya kōro,* the central figures in the hero's early childhood have been presented. They or their surrogates will reappear many times in the subjective accounts of his later years (both in the narrative proper of *An'ya kōro* and in other novels and stories), with the exception, noted above, that the thoroughly negative character of the grandfather is replaced by the wholly positive grandfather portrayed in other works. The role of Oei, originally the mistress of the "shabby old man," is also limited to *An'ya kōro.* Yet it becomes clear in the subsequent course of the narrative that she has been a kind of second mother to the hero over the years. This is a role which is filled in several other works by a doting grandmother, as it appears to have been throughout Shiga's youth by his own grandmother.

Here, too, some of the major recurrent themes of Shiga's works are set forth clearly or strongly suggested. These have to do in general with the changing nature of the hero's inner relationships to the figures introduced in the prologue, or to analogous characters who appear in other narratives. The "callous" mother, who has nevertheless loved him as no one else, and who is lost to him when he needs her. Another mature woman, strong and sensual, who treats him in a more warmly maternal fashion. And the cold, "predatory" father who is never to be trusted.

Already the notion of the unfairness of things has taken root in the young hero's mind, as well as the still more disquieting thought that in later life he is destined to repeat over and over again the same sort of bitter experience that he has had thus far, and in much "the same way." ("Repetition-compulsion" is the name which the psycho-analysts have given to this dismal mechanism, although from their point of view it is, of course, imposed from within, rather than by any external force or "destiny.") His childhood—that is, precisely what he feels compelled to remember of it—has become his fate.

We might pause for a brief reflection on this glimpse of the Shiga hero's beginnings, which we have been given in *An'ya kōro* alone. Within Shiga's career as a subjective and personal novelist this work represents not a beginning but a summation. And we may be so struck by the literary qualities of the opening passage (the stylistic virtuosity, with the overtones of a child's echolalic speech) that we overlook the substance of what is being said.

Whether one chooses to follow the Japanese critical approach and see Shiga's works collectively as a kind of autobiography or rather to consider them a loosely unified life history of an independent hero, one cannot help but have a few misgivings about this child's future. To be sure, these are doubts of the sort that may be raised by an unsentimental scrutiny of any childhood (and might be reinforced by the mechanistic formulas of orthodox psychoanalysis). Yet we know that the austere beginning of *An'ya kōro* is to inaugurate an ambitious "portrait of the artist," a type of modern myth of the hero with which we in the West are familiar from various literary encounters. It is not to be a case history, although the severe realism of the hero's confession may invite such an interpretation.

Nowhere in the prologue do we find those auspicious signs which mark the child hero in traditional myths.[6] More to the point, as this is clearly to be a modern, realistic account of a purely mortal life, neither does the passage convey any sense of an idyllic childhood (in contrast to the childhood portions of the portraits of young artists which Proust, Joyce, and Mann have given us) nor a trace of the child's own conviction that he is somehow specially favored.

The dominant tone is one of resignation, if not despair: a premature recognition of the darkest side of life. The hero is at this stage still too young to see his particular experience within a universal scheme of things. But already he has come to know and, ostensibly, to accept for himself a large measure of frustration, lovelessness, and irreparable loss.

There are, finally, only two bright moments which briefly illuminate the hero's reminiscence of his early years. One is the recollection of the times when he felt "transported" in the firm embrace of his grandfather's mistress. The other is the memory of what was already only an ill-defined memory of his mother's love, made all the more vague by the seemingly contradictory testimony of the specific events that he recalls. Yet in these few moments, if anywhere, we detect a glimmer of the "verts paradis des amours enfantines" that Sartre ascribes to Baudelaire in the epigraph to this chapter.

For our only view of the child hero as a developing artist as such we must look to the short story *Seibei to hyōtan* (Seibei and Gourds, 1912; translated below), one of several slender but vital works that may be considered somewhat apart from the life history contained in the longer works. The events of this finely wrought story and a few others of a similar type clearly take place in a realm which is rendered more objectively than is the world of the trilogy and *An'ya kōro*. It is possible to see such tales as a form of wish fulfillment within the total context of the Shiga hero's life—a realization on a more detached plane of those dreams and fantasies which abound in the subjective narratives.

Seibei to hyōtan is about a twelve-year-old boy who lives in a provincial port. (Although the town is not named, it would seem to be on the Inland Sea coast, judging from the snatches of dialect scattered through the dialogue.) Seibei has a consuming passion for gourds, which he has been collecting for some time in spite of his father's contemptuous disapproval. One of his father's cronies expresses surprise at the simple, ordinary shapes which the boy seems to prefer in his collection. By the same token, the boy is not in the least attracted, we are told, to the rare and misshapen varieties that adult connoisseurs fuss over. At a recent exhibition of local arts and crafts, he took but a single look at a famous gourd—known as "Bakin's gourd," after the Edo period writer—and concluded that it was "ridiculous."

One day Seibei comes upon a particularly fine specimen in the marketplace. Thoroughly enchanted with his find, he rushes home to fetch some money and soon returns to buy it. He is so pleased with his new gourd that he is reluctant to part with it even when he goes to school. Soon afterward he is caught polishing his prized possession under his desk by a stern teacher of "morals." (An outsider, the teacher utterly disdains the local interest in gourds.) Seibei's gourd is confiscated and his "misconduct" is reported to his parents.

Like the morals instructor, Seibei's father sees in this consuming passion proof that his son "will never amount to anything." He gives Seibei a sound thrashing, then takes up a sledge hammer and smashes the remaining gourds.

But Seibei, we learn, has long since forgotten about the incident and has forgiven his father. He now devotes all of his energy to painting—a pastime for which his father has already begun to show renewed disapproval.

A simple story, then, which portrays in a few deft strokes the emergence of æsthetic awareness in the young artist—a creative zeal strong enough to resist the philistinical opposition of the adults around him. The most obvious link to the subjective world of the Shiga hero's life history is found in the clash between Seibei and his father. As we shall see, in the longer novels the father repeatedly expresses contempt for the hero's literary aspirations (and in *Aru otoko, sono ane no shi* [A Man and the Death of His Sister, 1920], the son replies with a disparaging reference to the ponderous works of Bakin—apparently his father's favorite writer—which is reminiscent of the silent resistance recorded in *Seibei to hyōtan*).

But the conflict between Seibei and his father is relegated to the background for the most part, in a manner which is appropriate to the objective outlines of the tale and to its setting toward the close of the so-called "latency period" of the young hero's life.

The figure of Seibei himself is sketched with an ironic detachment seldom found in Shiga's treatment of his alter ego, so that the central image of the gourd looms very large on the surface of the work. And what a wonderful, all-purpose image it is! Hereafter in Shiga's works and in the life of his hero, the gourd will recur as an object—it is almost a character in itself—which carries with it a wealth of associations and comes to stand for all that is full and simple in art, nature and human life alike.

In *Seibei to hyōtan* the boy's life centers entirely on his fascination with gourds—those curious fruits that grow on vines yet look like primitive artifacts. He seems so deeply under their spell that, as Kobayashi Hideo has suggested, we can imagine him "tracing the pattern of their cracks" as he runs home to fetch some money.[7] Indeed, much later in his life, during a journey through the Inland Sea, the Shiga hero is reminded of the cracks on a gourd's shell by the "beautiful, strong lines" of the island peaks and marvels at the "grand design" that exists in nature (5:177).

Once they have been plucked from their natural state, gourds need only be slightly touched up by human hands (in Japan they are hollowed out, treated with sake and hung out to dry) and they become the simplest kind of art object. As such, they will serve as a prime example of the mature hero's æsthetic ideal: a subdued and spare kind of beauty that reflects an essential unity of the natural and human worlds.

The sexual symbolism of gourds is strongly suggested by Seibei's fetishistic attachment to them, the constant fondling and polishing. Yet nowhere in Shiga's works is the gourd established as pertaining specifically to one sex or the other. In one context where it occurs, we shall note that it has been attached to a woman; elsewhere it is clearly phallic (the "well-formed penis, no longer than a half-inch gourd" of the rescued boy in *Dekigoto*); but the variety of shapes that nature gives to gourds would itself indicate a bisexual or pansexual symbolism.

Seen in this light, a conventional psychoanalytic interpretation of the father's destruction of his son's prized possessions becomes almost inescapable. Now on the threshold of adolescence, the young hero experiences in the final scene a sudden, momentary return of the castration complex, to invoke its cumbersome name—fears which are objectified in the narrative through the father's smashing of the gourds.

According to the psychoanalysts, the original onslaught of this complex brings to an end the first act of that oedipal drama which forms the core of their view of human development, to be followed (after the "latency period") by a renewed struggle inside the family circle and, greatly intensified, within the young man's mind. We shall see in the second act of the Shiga hero's life drama that an inner struggle involving his shifting relations to father, mother, grandparents, and their substitutes (or his selective childhood memory of them) consumes much of his psychic energy, driving him at times into deep depression, disturbing fantasies and recurring nightmares.

In contrast to the introspective gloom and stark terror which often characterize the second, adolescent stage of the hero's development, *Seibei to hyōtan* is suffused by a gentle humor: the "redeeming human specialty," Erikson has called it, which enables a few gifted minds "at rare moments to play with and to reflect fearlessly on the strange customs . . . by which man must find self-realization."[8] If there is any single quality that is sorely lacking in the Shiga hero's subsequent portrayal, it is this fearless disposition to play with serious matters which Erikson has admired, as Freud before him considered humor to be "fine and elevating," "the triumph of narcissism" and "the ego's victorious assertion of its own invulnerability."[9]

In another short story, *Manazuru* (1920; translated below), we encounter the hero once again on the eve of his adolescence. As in *Seibei to hyōtan,* the story's events are cast in the clear light of a detached sketch and set against the background of a serene seascape (here it is the Izu Peninsula). The narrative begins: "The sun had gone down, leaving the world in bluish shadows. A boy of twelve or thirteen was walking down the high road that overlooked the deep sea, leading his younger brother by the hand. The boy's look was pensive. He was thinking very hard about love, although the word itself meant nothing to him" (3:129). He has, we are told, at least heard the word. Recently one of his teachers hailed him after school and, addressing himself as much to a woman companion as to the boy, taunted him gently with the poem: "My love is like a skiff / Cast adrift on fathomless seas / No safe harbor bids me rest / I am at the mercy of the waves."

"The boy," as he is called throughout, is now on his way back to his village from a neighboring town where he has spent the day with his brother. We learn of the day's events in a long flashback—a device often adopted by Shiga and several other modern Japanese writers, perhaps for the oblique perspectives which it affords. Having received a small sum of money from their father, the boy and his brother set off to buy some geta. But before they reach their destination, the boy discovers a splendid sailor's hat in a display window and buys it on the spot, although it requires all the money he has been given—and even though he has cause, the narrative states, to fear the reaction of his short-tempered father.

Later, the boy is on his way to pay his respects at a shrine to Ninomiya Sontoku when a troupe of minstrels comes clattering down the street. The boy is bewitched by the grotesque beauty of one of the minstrel women. "White with paint and powder from forehead to fingertips," she accompanies her shrill song on a "moon-shaped lute." The boy trails about after the troupe for the rest of the day, pulling his brother along by the hand. At one point he is forced to wait outside a restaurant where they have entered, and must brave the accusing looks which a young female member of the troupe casts his way.

That evening, on the road that leads back to the village, he can still hear the rustle of the lute and the woman's shrill voice in the sound of the waves washing against the rocks below. Her vigorous, erotic dancing and miming is recalled in detail. When a train passes by close to the road, his younger brother announces that he has seen the minstrels in one of the coaches. This provokes a vivid fantasy in which the boy imagines that the train goes off the track on a curve some distance ahead, throwing the minstrel woman to the side of the road.

Carrying his weary brother on his back, the boy struggles on under his heavy load until he has rounded the bend where, in his fantasy, the train was to have derailed. He is astonished to see a woman approaching through the darkness, holding out a lantern before her. But it proves to be only his mother. She takes the younger brother in her arms and tries to comfort the complaints that he has begun to utter upon awaking to find her. The older boy suddenly has an idea:

> He took off the sailor's hat and put it on his brother's head.
> "Hush up," he said. "You can have it for keeps."
> At the moment, he did not particularly mind parting with his new hat (3:134).

"The hat has been adequately established as a symbol of the genital organ, most frequently male, through analyses of the dreams...of young people or dreams occurring during the period of youth which concern the subject of castration."[10] So states Freud, with a certain Teutonic solemnity (one wonders if he did not sometimes have a twinkle in his eye when he was writing such things).

As in the case of Seibei's gourds, the bright surface of the work itself should be sufficient to convey in an intuitive fashion the "Freudian" overtones of the central image of the hat, which are here made explicit only for the purposes of the discussion. We are, of course, more or less aware that in traditional cultures, as until recently, at least, in our own, the wearing of various kinds of hats and caps has not only served as an emblem of specific professions and social classes, but has in general functioned as an outward sign of maturity or as a token of aspirations toward this identity.

In *Manazuru,* the symbolism (if such it must be called) of the boy's new hat is rendered a fortiori by his choice of a sailor's hat. The narrative comments that he has long been attracted to this most virile of callings, and that he has an uncle in the navy who has always encouraged him to be a sailor when he grows up. The uncle is sketched as a hearty, generous sort of man, in contrast to the "short-tempered" and (with his practical New Year's gift of a little money for geta) rather stingy father. There is likewise an implied contrast between the hero, who takes his first tentative steps into manhood in the course of the story, and the younger brother, who is still a mere infant in the boy's eyes. A final pair of contrasting figures is represented by the woman with the "moon-shaped" lute, the object of the boy's vague desire, and the other female minstrel, the young girl who tries to chase him away with threatening looks.

As a complement to the hat, the image of the lute suggests the mysteries which the woman holds for the boy. Originally a Chinese instrument, it is well-suited to her exotic charms. Both the rounded, concave shape of the lute and its low, resonant sound (a basso continuo for the woman's shrill song) contribute to the pervasive impression she produces on him. He even hears her in the waves! There is naturally some ambivalence in the twelve-year-old hero's attitude toward the woman, which is reflected indirectly in his envy of the hostile young girl—presumably the woman's daughter. And clearly there is an echo of the Shiga hero's earlier memory of his grandfather's mistress in the minstrel woman's description: the "thick paint and powder," her "glistening white arms," which she throws up in the air while she sings. Mysterious woman, prospective lover, substitute mother—she is perhaps some of all of these in the boy's mind.

But as he retraces his steps down the dark road that leads homeward, the day's events begin to blur. Then the glimpse of the minstrels which his brother claims to have had as the train passed by evokes the vivid fantasy in which he sees the woman emerging from the darkness at the side of the road. Yet, when he reaches the imagined point of encounter, it is only his mother who awaits him. Exasperated by his brother's tantrum and still afraid, no doubt, of his father's anger, the boy gives up his manly sailor's hat to the bawling child. He does not mind parting with it, we are told, at least for the moment.

ADOLESCENCE

Inasmuch as a thoroughgoing love of self serves as the
foundation of all Shiga's major works, his is essentially
an adolescent literature. . . . I consider him a writer
who has given expression to his adolescence through
his novels but has failed to express his maturity.
                                        —Nakamura Mitsuo

The neurotic is the victim of a soul struggle which
takes place in the amphitheatre of the mind. It is a
Narcissistic struggle with the self, and whichever way
the issue turns it is he himself who is the victim.
It is a sacrificial struggle waged by our highest types. . . .
                        —Henry Miller, *The Cosmological Eye*

THERE IS SOME TRUTH in Nakamura's sweeping evaluation of Shiga's
works, the bulk of which indeed center rather narrowly on a single
adolescent character—his inner life and the immediate reality of family, a small circle of friends, and various women toward whom he
remains radically ambivalent throughout much of his youth. But the
ruling passion in the portraits that we have of the Shiga hero at this
period of his life is as much self-hate as it is "thoroughgoing love of
self." Through an alternation between vividly described dreams,
memories and fantasies within the hero's private world, followed by
impulsive action in the outside world (though we are not always sure
on what plane such action takes place), these narratives give a profoundly realistic impression of a young man often divided against
himself.

Aru asa (One Morning, 1908), Shiga's first published work, is also
where we first encounter the Shiga hero as a young man. Here,
although he is called Shintaro, it may be conceded that he is but a thin
disguise for his author. This slight story represents Japanese personal
fiction *(shishōsetsu)* at its most limited. Only a few pages long, it
describes in seemingly pointless detail a painful scene in which the
adolescent hero clings stubbornly to his bed one morning while his
grandmother, with whom he shares the room, pleads with him to get

up. It is the anniversary of his grandfather's death; the priest is about to arrive for the memorial observance; and the hero has earlier promised his doting grandmother that he would be dressed and ready by the appointed time—in spite of which he stays in bed. At length, after several childishly cruel retorts to her pleas, he gets up. As he is putting away the bedding he begins, unaccountably, to cry.

Is it, we wonder, a sudden grief for his dead grandfather that has elicited his tears? Remorse for his treatment of his grandmother? Or perhaps he has been upset by a brief reference to his father that she makes at one point, provoking at first a particularly ill-tempered outburst on the hero's part. Most of those who read *Aru asa* when it was first published in *Shirakaba* did not, presumably, make much sense of it. Indeed, they could not, without some "inside" knowledge of the author's life and personality on which they might draw to complete the story. And so they may well have felt justified in not, finally, caring too much what it is that makes the hero cry.

If at the time of its initial publication *Aru asa* clearly deserved such a reaction from the reader, Shiga has since provided a suitably wide frame of reference in which to make some sense out of this and several similar stories. One need not consider *Aru asa* a polished work of literature in itself, which it obviously is not, nor fall back on some extraneous knowledge of its author, to recognize in it a partially coherent, though very fragmentary, presentation of the hero and *his* private world. These some readers will have come in time to know quite intimately, while, as I have suggested, they themselves must do the work of reconstruction.

The only features of this story that are worth noting here are the particular feelings or moods through which the hero passes in the course of the brief narrative and the introduction (or, from our point of view, the reintroduction) of characters other than the hero. His progression from a state of somewhat irritable passivity, through uncontrolled anger, to sudden sorrow and, in the end, a faintly smiling resignation not only describes a certainly volatility, which is no doubt common enough among adolescents in general; it also reveals in a more specific manner what might be called the emotional dynamics of the Shiga hero's youth. With the addition of two strong emotions which are missing here, fear and desire, these are the feelings that, to varying degrees of intensity, prevail throughout the narratives of this "period."

The indulgent grandmother reminds us of the comforting older woman who has filled an important role in the child hero's life, while the several allusions to his late grandfather are in a real sense our first introduction to a benevolent figure (in contrast to the evil old man evoked in *An'ya kōro*'s prologue) who will hereafter appear from time to time, both in the flesh and as a reassuring memory. Finally, the single, brief mention of the father produces an almost violent effect upon the hero that prefigures a renewal on a far wider front of the recurring conflict which we have already seen in his childhood.

Ōtsu Jun'kichi (1912), the first short novel of the so-called trilogy, provides a more extended preface to this phase of the Shiga hero's life. Like *Aru asa,* this work is decidedly juvenile: "shallow and sentimental," Masamune Hahuchō once called it.[1] Yet it recapitulates the strong theme of the hero's fear and mistrust of his father, one of the two most pervasive themes in his adolescent scenario, and more than any other work (except for the brief, openly confessional *Sōba no tame*), it fleshes out the figure of his grandmother. Finally, it introduces a few preoccupations outside of the "emotional tangles of the family situation," which include an unsteady faith in Christianity and an initially cautious curiosity about women.

The narrator-hero indicates that he has been attracted to the foreign religion less by the doctrine than by the charisma of his minister ("U"), which is concentrated in the man's face ("a dark complexion, large features—altogether forbidding at first glance, yet truly very appealing"; 2:242). Early in the narrative he explains that the impasse in his life at which he has recently arrived results from a contradiction between certain tenets of his adopted faith and various inner needs, some of them quite specific and urgent, others still vague and ill-defined.

He has been especially troubled by the stern commandments against sexual incontinence which, as the minister has proudly pointed out to his followers, are thoroughly original with Christianity. Until his conversion, the hero tells us, he has "freely practiced" homosexual love with his friends. But he has since abandoned the love of boys and, in obedience to St. Paul's dire warnings, has "kept apart" from women. Indeed, he has almost come to embrace that puritanical revision of early Christian teachings which may be traced in part to Pauline orthodoxy, namely, a rejection of the notion that men will be resurrected in the flesh, not merely as disembodied souls. Rather pathetically, the hero confesses to some of his fellow Christians that if, nevertheless, there must be a resurrection of the body as well, he would prefer to be reborn in paradise only from the neck up.

Of late, however, he has developed healthy doubts about this goal of self-mutilation which latter-day Christianity has suggested to him, while he recognizes the difficulties that he will face in attempting to fulfill his repressed needs: "I have grown stubborn and peculiar. I am repelled by my own perversity and sometimes feel that I would like to be a freer sort of man. But I know that, as I am now, it will take a long time and much experience before I can change my faith and satisfy my desires" (2:241).

Throughout the novel's first section we are given the general impression that the hero, now in his early twenties, cannot make up his mind about anything. In a pattern which is common to the three novels of the trilogy and the first part of *An'ya kōro* alike, only toward the end of the narrative does he gather up his resolution and take some action to change the course of his stagnated life. But in *Ōtsu Jun'kichi*, the decision so long in the making is not very resolute. It takes the form of a somewhat equivocal proposal of marriage which the hero extends to a family maid, after he has seduced her (the seduction itself is his most decisive action). We shall see this affair with a family maid later repeated in other stories, although elsewhere it is the woman who assumes the aggressive role.

The hero's proposal results in a direct confrontation with his disapproving family, represented by his father and grandmother. (Both here and in several other stories, his stepmother figures as a sympathetic but minor character: it is clear that she cannot take the place of the lost mother.) The narrative focuses for the most part on the hero's relations with his grandmother and, indirectly, those with his father—far more closely than on his affair with the maid. The reader may conclude that the affair is only an immediate pretext for a new outbreak of longstanding conflicts.

The hero recalls life with his grandmother as having been a constant battle of wills, a mixture of love and scorn, from the early years of his childhood. Since that time, she alone has always seen to his needs, and even now, "the peculiar fragrance of her body" brings back to him the nights in the past when he would fall asleep clasped in her arms. He is currently attending college but is never very explicit about his activities. Though he alludes vaguely to grandiose plans for the future, his grandmother remains skeptical. In an amusing scene (one of the few to be found in the somber trilogy) he says to her haughtily, "Have you any idea what I do, what I think about?" "Yes, I know," she replies. "You sleep late in the morning and skip classes all the time. You meet with your friends somewhere and talk about plays and storytellers—that's what you're up to!"

The proud, strong-willed woman is utterly opposed to the prospect of her grandson marrying a servant. After a quarrel in which he refuses to renounce his intentions, the grandmother leaves him with a veiled threat of suicide and goes out toward the storehouse where the swords are kept. All but sure that she is bluffing, he is nonetheless relieved when she is persuaded to emerge from her hiding place.

Throughout the family crisis brought about by the hero's proposal, which is meaningless in the traditional scheme of things without parental consent, the father remains ominously in the background, sending out autocratic directives from time to time that indicate his total disapproval. Annoyed and uneasy, the hero observes that his father "has not shown his face once." Eventually the maid is sent back to her country home under cover of night—by his father's orders, he is convinced. The hero is enraged. He vents his frustration and anger in a tantrum that proves mildly destructive to his room. (Yet the reader may note with some surprise that afterward he sums up his contempt for his father's conduct by declaring it "in bad taste.")

The novel ends with the same rapid transition from rage to tears and a final resignation that we have seen in *Aru asa*. The hero writes a letter to a friend in which he sadly acknowledges that he is "not the sort of human being who can be contented all alone." He has a few friends, of course, besides the maid. "And there is one other I would like to include," he adds. "My grandmother" (2:319).

In several shorter works which belong to this youthful period (both of Shiga's career and his alter ego's life), the specific nature of the vague needs and the "peculiarity" that the hero has observed in himself emerge in a clearer light. His psychological anatomy is revealed in a fragmentary manner and on various planes of reality, all of them remote from the humdrum domestic world of *Ōtsu Jun'kichi*. Like *Seibei to hyōtan* and *Manazuru*, these works may be considered realistic fantasies, either partially or wholly objectified "daydreams."

The anger and frustration which have so far ended in an impotent rage, whose origins we may suspect but are not told in *Aru asa* and *Ōtsu Jun'kichi*, here reach proportions that threaten to consume the hero. But they are instead deflected outward onto others, and the hero, now purged of his destructive impulses, is often permitted a special immunity.

Nigotta atama (Dementia, 1910) is one of these realistic fantasies, though in this instance an only partly convincing mélange of sexual aggression, murder, and insanity. As in *Ōtsu Jun'kichi*, the hero enters into an affair with an older woman. Named Onatsu, she is described as a relation of his mother, and it is clearly she who instigates the relationship. At the outset of the narrative he is once again engaged in somewhat callow musings on Christianity and its condemnation of nearly all forms of sexual gratification. But in the past, we are told, he has taken these matters quite seriously. He has even applied lighted matches to his crotch (and has contemplated using a knife) at moments of extreme desire.

Then he recalls the scene of his seduction:

> Onatsu suddenly wrapped her fleshy arm around my neck and pulled me toward her. As we lay together on the mats my mind worked coldly and sharply. All the while, I let her do what she would with my body and received her kisses.
>
> It was my first time with a woman; but before I encountered Christianity, I had learned a good deal about love from men. (1:216)

In the self-recriminations that follow on the hero's involvement with his mother's relative—which he does not, however, abandon—the notion of wholly individual and private "problems" beyond all conventional morality is introduced, an idea which comes to form the cornerstone of the Shiga hero's personal moral scheme. At this stage, he is in retrospect far from sure that he has been justified in pursuing his own instincts alone. "My despair," he comments, "has been the kind that serves to excuse and to explain away the problems one cannot face. Everything is exaggerated until one can only throw up one's hands 'in despair.' And so one's problems are placed outside the realms of religion, morality, society, and family" (1:220). Yet, in several critical situations which we shall observe later, the Shiga hero finally places full trust only in the dictates of his innermost urges, disregarding all other sources of moral direction.

The most striking sequence in this curious early work takes place toward the end of the narrative. The hero and his seducer abscond from Tokyo and wander about the country for a year or so. In time they become emotionally exhausted and filled with mutual mistrust. While they are staying in a small resort town, a violent scene erupts in which the woman all but assaults the hero, as appears to be her habit, and he in turn gives her a savage beating:

> Onatsu suddenly rose up from her bed and threw herself on top of me. She had done this often enough since she began to lose control of herself. But for the first time I was frightened by her violence. I was convinced that she meant to kill me.

When I tried to get up she pressed me backwards with a kiss. I
told myself that I was exaggerating—why should she want to
kill me? Yet my anxiety quickly grew to terror.

As I lay there, motionless, she began sucking on my tongue.
I was sure that she would bite me. Unable to bear it for
another moment, I tried to push her away, but she pinned me
down with her heavy body and sucked all the harder at my
mouth. I was desperate now. Placing my hand on her face, I
pushed up with all my might. The force of the thrust caused
her to bite down on my tongue.

It was not until her moans and shrieks brought me back to
my senses that I realized I had been beating her blindly about
the face. Blood was streaming from her nose. Onatsu fell
strangely silent as she began to wipe her face with tissue.
(1:235)

Shortly afterward, while in a dreamlike, somnambulent state, he
murders Onatsu—this woman who has defiled him and would muti-
late his tongue (as in his traumatic childhood memories his mother had
cruelly "assaulted" him there with a stick of candy). Or rather, when
he awakes one morning to find his clothes bloodied and his memory of
the previous night almost blank, he gradually concludes that he must
have killed her. But he still has no clear recollections of the circumstances. (The facts of the matter are left in question, as we learn at the
end of the story only that he has subsequently been committed to an
insane asylum.)

The hero's unsuccessful attempts to recall the previous day's events
revolve around a sharp steel awl which he remembers having seen
"glinting coldly in the sunlight." It was out in the garden, where a
tatami maker was at work mending the inn's mats. "After the barren,
senseless existence I had been leading," the hero tells us, "I wanted to
live a life full of the wonderful sensation which the long, sharp awl
gave me—gleaming in the sun as it cut through the thick mats with a
slight crackling sound" (1:181).

This is the first appearance of a vivid image which recurs in other,
more skillfully executed stories that treat of this phase of the Shiga
hero's inner development. Knives and razors, sharp objects of cold
steel, play an almost æsthetic role in a few of these stories, in addition
to furnishing an instrument with which the hero may realize the
powerful aggressive impulses that well up inside him at unpredictable
moments. And, as mentioned above, we have been presented with an
idea (or a strong "feeling") which becomes a mainstay of the hero's
private morality: the proposition that when a man commits what the

world calls a crime out of deep-rooted and largely unconscious motives, there can be no guilt and there should be no punishment.

While the proposition is articulated in an unusually lucid, formal fashion in *Han no hanzai* (Han's Crime, 1913), the most brilliant crystallization of the cold steel image and its psychological counterpart, the blind aggressive instinct, occurs in a short story entitled *Kamisori* (The Razor, 1910; translated below). In contrast to the rambling first-person narrative of *Nigotta atama,* which was written at about the same time, *Kamisori* is succinctly and anonymously told. It is also one of those relatively rare works in which the familiar figure of the Shiga hero does not appear in any clearly recognizable form. I would suggest that here he may be seen in both the aggressor and the victim, if anywhere. But as the title indicates, this brief tale focuses in a microscopic manner on one central image and on the involuntary act for which it becomes the instrument. The characters themselves are by comparison unimportant.

A highly accomplished barber by the name of Yoshisaburo lies sick in bed at a particularly busy time of year. We learn that he has recently had to dismiss his more able assistants, who had fallen into dissolute ways, and must now make do with incompetent apprentices. Much of the narrative is devoted to building up an impression of the annoyance that Yoshisaburo feels as he hears the customers come and go and imagines to himself the clumsy performance of his employees. Late in the evening, a razor which was to have been sharpened for an important patron is returned with the complaint that it is still too dull. In spite of his high fever and his frayed nerves, Yoshisaburo gets up and applies the razor to a leather strap.

When he has finished the job and is about to return to bed, a coarse-looking young man enters the shop and asks for a shave. Ignoring the strong objections of his wife, Yoshisaburo picks up the razor and starts to work on the young man's swarthy face. The fatigued barber struggles over the task with mounting irritation. He comes to feel a visceral loathing for his ungainly customer, who, after boasting of a rendezvous that he has arranged for that night, promptly falls asleep.

Suddenly the razor nicks the young man's throat. Never before has Yoshisaburo so much as scratched a customer. He watches spellbound as the blood begins to ooze out. Then, razor in hand, he feels himself being "drawn into" the thin cut:

> He changed his grip so that the tip pointed downward and in
> one swift thrust plunged the razor into the young man's

throat. It penetrated the length of the blade up to the handle. The young man did not move a muscle.

Presently the blood came gushing out from the deep wound. The young man's face rapidly turned an ashen hue.

Yoshisaburo sank into the adjacent chair as though in a faint. All the tension drained out of him. At the same time, the fatigue that he had felt before returned with a vengeance. With his eyes tightly shut, his body limp and motionless, he too looked dead. Even the night grew still as death. Nothing moved. The world had fallen into a deep slumber. Only the mirrors looking down on three sides of the room reflected this scene in their cold, impassive gaze. (1:192)

There is a chilling clarity in this final tableau of triumphant death, frozen as though forever in the barbershop's mirrors. But there is also some ambiguity about the act and its outcome. Are we to infer from the sudden drain of all Yoshisaburo's vitality after the deed is done that he has in a sense killed himself as well? The story could be interpreted in this way, whether the barber's "death" were considered to be mainly psychological or attributed more literally to a swift retribution which one might read into the tale's ending.

Yet there is an equally strong implication that the act justifies itself and therefore exonerates Yoshisaburo. On the one hand, the victim has been depicted in a few deft strokes as an utterly worthless creature; he is dissolute—like the barber's former assistants, though without any of their redeeming features. From Yoshisaburo's fastidious point of view (the only one that we have here, except for the reflected view in the mirror) this fellow deserves his fate, of which he himself is merely an agent. But apart from such hypothetical moralizing, the narrative itself would finally suggest that the murder is made inevitable by the innermost workings of the barber's mind, which culminate in the irresistible impulse that comes over him as he stands in front of the loathsome youth.

Gratification of these powerful urges is here placed (as it has some-times seemed to the hero of *Nigotta atama*) "beyond the realms of religions, morality, society and family." And so the mirror simply contemplates the scene and, however cold its gaze, does not condemn.

In contrast to what we find in the slice-of-life narratives of "naturalist" epigones, whether Western or Japanese, Shiga's stories are seldom devoted to a merely realistic, exterior description of blind instincts and compulsive drives, although his hero is richly endowed with them. Nor, despite the rather unsubtle insinuations of some of his more outspoken critics, does the author appear to be glorifying his own instincts through those of his alter ego. By this point in our cursory reconstruction of the Shiga hero's life it should be clear that he is more often shown to be victimized by unconscious impulses, both his own and those of others, than he is to revel in them.

We have seen in *Nigotta atama* that the hero remains ambivalent toward the aggressive forces within himself and is driven temporarily insane by their invasion of his consciousness. Similarly, even with the more detached and objective treatment of the characters in *Kamisori* it is possible to recognize traits of the recurring central figure in the barber, with his fastidiousness and his irritability, as well as in the dissolute youth, who is murdered (or "repressed") for offending the barber's inner sense of propriety.[2]

Before turning to *Han no hanzai,* which contains a clear-cut statement of the Shiga hero's "theory of instincts" (rather, his simple affirmation of them), we may briefly consider two further works that are in the general nature of adolescent fantasy: *Araginu* (1908), an early short story, and the somewhat longer *Ko o nusumu hanashi* (The Kidnaping, 1914; translated below).

Araginu is perhaps Shiga's only excursion into a type of modern fable which has become almost a subgenre in the literature through the contributions of various authors, most notably, those of Akutagawa Ryūnosuke. But unlike Akutagawa's cleverly contrived historical fables, with their inevitable moral lurking just below the surface, Shiga's tale does not ostensibly seek to elucidate anything. Set in the timeless realm of pastoral mythology (Shiga tells us that the initial inspiration owes to a German illustration of a scene from Greek mythology; 7:4), *Araginu* presents us with a miniature version of what Jung has described his "visionary" works to be: "a grimly ridiculous sample of the eternal chaos, . . . a disturbing vision of monstrous and meaningless happenings."[3]

"Long ago," the fable begins, "a beautiful goddess dwelt upon a certain mountain. She was not only the goddess of beauty and love, but of jealousy as well. At the first pangs of love, all the young men who lived within sight of her peak, even those who could only glimpse it on clear days, would ask her blessing for their courtship" (1:69). But as she is also the goddess of jealousy, no sooner do the lovers find happiness together through her favor than she turns against them and plunges them into despair and destruction. The old men of the region are sympathetic to the plight of the young lovers but can do nothing to prevail against the jealous wrath of the goddess.

The hero (he is, of course, a truly mythological figure here) makes his appearance: a handsome cowherd by the name of "Adoni" (presumably a Japanese rendering of Adonis). As a boy, he has faithfully honored the goddess with constant offerings of flowers. But when he reaches young manhood he falls in love with a weaving girl called Araginu (Arachne?), who is described as a few years his senior, and he soon begins to neglect his attentions to the goddess. She sends one of her informers down to the village to discover the cause of Adoni's defection and is much chagrined to hear of his new love.

The goddess further learns that his union with Araginu will be consummated as soon as the maiden has finished weaving a splendid mantle in which the lovers intend to wrap themselves each night, to ward off all harm and temptation. She is determined to disrupt Araginu's weaving before the charmed mantle is completed. Araginu, in her eagerness to be done with the labor of love, sits at her loom day and night, constantly passing the shuttle back and forth through the fine threads.

In the still of the night she begins to hear a "low, hoarse voice"—it seems to be a man's—muttering at her in threatening tones. Eventually she catches the drift of the ominous words. If she does not abandon her weaving, they say, she will be transformed into a spider. Yet Araginu perseveres in her task, in the hope of finishing with it before ill fate befalls her.

One day, an old uncle, who has earlier cautioned Araginu to keep her love secret, comes to call on her and finds the room empty, except for an oddly woven length of fabric. It is gorgeously embroidered with brightly colored birds and flowers that cover over half of the cloth. But toward the unfinished edge, the beautiful mantle is sullied by a "foul color" which begins to show in the fabric. Then the uncle discovers a trail of thread that leads out from the house and up toward the mountain. He follows it up the slope until he comes to a shrine which has been erected to the goddess at the mouth of the cave. "In front of the mountain shrine he found shreds of Araginu's clothes scattered about as though they had been torn from her body. The thread trailed onward into the cave. When he reached the entrance, all he could see of Araginu was a large pair of terrible eyes looking out at him from the murky depths of the cave. After he took a few more steps he saw an enormous spider web stretched before her, filling the entire passageway. As if she were still at her weaving, Araginu clutched a threadless shuttle in her hand and moved her arm back and forth across an imaginary loom. With her great, vacant eyes, her spindly arms and legs, and besmirched, lackluster skin, she now appeared very like a spider" (1:75).

Although this strange fable has been ignored by most Japanese critics, perhaps because it seems so far removed from the true-to-life myth of the author-hero which they prefer to pursue, it can surely be seen as a "vision" from the Shiga hero's inner world that has been cast within a mythic or archetypal framework. Once again we encounter the opposing figures of the two older women, one of them thoroughly tender and loving, the other a "goddess" of both love and cruel jealousy. The two women engage in an unequal contest for the hero, "Adoni," while he—more like Narcissus than Adonis, we may conclude—remains aloof from the struggle. In contrast to *Nigotta atama*, where the hero retaliates against his menacing seductress by succumbing to a murderous impulse, Adoni passively allows the jealous goddess to transform his love into a spider.

Various psychoanalytic interpretations of this rare venture by Shiga into modern myth could no doubt be made in a rather schematic fashion. For example, Erikson's discussion of the view of adult sex formed by children at the oedipal stage would suggest that the dominant image of Araginu possesses a certain universality. "The child seems to interpret the sex acts of his elders as intrusive on the part of the male," Erikson states, "and incorporative *in a spidery way* on the part of the female; and this especially where darkness surrounds adult sex life" (italics mine).[4] One would perhaps want to emphasize the tension between positive and negative aspects of the female archetype ("anima") which, according to Jung, exists within men's minds; or, similarly, the conflicting influence of the "oedipal" mother images of the Freudians.[5] And one might also mention the narcissistic nature of the hero's charmed existence and the auto-erotic implications of the labor of love lavished upon him by the "weaving girl" at her loom.

Yet the fable is sufficiently clear in the light of Shiga's intuitive depth psychology to compel recognition of certain obsessive memories from the past and continuing conflicts in the present which all but paralyze his hero as he approaches manhood.

Ko o nusumu hanashi exhibits a few of the best and several of the worst features of Shiga's writing combined in a single short story that is on the whole quite unsuccessful. As always, the style is even and measured throughout, and there are isolated lyrical passages which remind us of his fine short sketches, as well as some of the extended lyrical interludes in *An'ya kōro*. (A few passages have in fact been borrowed from *Ko o nusumu hanashi* and placed almost without alteration into the context of *An'ya kōro's* first part.) The plot contains both elements of more or less autobiographical material and incidents that are clearly in the nature of fantasy or "wish fulfillment," such as we have seen put to good use in earlier stories.

But here the manifest content of the fantasy, in which the hero kidnaps a young girl and holds her captive for several days, clearly derives from an episode in Saikaku's *Shōkoku hanashi* entitled "Otoko Jizō" (the sixth story in the second chapter). Inevitably, this invites a comparison between Shiga's "modern," subjective treatment of the incident, which has been transposed, so to speak, into his hero's life, and Saikaku's garrulous, anecdotal approach to his cheerful psychopath.

The comparison is not likely to prove favorable to *Ko o nusumu hanashi*. In the Saikaku story, after the culprit is finally caught (having abducted and, in contrast to Shiga's hero, also molested "several hundred" children), he confesses to the authorities, "Whenever I see these little girls I can't resist. So I take them home for a few days and love them, then I send them back to their parents."[6] As both Shiga and his hero elsewhere observe of other Saikaku stories, there is something quite compelling about the dispatch with which the acts are carried out, however objectionable one may find them. During this period of crisis in his life, the Shiga hero often strives, as we have seen, for a similarly bold realization of his inner promptings. If *Ko o nusumu hanashi* is a failure as a short story, it throws further light on his attempts to find a way out of his adolescent impasse.

It begins with a bitter quarrel between the hero and his father. The father is brutally frank in his expressions of contempt for his son. He wonders aloud what sin he could have committed to deserve such offspring—this "lazy punk" who has absorbed "all the evils of the modern world." It is clear that, as in *Aru asa,* the reader is assumed to know about the conflict with the father and to commiserate with the hero. As if to elicit this sympathy, the narrator-hero becomes almost mawkishly sentimental when he describes his futile efforts to return his father's insults (he is instead reduced to tears) and his subsequent flight from home that takes him to a small port on the Inland Sea coast.

This is the first of several journeys on which the hero embarks in the course of the life history that Shiga's works have presented to us. There will be a later occasion to speculate on the significance of these voluntary exiles that the hero imposes on himself. Here we need only note that he initially experiences a sense of new-found freedom in the quiet, verdant surroundings of the provincial town; but he is soon betrayed by his own troubled consciousness and ends up faced with a choice between suicide and a form of madness.

In *Ko o nusumu hanashi* the reader encounters that problem of self-expression which elsewhere the Shiga hero himself remarks upon, as cited in the introduction. ("He tried to describe his recent state of mind . . . but he came to realize that he did not know how to write about such things.") The narrator of this story is able to describe in detail the arrangement of his small cottage, the gentle seascape that he contemplates from time to time, and the exhilaration he feels when he sets to work on a long novel which he has planned. (This is the first story where we are told that the hero is a writer.) The narrator states that his thoughts were so clear then that he felt as though he could "see" them before his eyes. But as he quickly falls into a state of depression and anxiety that force him to abandon his work and wander about aimlessly in search of distraction, the reasons for his sudden reversal are not at all clear to the reader.

Unlike the lucid thoughts that have seemed to stand out "before his eyes" while he works, which we imagine to be floating on the surface of his consciousness, the sources of his depression and his nameless fears no doubt lie on a deeper level to which he cannot penetrate directly. Such deep-seated feelings are not, then, described in detail. Either he alludes to them vaguely, through their outward ("psychosomatic") manifestation in fatigue and various aches and pains; or, in a more revealing fashion, they are evoked through vivid visual images observed in the outside world ("objective correlatives") and are rendered still more real and specific in the shapes that they assume in dreams. (In a later novel, *Wakai*, the hero will speak of the "great clarity" of his dreams, which suggests the important role that these projections of the unconscious play in his portrayal.)

The narrative treatment in this story, as in other works, may often remind us of the psychoanalytic techniques of free association, dream interpretation, and, where the emphasis is on pure visualization, "ink blot" tests—except that there is, of course, no interpretation, analysis or evaluation as such.

We notice that the particular objects which frighten the hero in *Ko o nusumu hanashi* are in some instances the same as those which, at an earlier or later stage of life, he finds wonderfully reassuring: various insects that startle him here (crickets and centipedes), the "rough bark" of an ancient tree that "attacks" his frayed nerves, and, although it is only conjured up in a nightmare, the image of the gourd which, as we have seen, is usually vital and beautiful. It is as if his innermost world has become seriously deranged and all of its intuitive values distorted, or even inverted.

The nightmare occurs early in the narrative and foreshadows the story's main events.

> A twelve-year-old girl, her face splotched like a gourd's skin before it has been touched up, sits on the porch of a small shrine in the shadow of a leafy tree. She is staring at me with an eerie smile. . . . She comes directly toward me. As she draws closer she grows larger and larger until she seems about to bump into my nose. All of a sudden I am overcome with horror. When she is close enough to touch me, abruptly she looks down at the ground. Her short hair, coarse and stiff like a straw bag, flops over as she lowers her head. I cannot see her face, but through the mass of tangled hair I catch a glimpse of an unnaturally red underlip drooping down as though she had her tongue out. She is no longer a girl but an aging hag of fifty or so. (2:102–3)

Once more we are confronted with a threatening female figure, here in a truly frightening form. In the brief montage where she rapidly transforms herself into an obscene old hag, the first "frame" has the quality of an idyllic scene that has just begun to go wrong. The gourd to which her face is likened, the small shrine underneath a leafy tree, the smiling, nubile girl herself—these are all images that, in a slightly altered aspect, would no doubt have the most pleasant connotations for the Shiga hero. The sexual details on which the succeeding frames focus are almost uncomfortably blatant—not because they are sexual, of course, but because the eroticism seems so malignant and clearly reflects childish fears.

The apparition comes looming up against his nose (a common upward displacement of the phallus) and he is horrified; her tangled hair is coarse and stiff; her "unnaturally red underlip" droops down. By the end of the montage she has turned into another one of these evil older women (negative anima figures) who would defile, if they do not devour him.

When the hero of *Ko o nusumu hanashi* later attempts to act out in the real world the initially positive aspects of his dream by kidnaping a young girl, he does not appear to be sexually attracted to her. Rather, while there is no doubt some desire in his conflicting attitudes toward her, this "aim," as the psychoanalysts put it, is "inhibited." His original plan is to abduct a bright, pretty child whom he has glimpsed at the local playhouse and to bring her up as if she were his daughter.

In his early deliberations, the emphasis is on proving his resolution to himself, fulfilling his strong need for someone to love, and asserting the validity (or the "morality") of his own instincts.

But he never has another chance to see the girl around whom he has elaborated these fantasies. Instead, in an almost accidental manner he kidnaps an unkempt little "country brat," and his dream soon reverts to a nightmare. He is at first elated by the force of will with which he has realized his designs, even though he has had to settle for a different girl. But he shortly finds himself "slipping weakly into a conventional view" of what he has done. Although he tries to justify his act by telling himself that it has been the only way out of his nightmarish existence short of suicide, which he has earlier rejected resolutely, he succumbs in the end to self-recriminations and resentments of the whining child. By the time the police, accompanied by the child's mother, arrive to arrest him, he himself has become like a frightened child. As they approach his door, he arms himself with a kitchen knife. But he surrenders without any pretense of a struggle and submits in silence when the enraged mother begins to strike him.

In Nigotta atama and Ko o nusumu hanashi, the hero's obedience to his strongest instincts have led him into what the world adjudges criminal behavior: murder and kidnaping, for which he has been duly punished by confinement to an asylum in one case, prison (presumably) in the other (though not in an earlier draft of this story, where he is a little distressed to learn he will soon regain his freedom; 2:606). These narratives obviously lack both tight structural unity and ambitious formal designs. Like Ōtsu Jun'kichi, beyond the single climactic events reviewed in retrospect, they are held together only by the narrator-hero's selective memory and the meticulous style in which his monologue is delivered. Yet it should be granted that they also contain a convincing, if wholly interior, characterization of the solitary central figure. Partly in spite of ourselves, perhaps, we become thoroughly acclimated to the close atmosphere of the hero's inner world. This is, of course, one of the insidious aims of "modern subjective fiction."

As in the more objectively portrayed realm of Kamisori, the main character of Han no hanzai, a Chinese circus performer named Han, is not presented as a many-sided being and is not, perhaps, of prime importance in himself. It is rather an idea which is to be set forth in this carefully constructed piece. And so the author has deliberately conferred on his protagonist a theatrical profession and a somewhat exotic identity, as if to emphasize the allegorical overtones of his story.

The setting for Han no hanzai is a courtroom. In Western literature, at least, this has long been a common device in both novels and plays and has proved itself a dependable device for furthering the plot, as well as assuring a certain amount of drama. Akutagawa likewise employs a courtroom setting in his well-known *Yabu no naka* (In a Thicket, 1922)—a story which also bears a superficial thematic resemblance to Shiga's tale, though it is not so strong as to suggest a definite "inspiration." In any case, Akutagawa himself once remarked rather playfully that, despite certain similarities which might be detected between *Han no hanzai* and "a story by Maupassant entitled 'L'Artiste'" (a misattribution, according to Yasuoka), there is no possibility of Shiga's having been influenced by it.[7] "In the course of a circus performance, a young Chinese juggler by the name of Han severed his wife's carotid artery with one of the large knives employed in his act, causing great consternation among the spectators. The young woman died instantly. Han was arrested on the spot" (2:75). So the story begins, almost like a newspaper article. The narrative then proceeds in the formal tones of courtroom testimony. The judge briefly questions the head of the circus troupe, interrogates Han at some length, and arrives at a verdict.

According to the head of the troupe, Han's act is not too difficult for a practiced performer. It requires only a robust constitution, steady ("taut") nerves and "a kind of intuitive skill." The judge inquires into Han's relations with his wife and discovers that, although they were always on good terms with outsiders, they did not seem to get along well with each other. From Han's own testimony it becomes apparent that there had been no love between them and that he had, indeed, hated his wife, for quite specific reasons. She was once unfaithful to him through a brief affair she entered into with an old friend. When a child was later born from the adulterous union, she "accidentally" smothered it at her breasts. And still, Han tells the judge, the baby's death had not seemed to him "an adequate atonement" for her sin.

A rather narrow notion of sin and of the necessity for swift and sincere repentance by the sinner become ostensibly central themes in *An'ya kōro,* where again the "sin" is adultery and the sinner a woman. In *Han no hanzai* the focus is not on the transgression itself (nor is it in *An'ya kōro*) but on the attempts of the wronged husband to come to terms with the violent resentment which it has provoked in him. Han's testimony about his experience provides an articulate restatement of the Shiga hero's views on powerful inner urges which cannot be repressed.

What he says, in effect, is that he found himself faced with a choice between consciously directing his aggressive impulses outward against another (in this case his "treacherous" wife) or turning them inward against himself. In short, murder or suicide. Then he tried to reject both of these alternatives as "evading the real issue," supporting his argument partly with newly acquired religious scruples. (We learn that he has been studying Christianity, as in other novels the young hero is attracted to this religion for a while.)

But in the end, Han recalls, the suffering became unbearable. His attempt to deny his innermost instincts brought him to the brink of a kind of death. "I was being progressively poisoned by the revulsion and pain within me," he says, "I knew that when the poison had spread through my whole system I would die. I would survive only as one already dead." In the hero's eyes, then, this is the fate that awaits him should he continue to repress his vital unconscious needs: a living death.

And so he decided not to decide consciously but to allow his instincts to determine his actions. Han cannot honestly say whether he has deliberately killed his wife or not, for he has never knowingly made up his mind. Only at the last moment, just before he threw the knife that lodged in her throat, did he feel a strong presentiment of what was to happen, which he experienced as a sudden dizziness. "I felt as though I were in a faint," he remembers. "Then I went ahead and hurled the knife with all my strength, although I could not even see the target. It was as if I were aiming into thin air" (literally, "into the dark void"; 2:88). The judge tells Han to stand down. He picks up his pen. "Conscious of a strange elation stirring within him," he writes down the verdict: not guilty.

More than the precise words with which Han explains the tortured train of thought leading up to his "guiltless" crime, it is the clear metaphor that Shiga has given us in this story which illuminates the hero and his private morality, the metaphor of a man who must live by throwing knives at those closest to him. On the one hand, this extraordinary way of life requires of him both great psychological control ("taut nerves") and constant reliance on his instincts ("intuitive skill"). On the other hand, it provides him with a special immunity in the event that his instincts compel him to transgress conventional morality by hurling himself outward into the "dark void."

The metaphor of the Chinese juggler who kills with sharp knives and without premeditation, thus saving himself from a living death, sums up the ideal solution to deep-seated problems at which the adolescent hero has arrived. But for the hero of the more subjective and "personal" narratives, it is only an ideal, as yet unattained—and for him ultimately unattainable in any literal form. Before he can find some lasting peace with himself and maturity in his relations with others he must cover much of the same ground all over again, in keeping with his resigned reflection while still a child that "in later life the same kinds of things will go on happening, in the same way."

In the slight but engaging *Dekigoto* (An Accident, 1914; translated below), published only a month after *Han no hanzai*, there is a rare example of an adolescent character, here at most a two-dimensional embodiment of one facet of the Shiga hero, whose outward expression of a strong inner impulse happens to coincide with conventional morality. Yet, though he ends by doing a "good deed," the goodness is portrayed as welling up spontaneously within him, not as the result of some externally imposed ethical code.

The setting and the essential elements of the simple plot are strikingly similar to those of two other stories, *Seigiha* (The Righteous Ones, 1912) and *Haiiro no tsuki* (Under an Ashen Moon, 1945; translated below), which attests to Shiga's economy of means praised by Akutagawa, also to a certain poverty of imagination, others might say. The narrator is riding on a streetcar one blazing hot summer day when an accident occurs. A little boy wanders onto the track and is very nearly run over; in fact, he disappears from sight under the front end of the car, but is saved by a recently installed catching device. In the emotion-charged aftermath of the accident, while the streetcar personnel, passengers, and onlookers rush about exclaiming to one another, it is on the stalwart figure of a young electrician, previously noticed by the narrator for his unpleasant, sullen air, that the story comes to focus. Unsolicited, he more or less takes charge of the frightened child, and does not hesitate to berate the mother, when she arrives on the scene, for her wanton carelessness. As he sternly fulfills his intuitive sense of duty by examining the child for injuries (there are none; the boy has only wet his pants) and rather savagely admonishing the mother, his reactions are implicitly contrasted to the fussy, semi-professional expressions of goodwill on the part of another passenger, a middle-aged petty bureaucrat who emerges as a sympathetic self-caricature of his kind (somehow suggesting a minor character in an Ozu film). The story ends with a vivid, intensely physical still-shot of the manly electrician, stripped to the waist, wiping the boy's urine from his torso, which is registered by the admiring gaze of the narrator. Characteristically, the narrator has already ratified his own "essentially self-centered reaction of relief" after the accident as "nevertheless good and right." But in his final visual embrace of the electrician, who beams back at him and cracks a joke, he implies that the young man's reaction, equally true to his own inner urgings, has been the more powerful and admirable. The other passengers too bask in the glow of his unaffected goodness. And a frolicsome butterfly that, before the accident, served as the only bit of hopeful life among the half-dead human cargo, is discovered to have flown away, now liberated from its thankless task.

Seigiha likewise treats of a streetcar accident involving a child, but in this case the accident is fatal. The reactions of three of the passengers, which again form the burden of the tale, are shown here to be quite unspontaneous and therefore quite wrong, even though they reflect what in the conventional scheme of things would pass for righteousness (the *"seigi"* of the ironic title) of a particularly brave sort. For these passengers, who angrily testify to the police against the negligent driver, are themselves employees of the streetcar company and stand to lose their jobs. The last pages of this relentless little study of the psychology of false moral consciousness and its consequences are devoted to the three men's vain attempts to win recognition for their good deed, which end in a drunken insight into the folly of what they have done. There is more than a suggestion that because they have acted in concert, and after much consultation, they have acted in bad faith, forfeiting in the process whatever strength and true "rightness" there might have been in each one's spontaneous individual reaction.

In *Haiiro no tsuki,* perhaps Shiga's only postwar piece of any interest, he again makes use in a distinctly fabulistic way of a disturbing incident that takes place in the midst of a crowded vehicle. On boarding a train at the half-ruined Tokyo Station, the narrator finds himself forced to sit beside a disheveled young man who appears to be semiconsciously engaged in alarming convulsive motions. A group of loud, cheerful businessmen point out the youth's strange behavior to one another and speculate aloud on whether he is sick or merely drunk, until they are interrupted by a stalwart-looking fellow passenger, very reminiscent of the electrician in *Dekigoto,* who abruptly signals to them with gestures that the butt of their loud jokes is on the verge of starvation. In a guilty, less than spontaneous impulse to "help out," the businessmen then rouse the young man from his troubled sleep and ask him where he is going. It becomes apparent that he has missed his stop, and will soon have made a complete circuit of the loop line. When the young man at length realizes his own mistake, he only mutters despondently that it really doesn't matter at all. In his initial consternation, however, he has lost his balance and keeled over against the narrator, who fends him off with curt, reflexive force. Afterward the narrator voices to himself mild regret over his treatment of the starving youth. But in the end he gets off the train with a mixed sensation of pity and relief: there would have been no use in giving the fellow money, he tells himself, what with the acute shortage of openly available food.

When first published, a few months after the end of the war, this gloomy fable appears to have been read by some (Dazai Osamu, for example) with considerable distaste. Given the particular circumstances it portrays (and the widespread assumption on the part of Shiga's Japanese audience that things had happened in reality just as in the story), it no doubt is distasteful. Viewed as a final variation on the theme first set forth much more vigorously in Dekigoto, and its obverse in Seigiha, it does provide, at least, one last confirmation of the Shiga hero's supreme faith in the ineluctability, and the rightness, of acting on one's strongest inner impulses, wherever they might lead.

A RIDDLE AND A DREAM

If a person has a nightmare, it means either that he is
too much given to fear, or else that he is too exempt
from it; and if he dreams of the old wise man
it may mean that he is too pedagogical, as also that he
stands in need of a teacher. In a subtle way both
meanings come to the same thing, as we perceive when
we are able to let the work of art act upon us
as it acted upon the artist. . . . Then we understand the
nature of his experience. We see that he has drawn upon
the healing and redeeming forces of the collective
psyche that underlies consciousness with its isolation
and its painful errors; that he has penetrated to that
matrix of life in which all men are embedded, which
imparts a common rhythm to all human existence,
and allows the individual to communicate his feeling
and his striving to mankind as a whole.

—C. G. Jung

I lay down and began to read *An'ya kōro*. I followed
each step in the hero's inner struggle, thinking to
myself: compared to him, what a fool I have been!

—Akutagawa Ryūnosuke

WE HAVE SEEN SHIGA often subject his single central character to a
process of intuitive psychoanalysis throughout the various stages and
situations in which he has placed him. The parallel project of the Shiga
hero as he approaches the prime of life (according to conventional
reckonings) is to come to terms, however belatedly, with the basic
realities of his origins: his birth, the ensuing separation from his
mother's body and the irretrievable loss of her love; and also, as the
narrator so simply states it in one novel, with "the riddle which a
father as a father poses to his son" (2:446).

In the concluding works of the "trilogy," *Wakai* (Reconciliation,
1917) and *Aru otoko, sono ane no shi* (A Man and the Death of His
Sister, 1920), Shiga has presented us with two alternate resolutions of
that conflict with the father which has rankled more or less constantly
in the hero's mind during his childhood and adolescence. (Shiga himself has pointed to both the similarity and contrast between these two
works by describing *Wakai* as a "fresh fish, just caught" and *Aru
otoko* as "the same fish, dried"; 7:29.) The first part of *An'ya kōro*

(1921) contains still another denouement for this most conspicuous plot in the scenario of the hero's life at this stage.

Although the outcome which is set forth in *An'ya kōro* will perhaps strike us as a deus ex machina in the context of an otherwise realistic narrative, it is psychologically the most convincing of the three alternatives presented to us. (Shiga's statement to the effect that *Wakai* alone represents the "facts" of the matter in his own life need not concern us in our approach to his works as fiction or myth; 7:17.) In any case, Shiga's choice of this third resolution in *An'ya kōro,* his longest and his finest novel, offers ample grounds for considering it "definitive." Consequently, in the following discussion it will be given greater weight than the versions found in *Wakai* and *Aru otoko,* which may be briefly reviewed together.

Wakai is cast in the familiar form of a retrospective monologue spoken by the narrator-hero. He recalls for us recent events in his relations with his father leading up to the "reconciliation" of the title and interpolates an account of earlier occurrences that makes up much of the narrative. *Aru otoko* is also told in the first person, but by a so-called observer-narrator, the younger brother of the hero. He proposes likewise to review the relationship between the hero and his father to the extent that he has observed it over the years. In this case, the foregone conclusion revealed by the narrator at the outset is not a reconciliation but a final break in their relations, and the hero's subsequent flight from home. The narrator tells us that he has seen his brother only once in the ten years since, at the funeral of an older sister who has also been "cast out" by the father.

The knowledge which our reconstruction of the hero's life has given us of his childhood, as revealed in the prologue of *An'ya kōro* and several short stories, helps us to place in perspective the obsessive portrayal of seemingly minor episodes and disconnected scenes that fill these narratives. In *Aru otoko,* the hero himself apologizes to another character for his "fixation" on resentful feelings toward the father. But even should he try to forget them, he adds, he is sure to slip back into the "same mold": *moto no Mokuami* in the playfully ironic phrase that Shiga frequently uses to denote the kind of internal processes which the psychoanalysts have called the "repetition compulsion" and "the return of the repressed."

The hero of *Wakai* confesses that he lacks the necessary objectivity to examine impartially the whole history of the conflict with his father. In any case, he tells us, he has been concerned not so much with the origins of their feud in the distant past as with its disturbing effects upon him in the present. "The strong antipathy which I felt toward my father was no doubt part of the complex tangle of emotions that inevitably arise from the fact of being father and son. But by now, my feelings seemed to be dictated simply by the hatred that came from our total lack of rapport" (2:327). To reduce this comment to the tautology which it clearly implies, he hates his father because he has always hated him. We are aware that the "reasoning" behind this curious statement is rooted in childish passions, which are openly expressed in *An'ya kōro*, while in *Wakai* they remain concealed. And so we further deduce that the hero hates his father because the man has long ago become irredeemably "hateful, hateful, hateful" to his son.

Paradoxically, nowhere is the distinction that must be made between Shiga as author and his alter ego as hero so obvious as it is in this and similar observations by the narrator of *Wakai*—supposedly Shiga's most autobiographical work. If Shiga's "intuitive psycho-analysis" were indeed limited to such empty tautologies as the one quoted above, his characterization of the hero would not have much interest for us, neither on literary nor on psychological grounds.

Fortunately, Shiga is endowed with a more penetrating consciousness than is the hero as he has been presented in *Wakai* and *Aru otoko*. The probing sharpness of the author's mind, manifest in his relentless style, succeeds in bringing to light through almost tangible images a few real and (one assumes) recurring moments in the hero's inner life which he himself mistakenly imagines he can soon forget. These disturbing moments and other, happier memories that are recorded in the relatively unrewarding novels of the trilogy not only contribute to a fuller view of the hero, whose characterization culminates in *An'ya kōro;* they are also, we should not deny, of some interest in themselves.

It should be noted that the narrator-hero of *Wakai* is in a sense forcing himself to "regress." He revives the acrimonious feud with his father in order to tell his story. It is clear that even before the reconciliation is effected, he has overcome some of those nameless fears and uncontrollable urges which we have seen break out during his youth in fantasies of murder, dreams and fables of destructive women, etc. Indeed, he is presented in this novel as already married and the father of a child. Concerning "a certain attitude" (as he evasively calls it) which he has adopted toward his father in the past, he remarks: "As a father myself, the mere thought of becoming the object of such an attitude on the part of my own child was unbearable" (2:334).

While it is one of the axioms of the Shiga hero's world that "the same things will go on happening"—and the process will in fact begin all over again in *An'ya kōro,* though on a different plane—we may nevertheless recognize that the hero of *Wakai* shows a new measure of maturity in his eagerness to rid himself of the debilitating hatred of his father and to carry on with his own life and work.

Both in *Wakai* and in *Aru otoko,* the hero's late grandfather is evoked in memory and vivid daydreams as a very positive figure. From the hero's point of view he represents the most honest aspects of traditional morality. (Like Shiga's own grandfather, he has been an ardent disciple of Ninomiya Sontoku.) And he acts within the young man's still unsettled mind as the agent for a spirit of inward self-fulfillment and outward tolerance.

According to the retrospective account in *Wakai,* the principal motive behind the hero's growing wish for better relations with his father has been a strong desire to see his ailing grandmother more often. As she lives with his father, his visits to her must be made almost furtively. On his way to one of these clandestine meetings, the hero visits his grandfather's grave and silently communes with him. "As I walked about in front of his grave he came back to life in my mind. It occurred to me to tell him of my intention to visit my grandmother. 'Yes, you should do that,' my grandfather answered me directly. His response was quite natural. It seemed too immediate and too clear to be merely a figment of my imagination. The figure evoked then had the objective clarity of the people I see in my dreams and looked just like my grandfather when he was alive.... Although my side of the dialogue had unmistakably implied strong criticism of my father, in my grandfather's reply, which also came from within, there were no such overtones" (2:325–26).

The narrator is quite specific, we note, in stating that his grandfather has been called up in his own mind—the voice comes from "within." Here we may turn to Jung for a suggestion of some wider implication contained in the hero's reassuring vision (though we need not dwell on the theoretical details of the interpretation). "If an individual has wrestled seriously enough and long enough with the anima problem so that he is no longer identified with it, the unconscious changes its dominant character and appears in a new symbolic form representing the Self.... In the case of a man, it appears as a masculine guardian, a wise old man."[1] To restate the above rather too simply, no doubt, now that the full force of the hero's adolescent struggle has abated somewhat (if only to resume later with a vengeance), the grandfather has become part of him and is present in his deepest thoughts.

Granted that, in this instance, he may fulfill some symbolic role such as "the wise old man" mentioned by Jung, the grandfather is also, of course, a very real, fleshed-out memory for the hero. We would do well to reserve judgment as to how far and in what ways he identifies with his grandfather until we have glimpsed the specific content of his memory.

While in *Wakai* the grandfather is simply evoked as a benevolent ghost from the past, a much more concrete image of the man is built up through two recollections of him in *Aru otoko*. The first has to do with the grandfather's participation or, more precisely, his nonparticipation in a particularly ugly scene which erupts between the hero and his father. The immediate cause of the confrontation is a disagreement between father and son over a contemporary case of what we would now call criminal pollution. We are told only that the much-publicized case involved the contamination of the "W." River and the land along its banks by a large mining company, and that the hero (he is about twenty years old at the time) has arranged to accompany friends to the stricken area on a mission of relief. His father angrily refuses to permit the journey. After the son has argued his views of the case in vain, the project is dropped. The grandfather, who is a witness to this scene, remains silent throughout.

The narrator here provides an extended commentary on this episode, though not on the details of the pollution incident itself, for which he shows little concern. His interest centers rather on the hero's reaction to his father's conduct and on the grandfather's silent role in the background. In the course of this episode, we are told, "the riddle which a father as a father poses to his son" has been "shattered once and for all" (2:446). Although we may recognize much intuitive truth in the words with which the narrator describes the relationship between father and son, we may choose not to accept his claim that "the riddle" has been solved "once and for all." For in *Wakai* and *An'ya kōro* alike the hero is shown to be still agonizing over this riddle at a considerably later stage of his life.

The primordial riddle which so often preoccupies the Shiga hero does not lie simply in such basic questions as "Who is my father?" and "What manner of man is he?"—though we shall see it temporarily reduced to these rudimentary terms in *An'ya kōro*. It has far wider ramifications that are closely bound up with what Erikson has called the "psychosocial" development of the individual. Subjective notions of one's paternal origins clearly condition, while they need not wholly determine, one's view of the great "objective" world and of one's own place in it. This is borne out both by the hero's confession in *Wakai* that his deep distrust of his father has even impeded him in his career and, on a larger scale, by the uncertainty and apathy which on the whole the Shiga hero displays toward the paternalistic worlds of state and society.

The narrator of *Aru otoko* then comments at length on the "sad" silence that the grandfather has maintained during the quarrel between father and son. Only long after the episode, we learn, has it been revealed that the grandfather once controlled a large share of the very company which perpetrated the pollution, although by then he had disposed of his interests in the venture.

On the other hand, the narrator speculates, as a staunch supporter of Sontoku's agrarianist philosophy the old man has most likely sympathized with the peasant victims in this case; and perhaps he has secretly taken his grandson's side in the family dispute. Yet, upon further reflection, the narrator sees it in a different light. "To my grandfather the problem must have appeared as a tangle of divergent threads, all of which he could clearly distinguish. I can sense now, as I remember the episode, the great wave of sadness that came over him then" (2:450).

This, then, is one of the lessons that the hero learns from his old grandfather while he himself is yet a young man: a sad resignation in the face of the complexity of things. To the extent that he comes to identify with his grandfather in this respect, it does not presumably redirect his emotional energies away from the constant inner struggle toward strenuous efforts in the outside world; it must instead tend to discourage him from more active participation in the endlessly "complex tangle" that one finds there.

A final anecdote is told about the grandfather which suggests another kind of influence that he has exercised upon the hero and a deep bond that grows up between them over the years in the grandson's mind. Until the time of his death, a plaque inscribed in Chinese with a traditional exhortation hangs prominently in the grandfather's room. The narrator comments that, "in itself of the commonplace sort that one sees on the walls of country inns," the inscription has been given true meaning by the grandfather's understanding of it. "Though we store up wealth and bequeath it to our descendants, there is no assurance that they will preserve it. Though we accumulate books and pass them on to our progeny, it is far from certain that they will read them. The best course of all is to build up the latent reserve of virtue which lies deep within ourselves, that it may serve as a lasting guide for our descendants in their own lives" (2:451).

The hero, who has developed literary aspirations, remarks wryly on one occasion that the "accumulating of books" refers to him, while the "storing up of wealth" applies to his father (a successful financier). This remark implies, as does the inscription itself, a partial rejection of both gainful economic activity and endeavors in the realm of conventional "high culture": book-learning, literary creation, etc. And it affirms a reliance on the "latent" moral force that lies deep within the individual as the ultimate source of a good life for himself and his descendants.

Beyond the outward self-denial and resignation to the world as-it-is which, perhaps prematurely, the hero has begun to learn from his grandfather, through the "wise old man's" example he also confirms his inclination to seek a way of life that is rooted in his unconscious instincts, his own "latent reserve of virtue." The anecdote concludes with the disclosure that his father has disposed of the pregnant inscription shortly after the grandfather's death.

The rest of the narrative in *Aru otoko* is devoted to a painfully detailed account of the events that lead up to a final breaking off of all relations between the hero and his father. The last section of *Wakai* moves by contrast quite swiftly, even melodramatically, toward a total reconciliation. In either case, the exaggerated nature of the outcome and its effect upon the hero—nothing but despair and self pity on the one hand, all joy and self-congratulation on the other—may elicit a skeptical reaction from the reader. We are too familiar with the cyclical and recurrent character of such deep-seated conflicts in the Shiga hero's mind, as of those within ourselves, perhaps, to accept so final and absolute a resolution.

In both novels the denouement is preceded by further revelations of the violence and ambivalence underlying the relationship between father and son, which give us added cause for skepticism about the decisive endings. As mentioned in the introduction, the hero of *Wakai* tells us of past attempts at a kind of autotherapy in which he projects his own problems onto the chief character of a novel that he has been writing. It is to be about a young man like himself at odds with his father. According to a rough draft which he never finishes, the conflict will come to a head in a violent scene enacted by the "fictional" father and son at the grandmother's deathbed. The hero of *Wakai* recalls: "As I worked out the scene in my imagination I tried to decide whether the father would kill the son or the son would kill the father. When I reached this crucial point, suddenly a picture flashed through my mind in which the two of them embraced one another and burst into tears. This abrupt change caught me by surprise and I began to cry myself" (2:367–68). Unable to decide which of the two projected endings he should use in his novel, the murderous outburst or the tearful reconciliation, the hero has put the draft aside. It is, of course, the second, surprise ending that prefigures the reconciliation with the father which eventually takes place in his own life.

One day, "on an impulse," the hero seeks an interview with his father. He states a brief and cautiously worded apology for his role in perpetuating the conflict. The father in turn expresses his regrets, though without admitting any wrong on his own part. Then he breaks down and cries. The hero too is moved to tears. And the reconciliation has been effected. Afterward he tells us that he has come to love his father and has now forgotten all the old animosities.

At the close of the novel a kind of benediction is offered by an uncle who is a devotee of Zen Buddhism. (Elsewhere, as we shall see, the hero displays a certain contempt for the established Zen sect.) It is a passage from the *Hekiganroku,* which he quotes in a letter of congratulation to both father and son:

> From north, south, east, and west
> They all come home to roost. •
> Together once again in the still night,
> They gaze at the snow upon the craggy peaks (2:419).

In contrast to this harmonious conclusion with its suspiciously pious coda, *Aru otoko* ends with a gloomy picture of the forsaken hero after he has fled from his father's house. Although he leaves on his own initiative, he feels that he has been virtually driven out by certain cruel remarks which his father has reputedly made about him.

According to a tactless relative who comes bearing tales, his father has said that he no longer feels any love for his son and would indeed be happy to see him dead. Devastated by his father's alleged curse, the hero leaves home and disappears into endless wandering. The novel is brought to a close by a long letter in which the hero's tortured feelings toward his father are exposed once again, this time wholly from his own point of view. (The lengthy and redundant interpolation is only one of several awkward features that mar this most misshapen of Shiga's longer works.)

There is some pathos and much self-pity in his review of past attempts to come to terms with the remote and threatening figure that his father represents for him. He confesses that he has often felt a secret desire to please his father, even to overwhelm him by some heroic accomplishment. As an example, he recalls a recurring fantasy in which he imagines that he has constructed a giant dirigible and by means of this exotic craft transports an entire pine-clad island to his father's garden in Tokyo. As we shall observe in *An'ya kōro*, aircraft in general take on a shifting symbolic value in the hero's outlook on the world. (They were, of course, a new phenomenon at the time Shiga was writing these works.) But as it is conjured up in this childish fantasy, the image seems merely phallic, and pathetic.

Another pathetic attempt on the part of the Shiga hero—in this case, the "Shiga narrator" would be more apt—to placate the implacable father is to be found in the very curious short piece entitled *Kurodeiasu no nikki* (Claudius's Diary, 1912). Here the treatment of the father-son conflict takes the oblique form of a fanciful reinterpretation of *Hamlet* in which Claudius, appealing to us directly through his "journal" entries, emerges on the surface as the wronged party, not entirely innocent of rejoicing in his brother's death but neither guilty of his murder, and finally forced to dispose of his hysterical nephew against his own inclinations, out of self-defense. Assuming, as we certainly can, that Shiga was aware on some level of the oedipal motifs which Ernest Jones showed in his famous essay to be one set of "meanings" informing *Hamlet*, *Kurodeiasu no nikki* like *Aru otoko* would appear to represent a half-hearted effort to examine the other side of the story for once. And yet, though exonerated of actual murder, Shiga's Claudius has clearly wished for his brother's death; and wishing for something is, as we have seen, often tantamount to making it happen in the Shiga hero's dreamlike world. In the end, the dominant impression the reader gets from Shiga's quirky portrayal is one of still another cold, autocratic, and in all but deed murderous father-figure. (Shiga's boast in his diary that those who read his story with care "would no longer be able to take the tragedy of *Hamlet* seriously," since he has proven that there is no objective proof of Claudius's guilt [10:557], fails to take into account his self-incriminating soliloquy in the third act, as Mathy has pointed out in his discussion of this work.)[2]

The novels of the trilogy, in particular *Wakai* and *Aru otoko*, have been treated here as if they were in some respects preliminary drafts for *An'ya kōro*. In the case of *Wakai* alone this approach does not, perhaps, do justice to what is after all a short novel in itself—and a novel which appears to have been an object of considerable admira-

tion among Japanese readers. It is true that *Wakai* has a relatively
well-constructed plot, simple though it is. And the narrative control
which the author maintains in this first venture into novel-length
fiction since *Ōtsu Jun'kichi* (where such control is clearly lacking)
assures a certain dramatic impact on the reader when he reaches the
final scenes for which he has been carefully prepared.

It is also true that, seen in the perspective of our reconstruction of
the hero's slow development, *Wakai* reveals a measure of maturity
which would indicate that his nameless fears and uncontrollable urges
have been somewhat subdued. But we note that he has sought the
reconciliation "on an impulse." It remains a cardinal principle of the
Shiga hero's private morality that his strongest instincts cannot and
should not be denied. Through various kinds of autotherapy, the hero
hopes to avert their more destructive manifestations, while not pre-
suming to circumvent them when they arise in consciousness. "Things
must be allowed to take their natural course," he comments to himself
(2:397).

Yet our long-range view of the Shiga hero gives us some cause to
question the validity of the total reconciliation with which we have
been presented in *Wakai*. There is something quite unreal, even "unnatural," about the way he suddenly forgets "all the old animosities"
that have plagued him for so long. At the end of the novel he seems to
vanish into the otherworldly cloud of eternal harmony and light which
the closing benediction invokes, as if he has existed only to pursue
these ghosts from his past that have now been laid to rest.

Finally, we may conclude from the completely opposite outcomes of
the conflict which we find in *Wakai* and *Aru otoko* that there is still
much uncertainty in Shiga's own conception of his protean hero at this
stage. Whatever plateau Shiga's relations with his father might have
reached by this point in his own life (supposed by the biographical
critics to be reflected without distortion in *Wakai*), it is clear when we
next encounter his alter ego in *An'ya kōro* that he is still much troubled
by the open question of his origins. The prologue shows him to be obsessed with the shadowy figures who preside over his earliest memories.
And again in *An'ya kōro,* as throughout the trilogy, these fundamental
questions in the hero's mind, with all their wider implications for his
identity ("psychosocial," "psychosexual," etc.), form the core of his
story.

After the hero has delivered the monologue with which *An'ya kōro*
begins, the anonymous author raises the curtain of the narrative

proper to find him back "in character" on the more objectified stage of the novel. The composite protagonist made up of Seibei, "the boy," Ōtsu Jun'kichi, Adoni, Han, "the electrician," and various "I"'s here becomes Tokitō Kensaku. Still a bachelor, he appears to be approaching thirty, although his age is not specified, and he may strike us simply as a young man on the outer fringe of adolescence.

Of the four figures introduced in his childhood reminiscences, only Oei remains in full view. Mistress to his grandfather in those distant days, she now keeps house for Kensaku. The shabby grandfather is dead and apparently forgotten as well. Kensaku's mother is of course long dead. But he remembers her often, and especially at critical turning points in his life. The "hateful" father is still alive though he is completely absent from Kensaku's day to day life. In contrast to his central role in the trilogy, the father is only a vaguely menacing presence in the background of this novel's first part, at the end of which the riddle which he has posed will be "solved" by the hero in an extraordinary manner.

There is an opaque quality in the portrayal of the hero throughout much of the opening section. (Each of the novel's two parts is subdivided into two sections.) This no doubt reflects an authorial perspective which is more distant from those employed in the trilogy and other early works. But it would simply suggest that since his previous portraits the hero himself has grown up some. He has lost the transparency of childhood and early adolescence, while in the course of the narrative he will regain it from time to time.

Kensaku's characteristic pose in these early chapters is that of a disenchanted observer, a "dangling man" of the sort familiar to us from many modern novels, both Western and Japanese. The obvious difference between Kensaku and, say, Nagai Daisuke, the hero of Sōseki's *Sore kara*, is that Kensaku scarcely looks at the macrocosm of society at large and seldom engages in intellectual speculation for its own sake, as Daisuke does with a vengeance. Kensaku's apathy toward the great world stems partly from a lack of intellectual curiosity, we infer, and partly from the fact that he has in a sense been disillusioned from the very beginning.

Early in the narrative we find him perusing with disgust a "personal novel" by a friend named Sakaguchi. It relates in a frivolous tone an affair between the narrator (presumed to be Sakaguchi himself) and a family maid. As it is outlined for us here, this slight "novel within a novel" seems indeed very trivial. Yet it serves the purpose of establishing Sakaguchi as a kind of negative double or scapegoat for Kensaku, a role which assumes considerable importance at the close of the first section.

In Kensaku's vehement reaction against his friend's novel we may see a rejection of the shallow, exhibitionistic sort of *shishōsetsu* which it represents. (At one point, his father dismisses such works as "family novels, that is no novels at all"—perhaps with Kensaku's own publications in mind, although these are hardly mentioned in the narrative.) Sakaguchi's story of master and maid further suggests certain superficial parallels with Kensaku's feelings toward his housekeeper, feelings that he has so far been scarcely aware of. On the surface level of plot, then, the trivial novel within a novel introduces the main theme of the first part, as on a deeper level, it prepares for the climax.

Hakachō has justifiably remarked that the characterization of Oei is lacking in substance.[3] The prologue gives us a vivid glimpse of her as Kensaku remembers her in the remote past—still warm from her bath, slightly drunk on the wine, humming a popular tune. But hereafter she is never described in the flesh. Nor do we hear her speak at any length. Her conversations with Kensaku are restricted mostly to cheerful, sometimes almost silly, comments about his doings and solicitous, motherly advice. Whatever else we learn of Oei comes to us indirectly through his tangled thoughts about her. Gradually she is surrounded by a faint aura of mystery, and we are further mystified when the narrative states, without further elaboration, that Kensaku finds himself pausing outside her door late at night while she is asleep.

At the end of the first section we shall see the hero suddenly overwhelmed by a desire for this older woman which is of truly demonic force. He acknowledges to himself that there is nothing provocative about Oei's conduct toward him in reality. Yet in his fantasies she always appears as an aggressive seductress, while he is cast in the role of an innocent youth who tries to dissuade her from her wanton course. From our review of the hero's earlier life we are familiar with this ambiguous figure of an older woman, both frightening and fascinating, loving and voracious. Eventually, Kensaku himself comes to sense danger in these daydreams. "He shuddered at a presentiment of the destruction which, in one form or another, would surely result from relations with this woman: twenty years his senior and for a long time his grandfather's mistress" (5:133–134).

Prior to this point in the narrative, Kensaku occupies himself in rather aimless meetings with friends, passing flirtations with geisha

and cafe waitresses, and infrequent visits to a brothel in the Fukagawa
quarter. Such activities fill up his days and nights, but they seem to
hold little real interest for him. It is as if he seeks to ward off the
danger that he has begun to sense within himself by expending his
energies on these pastimes.

In his various encounters with women whose profession it is to
please men, Kensaku feels now awkward and self-conscious, now
disdainful and fastidious. While playing a game at a geisha party (akin
to "Button, button, who has the button?"), he becomes acutely embarrassed about his "large, bony hands, hairy as a bear's paws." And
when he first visits the brothel in Fukagawa, his experience with an
ugly woman—she is described only as having a "pale, flat face"—
leaves him dissatisfied and mildly disgusted with himself. It is rather
from watching a pretty young mother shower "little Japanese-style
kisses" on her baby that he derives his most unequivocal sensual
pleasure at this stage.

We learn in retrospect of an unsuccessful marriage proposal that
Kensaku has recently made to a girl whom he has known since
childhood. She is the daughter of a close friend of his mother. After his
mother died, this woman treated Kensaku with great kindness; and so
it is to her that he first confides his wish to marry the daughter. When
his proposal fails (for reasons that have nothing to do with the girl's
own inclinations), he cannot help feeling that he has been betrayed by
the mother—although he knows that it is generally fathers and elder
brothers who have the final say in these matters.

The unhappy experience renews in him that fundamental disenchantment with the world which has lurked at the back of his mind
from his early years. He falls prey to "the banal yet nonetheless
unsettling conviction that, underneath it all, men are not to be trusted"
(5:74). Then he retreats into himself and looks to his one source of
abiding consolation. "There was no one whose love he could depend
on. Again he wistfully sought out his long dead mother from the few
memories of her that remained. . . . Were she still alive now, it was by
no means certain that she would give him the comfort he needed. It
was precisely because she was dead and gone that he had come to
venerate her so" (5:63).

Precisely because she is dead and gone . . . , but his few memories of
her, in effect no more than memories of memories, as we have seen,
will not prove sufficiently reassuring as he approaches the life crisis
which divides still dependent youth from independent manhood. To
the above he adds that he is not, of course, completely alone. He

enjoys the affection of his older brother, Nobuyuki—a new character who is introduced here into the Shiga hero's world. And although hers is "not of the same magnitude as a mother's love," Oei has always cared for him.

At length it becomes apparent that in the living figure of Oei, Kensaku has partially and unconsciously revived his mother, or the chimerical image of her which was formed during his childhood. Oei too, as we have noted, seems at times to be more a figment of the hero's imagination than a flesh-and-blood woman, one whom, in moments of objectivity, he recognizes to be a generation removed from himself. The substitution, which has no doubt begun long ago, is evident from the close interweaving of his recollections of his mother and his daydreams about Oei. But he himself does not become aware of it until the onslaught of maturity, in conventional social terms, forces him either to break with his distant past or be engulfed by it.

Before his fantasies take on a nightmarish reality of their own that pervades the later chapters of the first part, there is a further interlude in which he attempts to satisfy his restive instincts through dalliances with professional women and, occasionally, to "sublimate" through intellectual endeavors.

We look over Kensaku's shoulder while he records in his diary callow speculations on the large questions: "I do not want the peace of mind that comes with premature resignation. I want the joy and satisfaction that one finds only in a constant pursuit. There is no death for those who have achieved something immortal in their lives. . . . I want to see what no one has seen, hear what no one has heard, feel what no one ever felt before" (5:114). Perhaps the most interesting reflections in this passage are his references to what he variously calls man's "blind strivings," "instinctual urges," and "the great common Will." The discussion begins by granting the hypothesis that the earth is eventually doomed to perish through natural processes. If we suppose that mankind's destiny is inevitably earthbound, he continues, then our descendants are likewise doomed. But in man's "instinctive and insatiable craving for work," Kensaku sees a "blind will toward self-preservation": "Men work. Women bear children. That is the sum of human life. In the early stages of mankind's development, men had only to work for the sake of their families and villages. Through progress, the communal sphere gradually extended beyond the village so that, in Japan, men came to satisfy their instinct for work by serving their feudal domain. Subsequently their allegiance widened to include the nation, the race, and finally the whole species" (5:115).

He concludes that men will strive together to avert the fate which appears to await them in their earthbound condition. As a specific example of his own participation in the "great common Will," he mentions the "involuntary thrill" that he experienced a few years ago upon witnessing a demonstration of an airplane in flight—the first to be held in Japan. (Here we recall the symbolic role which has been allotted to aircraft in Shiga's narratives.)

If only because such abstract speculation is so rare in the various portrayals of the hero which we have reviewed, we may suspect that some of these ideas have been less than fully digested into his own scheme of things, or into his author's conception of him. The passage seems at certain points to have been "pasted on" to the character, an impression one seldom gets in Shiga's works. And indeed we find in one of Shiga's essays, written long after the completion of *An'ya kōro*, a statement to the effect that as a young man he had been quite disturbed by a description of the end of the world and the death of the last human being which he had read in a novel by Anatole France *(Le jardin d'Epicure)*. At the time, he tells us, he had reacted by denying that man's destiny is inextricably tied to the earth, although he has since completely reversed his views on this question (7:461).

It may be surmised, then, that the optimistic notions of a benevolent common Will backed up by a beneficent technology have been somewhat artificially imposed on Kensaku's own view of the world at this juncture. In any case, we shall later see him reject these notions himself. Already, at the end of this brief consideration of the "large questions," he raises some doubts about the benevolence of the instinctual forces that he has postulated. "From another point of view," he remarks, "these instincts are totally blind and may affect men in a pathological manner as well" (5:115).

Although he cannot bring himself to abandon the whole idea of a collective striving for the preservation of the species, he has long ago given up his "childish hopes," as he calls them, for immortality of the individual soul. (From our knowledge of the hero's background we may conjecture that his former belief in individual immortality was part of an adolescent infatuation with Christianity which he has since repudiated.)

Finally, there are only two points touched upon in this passage which appear to be matters of more or less firm conviction with Kensaku. The first is the existence, in one form or another, of a "great common Will." The second is the assumption—the "feeling," as he expresses it—that some of the time, and "in certain situations," these

instinctual forces will function for men's benefit. But even this rather
tentative belief is further qualified: "Perhaps I shall in time become
more enlightened and shall free myself from this feeling. For there *is* a
more enlightened outlook." ("Enlightened" and "free myself" render
here a single word, *gedatsu,* which occurs twice in the text, with
slightly different connotations: originally a Buddhist term meaning to
extirpate the roots of desire, it also has the general sense of emancipation and enlightenment.)

On this somewhat enigmatic note, Kensaku concludes the lengthy
entry in his diary.

Not long after he has intellectually affirmed the existence of a blind
Will with a capacity to make men sick as well as to enrich them,
Kensaku succumbs to the demonic fantasies surrounding Oei which
were mentioned earlier. We are told that his own role in them has
grown increasingly active and aggressive. Then, one night, he has a
stark nightmare which takes the oblique form of a dream within a
dream and leaves him feeling purged (for the moment) of his nameless
fears.

In addition to Kensaku himself, the characters who appear in the
dream include Miyamoto, an acquaintance who otherwise figures
scarcely at all in the novel; Sakaguchi, his erstwhile friend who, as I
suggested earlier, has become something of a scapegoat in Kensaku's
mind, both for writing "frivolous" novels and for seducing a family
maid; and, finally, a deformed creature the likes of which Kensaku has
never seen before.

First, he dreams that he is dreaming:

> As he lay sleeping, Miyamoto entered the room, smiling
> eerily.
> "Sakaguchi has died on his journey," he announced.
> Oh, thought Kensaku, still asleep, so he's dead at last, is he?
> In the midst of his dream he was somehow aware that
> Sakaguchi had recently left home without a word to anyone;
> nor was he surprised by his friend's sudden death. Gaining no
> response from Kensaku, Miyamoto resumed talking.
> "I hear he did *harima*," he said with a knowing chuckle.
> "He actually went through with it."
> Again, Kensaku was not exactly surprised. He was not
> quite sure what to do *harima* meant. But he knew at least that
> it was a mortally dangerous technique which Sakaguchi had
> learned once in Osaka. Miyamoto had no doubt heard about
> it before from Sakaguchi. A cold shiver spread through his

body as he thought of how Sakaguchi had at last descended to *harima* after exhausting all possible stimuli in his search for carnal pleasure. But surely Sakaguchi himself had known full well the horror of it. He could not have committed the depraved act of his own free will.

Kensaku started to ask Miyamoto what was involved in doing *harima,* but he stopped himself before he had finished the question. If he heard, he was sure to do it himself. . . . He might survive—it was not impossible; yet most people died. The odds against surviving this awful technique were a hundred, or a thousand, to one. And so long as he was still subject to his evil fantasies, the prospect would be all the more terrifying. In this case, truly "ignorance is bliss," to know is certain death. (5:134–35)

Presently Kensaku awakes from his dream within a dream with a lingering sense of horror. Still dreaming (so the narrative states: we may imagine a somnambulent state), he gets up and goes to the toilet. From the window he sees a "rather comical goblin" about the size of a seven-year-old child, with an enormous head and a scrawny body, frolicking about in the moonlit garden. It occurs to him that this goblin must come to preside over men's depraved dreams in the still of the night: "To think that in its true form the spirit of depravity was such a vulgar, silly little creature—it made one feel almost pure." Here he becomes fully awake.

From a strictly literary point of view, Kensaku's strange dream will not bear much analysis. If it is to have the impact which, perhaps only semiconsciously, the author no doubt intended it to have, the dream should be understood in its own intuitive terms. Or, as Jung has stated, "A suitable warning to the dream-interpreter—if only it were not so paradoxical—would be: 'Do anything you like, only don't try to understand!'"[4]

What is *harima,* the "mortally dangerous technique" about which "ignorance is bliss, to know is certain death"? It is obvious that Kensaku himself has no clear understanding of it, but only a feeling of purity on seeing that "the spirit of depravity" is such a "silly little creature." The hero's refusal to examine the content of his dream, to analyze it intellectually, is in keeping with Shiga's purely intuitive approach to his alter ego's troubled inner world and to his eventual "cure."

Yet a purely intuitive approach is not at all the same as random and arbitrary invention. Freud inquires apropos of dreams which authors have made up for their characters ("those dreams which have never been dreamed," as he calls them): "If actual dreams are considered to be unrestrained and irregular phenomena, what about the free recreations of such dreams? But there is much less freedom and arbitrariness in psychic life than we are inclined to believe, perhaps none at all."[5]

We may assume, then, that Kensaku's dream is determined by the author's total conception of his hero and draws on the deepest source of his creative imagination. The prominence accorded to this and many other dreams in Shiga's works would in itself argue that they should not be dismissed or passed over in silence (as for the most part they have been in Japanese critiques, which tend to dwell on the supposed autobiographical outlines of the plots).

The ensuing course of Kensaku's "cure" is somewhat perplexing. The manner in which the disturbing implications of his dream are worked out toward the end of the novel's first part places a severe strain on our disposition to believe. We may nevertheless accept the sudden denouement that brings to a close this penultimate stage of the hero's journey, though in a less than literal fashion, and in a perspective which is more consistent with the dominantly psychological realism of the novel.

In spite of Jung's warning against facile interpretation, one should perhaps overcome one's own scruples and take another look at the hero's dream. For it unmistakably marks a turning point in his inner life, even though its initial effect upon him is only temporarily cathartic. And I would suggest that the subsequent denouement on the level of "plot" may be viewed as if it occurred wholly within the hero's mind, in response to a growing self-awareness that is fostered by his dreams and fantasies.

Yasuoka, who recognizes the large significance of this particular dream, states that, to the best of his knowledge, the word *harima* is a neologism of Shiga's own devising.[6] (It exists in the language only as a proper noun: Harima, the name of an old province on the Inland Sea coast.) As an almost concrete word picture, rather than an abstract symbol, *harima* conveys both the terror and the intense pleasure associated with the arcane sexual practice to which it alludes. Although he does not know in detail how it is done, Kensaku is instinctively aware of *harima*'s dangers and its "depravity." It is as though he has always had a certain acquaintance with the general nature of *harima*—its fatal attractions and his own susceptibility to it. He is not in the least surprised to learn that Sakaguchi, his amoral friend (and scapegoat), has finally committed the act in his constant search for the ultimate satisfaction; nor that the indulgence has cost him his life. And still Kensaku is strongly tempted himself.

The incestuous implications of his desire for Oei are here made devastatingly clear to him, if only momentarily. In the unconscious, where this desire arises, there are, of course, no "implications"—only inchoate urges and infantile instincts. In their primal terms it is incest that he wants. But how devious are the channels which the unconscious uses to make its wishes known! The true nature of his fantasy is temporarily revealed to him through a rumor about a friend that comes to him in a dream within a dream. It reminds us of how remote from him his mother has been: no more than a memory of a memory. (Likewise, in the confessional *Sōbu no tame*, it is precisely in a two-layered dream that he momentarily conjures up his grandmother in a monstrous aspect.)

And what of the goblin that he later sees cavorting in the garden? It is described as "about the size of a seven-year-old child," that is, at most a year older than the age to which he has attributed the traumatic episodes in his early childhood. The creature strikes him as vulgar and silly. So, to some extent, must all men see themselves when, whether from simply curiosity or neurotic compulsion, they look back on this period in their past: the stage at which biological facts, as well as fear of the father, force the child to abandon his attempts to grow up ovenight and make himself master of the home. The psychoanalysts tell us that these attempts are never merely forgotten. Along with the rage and pain that accompany their defeat, they are driven underground into that mysterious entity known as the id, which no one has ever seen. Jung and others have maintained, however, that the id (in Jungian terminology, "the shadow") is often projected onto the outside world in the form of monsters, wild animals, etc. This is an interpretation which would clearly apply to Kensaku's goblin—"the spirit of depravity."

Now that he is vaguely aware of what has been troubling him so, Kensaku embarks on a more decisive phase of his autotherapy. As in several of Shiga's works, the dramatic climax of the first part takes place within the context of a journey. Like the disturbed hero of *Ko o nusumu hanashi*, Kensaku travels by boat to a small town on the Inland Sea coast (here it is specified as Onomichi) where he hopes to regain his emotional equilibrium and complete a novel which he has planned. Standing on the deck one night, he has "a not unpleasant sensation" of being swallowed up by the boundless nature that surrounds him—a foreshadowing of a far more intense experience of this

kind which the hero will have at the end of the novel. Here he is still in
an unsettled state, and we observe him indulging again in childlike
daydreams of an aggressive character. As the boat passes by a mountain called "Elephant's Head" (Zōzu San) he imagines himself to be an
elephant which has been provoked into a destructive rampage. He
tramples thousands of men in a few steps and floods whole cities by
snorting water from his trunk. Kensaku comments to himself that such
fantasies have served him as a useful outlet since childhood and are
essentially harmless. We may agree, while taking note of his distinctly
"regressive" frame of mind on the eve of his final adolescent crisis.

Kensaku's sojourn at Onomichi begins happily enough. He finds the
people friendly and the scenery beautiful. But as we have seen in *Ko o
nusumu hanashi,* the very beauty of the surroundings becomes oppressive to him, and he soon sinks back into moody introspection. He
begins preliminary work on his novel (predictably, it is to be semi-
autobiographical) by looking back on his life as far as his memory
will take him. His father is virtually absent from his earliest recollections, most of which appear "quite innocuous" to Kensaku. There is,
however, "one exception":

> Once—it was while they were still in Myōgadani, he was lying
> beside his mother. After she had fallen asleep, he saw his
> opportunity and burrowed way down under the covers. Pres-
> ently his hand was thrust aside with violence. His mother,
> whom he has supposed to be fast asleep, seized him cruelly and
> dragged him back up to the pillow. She kept her eyes closed
> and not a word was spoken by either of them. At the time, his
> understanding of what he had done was no different from an
> adult's: he was ashamed. The memory now affected Kensaku
> strangely, with mingled feelings of shame and wonder. What
> could have made him do such a thing? Had it been no more
> than curiosity, or an involuntary impulse? Mere curiosity
> could not account for the shame which he had felt then. Nor
> could he imagine that such impulses were at all common in a
> child of three or four. It occurred to him that it was perhaps a
> deeply ingrained tendency from a former life which had been
> passed on through the workings of karma. Even sins of this
> nature will be visited on a small child. So he reflected, with a
> momentary sense of despair. (5:168)

This, then, is the Shiga hero's definition of original sin: "a deeply
ingrained tendency from a former life which has been passed on
through the workings of karma." Inasmuch as the tendency to which
he refers here is none other than the incest wish, his view seems close

to the psychoanalytic redefinition of original sin. Yet it should not be overlooked that Kensaku's thoughts on the subject are again couched in Buddhist terms, as in his speculations on mankind's fate he has alluded to a more "enlightened" outlook. It is not the "sins of the fathers" that are visited on the sons, as it is in the Judeo-Christian notion to which Freud gave a new and more "scientific" interpretation in modern times (while attributing to psychoanalysis itself something like the redemptive role which the religions had traditionally fulfilled).

Contained in Kensaku's view of the question, or in the words used to express his view, is the Buddhist idea of the cosmic process of karma—a concept of "sin" which is less oppressive to individuals than the Judeo-Christian doctrines. For ignorance and desire, the cause and effect of "sin," are considered to be inherent in all organic existence. On this vast, all-encompassing scale, variations in the amount of karma accruing to a particular soul are insignificant. But, with the important exception of Zen (and perhaps some other late Mahayana doctrines), the Buddhist scheme of things is also ineluctable. There is no redemption other than through total release from the process, that is, cessation of all organic functions in nirvana.

I do not mean to assign any specific religious quality to the hero's growing self-knowledge. We may infer that, as at earlier stages in the development of his consciousness, there are still contradictory and barely articulated assumptions underlying both his self-perception and his view of the world outside himself. These intellectual conflicts, as they may be loosely called, continue to appear in his rare moments of speculation on the "large questions" of culture, religion, art, etc., and no doubt reflect the influence of opposing elements in his education: those of a traditional Japanese and (broadly speaking) Buddhist outlook and isolated aspects of a Western and partially Christian world view.

Yet we have seen that the Shiga hero tends less to think things through on a sublimated level than to feel his way intuitively toward a solution of deep-rooted problems. During his stay at Onomichi, Kensaku suddenly arrives at an astonishing decision. He makes up his mind to marry Oei. He will overcome his disquieting fantasies and nightmares by acting them out in broad daylight. He will transcend the only dimly perceived implications of his dream of *harima* by realizing his designs on the older woman and (like Han after he has hurled himself into the dark void) getting away with it in the eyes of the world. The narrative laconically states that in his excitement at the mere prospect he indulges himself repeatedly.

Kensaku's proposal, which he communicates to Oei through his brother, does in fact lead to a resolution of his innermost conflict. But instead of the outcome he has ostensibly hoped for, he is again forced by circumstances to abandon forbidden desires and to accept the irretrievable loss of a child's imagined paradise.

A letter arrives from his brother in which it is revealed that Kensaku is in reality the offspring of a brief union which his (supposed) grandfather had forced on his mother while his (presumptive) father was abroad. Somewhat superfluously, Nobuyuki adds that for Kensaku to marry Oei, the former mistress of his true father, would be to tempt an already unkind fate. "Questions of morality aside," he writes, "the very thought of it is somehow terrifying."

Kensaku is stunned, revolted, and finally moved to pity by the disclosure of his origins: "That base, shriveled-up old man, without a single redeeming feature—and his mother. What an ugly coupling! How defiling to his mother! He felt immense pity for her. 'Mama! Mama!' he called out, like a child drawn to its mother's breast" (5:199).[7] As soon as he has recovered from his initial shock, he resolutely comes to terms with the "true circumstances" of his birth. In a letter to his brother Kensaku states that he is determined not to dwell on the matter. "Some would no doubt consider it frightening," he writes, "but whether it is or is not, *it was not of my doing. It has nothing to do with me. And I cannot be held in any way responsible for it*" (5:201; italics mine).

Kensaku protests too much. I suggested earlier that we need not accept this abrupt development in the plot literally. It is not the "true circumstances" of his origins that the deus ex machina reveals, we may conclude, but wholly imaginary circumstances representing a compromise solution at which he has arrived after his long struggle with this primal question. In his mind the hero has at last done away with the cold and menacing figure in his childhood memories by establishing that this man is not his father after all. He further determines that the money he has received from the "false" father has in fact come out of a legacy left to him by his "real" father. By an only partly conscious act of will, then, he has broken both the ties of blood and the economic nexus with the hateful father.

As stated before, of the three "solutions" to the riddle of the hero's origins which we have been given in three different works, this one has the greatest psychological validity for the character whom we have come to know so well. Yet it cannot be considered any more final and true than the others. For in a real sense there is no solution to this primordial riddle.

Concerning the most various manifestations of the universal oedipal wishes (here with an emphasis on the mother-loving aspect), Lévi-Strauss has written: "The correlation between riddle and incest thus seems to obtain among peoples separated by history, geography, languages and culture.... Let us define it as a question to which one postulates that there is no answer."[8] In his attempts to solve the insoluble riddle, the hero has simply substituted a new enigma: the almost subhuman figure of the "grandfather" who appears only briefly in his earliest recollections, who is totally unlike the wise old man evoked in other works, and whose existence we may therefore doubt.

It will become apparent that, as a desperate, pragmatic measure, the hero's revision of his own beginnings has achieved a certain success. We may even conjecture that it has saved him from the insanity or self-destruction implicit in some of his adolescent fantasies. But it is hardly to be expected that he has laid to rest all the feelings of guilt and anxiety which have clung to the riddle of his birth, even though he now bravely denies all responsibility. Freud tells us that "it is not really a decisive matter whether one has killed one's father or abstained from the deed. One must feel guilty in either case."[9]

Reluctantly Kensaku gives up all thought of marriage to Oei. He does not renounce all dependence on her, and she will reappear in an ambiguous role on the periphery of the new life that he makes for himself in the novel's second part. But it is a condition of the compromise by which he frees himself from his past that he recognize the futility of his attraction to this woman—mistress to the father, second mother to the son.

Now that Kensaku has at last turned away from the shadowy figures of his childhood, he faces the more positive task of making a new identity for himself. He wants to transform himself completely, we are told, "so that he will no longer know this person he has been in the past, Tokitō Kensaku" (5:269). The psychological pain of his separation persists awhile. He is often depressed and experiences mild delusions of reference, imagining insults where none could be intended. (He even fancies that people can see the "truth" of his origins looming over him like a hideous ghost.) At the same time, he begins to devote some of his energies, until recently sapped by his inner struggle, to more resolute, outward pursuits than he has engaged in before.

Nobuyuki observes the change in Kensaku and expresses admiration for his self-reliant spirit. "You have a strong ego," he tells him. "When you make up your mind to do something you carry through with it. I don't have that kind of strength" (5:236). Nobuyuki has recently abandoned his career in business in order to practice Zen. He hopes that the religion will bring him a strength of purpose and a peace of mind that have so far eluded him. Kensaku is skeptical that institutionalized Zen will have the desired effect. He cannot help being cynical about "the recent Zen boom," as it is described. Nor does he approve of the teacher whom Nobuyuki has chosen, a well-known Kamakura master who is "always giving speeches to Mitsui employees and the like" and has impressed Kensaku as "rather wasteful of his spiritual gifts."

We may see in the hero's disparaging attitude toward established Zen an implied contrast between his own intuitive autotherapy, which has only of late given him a firm grip on himself (by a very devious route), and the religion's formal approach to self-regeneration through a method that is both ascetic and (at least initially) imposed from the outside. There is, however, a superficial similarity in that Kensaku's self-emancipation from obsessions with his origins represents a form of rebirth, as does the Zen experience of enlightenment.

This aspect of his own makeshift cure for the universal human neurosis with which he has been acutely afflicted becomes fully apparent in a subsequent passage. While on a short visit to the small town where his mother's family had lived for many generations, Kensaku tries to locate the ancestral home. But no one can tell him where it is. "It really doesn't matter," he comments to himself. "In fact it is better that way. Everything begins with me. I will take the place of all my ancestors" (5:340).

The first part of *An'ya kōro* ends with a simple and beautiful postlude. Like the prologue with which the novels begins, it was first published separately as a short story. (The mawkish title that Shiga gave to it then, *Aware na otoko* or "An Unfortunate Man," scarcely does justice to this fine prose poem.) The closing sequence takes place at the same Fukagawa brothel where he has earlier had his unsatisfying experience with an ugly woman. More recently he has discovered a plain but somehow beguiling, countrified woman. While waiting for her to be free on one of his visits, he practices his calligraphy by copying out a verse in praise of Kannon, the most maternal deity in the Far Eastern pantheon: "She embraces all sentient beings in her merciful gaze, the store of her blessings is boundless as the seas" (5:266).

Later he peruses a book of Chinese poetry and daydreams about Li Po: the sublime stupor in which, according to tradition, he created his art; his buoyant existence, untrammeled by guilt and fear. Kensaku would wish such a life for himself now. But he knows that it is beyond him: he is made of "very different stuff." In the same book he comes

across the famous anecdote about Chuang Tzu's dream of a butterfly
(or the butterfly's dream of Chuang Tzu). And finally his woman
arrives.

He fondles her ample breasts, delighting in their weight. He
squeezes them and shakes them and cries out joyfully: "Hōnen!
Hōnen!" (literally, "Good harvest!"—but it is untranslatable). Kensaku wonders why the woman's breasts mean so much to him: "What
was it about them? He could not be sure. But at the moment they
stood for the one precious thing that could fill the void" (5:275).

There is clearly nothing equivocal about the hero's desire for this
woman. Beginning with the couplet in praise of Kannon, the final
passage contains a lyrical celebration of a mother's love and a love for
mother that is here made universal in a way it has not been before. His
radical ambivalence toward women, founded on the dual character of
the mother(s) in his earliest memories, is nowhere apparent at this
point. And in the novel's second part we shall see Kensaku seek out a
mate with astonishing determination, even though when his search is
rewarded he is again disposed to attribute everything to "fate." Having also overcome fear and hatred of his father, by the drastic means of
denying his existence, he is now able to approach certain areas of the
"man's world of work" with a new enthusiasm. While he continues to
ignore the "real" worlds of society and state, he has already begun to
take a more active interest in the realms of art and religion.

At the same time, the conclusion of the first part is pervaded by an
air of unreality, a sense of euphoria created by the allusions to Li Po
and his revels, Chuang Tzu and his dream. We are not sure how much
of Kensaku's ecstatic experience will stay with him after he leaves this
rarefied atmosphere. But there is no doubt that he has left the murky
world of his prolonged adolescent struggle. And as if to underscore his
break with the past, at the opening of the novel's second part the
setting shifts from Tokyo to Kyoto.

Before proceeding to the final phase of the Shiga hero's inner portrait, it will be useful to review in the broadest outline some of what
we have seen so far:

As a young child the hero learns to mistrust his cold and distant
father. Although his mother often treats him callously, he loves her
and is sure that she, and she alone, loves him. After losing her at an
early age, he transfers some of his affections to a strong and maternal
woman who "sees to his needs." But he always longs for his true
mother and comes to "venerate" her, precisely "because she is dead
and gone."

While yet a child he has resigned himself to enduring the same kinds of bitter experience as those which he has already had. Later in his boyhood, however, he often sees the world in a brighter light. He devotes himself to simple things of beauty, such as gourds. On the eve of his adolescence he is drawn to an exotic minstrel woman, who rekindles sensual feelings from the distant past and arouses hopes of future pleasures. And throughout this period he manages for the most part to ignore the threatening figure of his father, who remains in the background.

After he has entered into young manhood, his fears of the father are revived and intensified. He seeks out his mother in his memory with renewed longing, while often venting his frustrations on his doting grandmother, who has always been a second mother to him. Later in youth he turns to Christianity, but he is unable to accept it completely. He objects in particular to its stern prohibitions on sexual fulfillment, although for a while he goes to great lengths to observe them.

Following several experiments with men, his sexual experience with women begins when he is seduced by a family maid who is several years older than he (and, according to one version, a relative of his mother). In one particular scenario she becomes increasingly aggressive and voracious, until he murders her (or imagines that he murders her) in a moment of panic. In another fantasy, he passively stands by while an older "goddess of love and jealousy" defiles a young maiden who has competed for his affections, transforming her into a "human spider."

During his adolescence his pent-up aggressions and frustrations break out in vivid scenes of spontaneous murder, which are illuminated by the cold glint of knives and razors. He comes to idealize these impulsive and destructive acts. They justify themselves and are beyond the realm of conventional morality. Similarly, he seeks to gratify his need for a docile object of love through fantasies of possessing a young girl, partly as a parent, partly as a prospective lover. But his dreams of passive feminine purity again turn into nightmares.

As his youth draws toward a close he reviews his inner problems in a more realistic light, with emphasis on the hostile relationship to his father that has rankled so in his mind. Yet he also recalls with fondness and admiration his wise old grandfather, who mitigates the pain of the memories which he has chosen to dwell on. His grandfather points the way toward an almost quiescent life, rooted in the soil of traditional culture but ultimately founded on one's innermost self. Though he is still too young and too disturbed to accept this vision, it begins to grow within him.

Still caught up in obsessive feelings toward his father, the hero poses to himself several alternatives for resolving the conflict: a fight to the death, complete estrangement, or total reconciliation. But in a real sense he cannot decide on any one of them. Instead, he adopts a compromise solution whereby he convinces himself that he is not the son of his father after all; he is the offspring of a subhuman old man—a demonic figure more or less invented out of his own fantasies, we assume—whom he imagines to have violated his mother. In effect he chooses, as he tells us, to become his own progenitor.

At the same time, he has continued to yearn for his mother. Over the years he has found a partial source of the unconditional love that he wants in the strong-willed yet indulgent woman who has looked after him during his youth. As he approaches the crisis of late adolescence, the more he is assailed by fear and self-doubt, the more he turns to her for comfort. But through dreams and fantasies he becomes dimly aware of the threat which his growing desire for her poses to his psychic stability. By a sudden act of will he makes himself fully conscious of his essentially infantile wishes. Then, after a last, vain attempt to realize them, he abandons them once and for all, though not without reluctance and a parting reproach for his cruel fate. Having achieved this separation from his past, he proposes to transform himself beyond recognition—to recreate himself in an image of his own choosing.

Two brief excerpts from Norman O. Brown's remarkable book *Life against Death* may cast some light on the path the Shiga hero has traveled so far. His words will certainly be more elucidating than anything I might add here, also, perhaps, more so than the bulk of the voluminous biographical studies of Shiga's works that have been written in Japan. Finally, Brown's general comments on what was once romantically called "the human condition" will suggest a very wide—but in my opinion, a proper—perspective in which to view the whole of the hero's journey when he has reached his destination at the end of *An'ya kōro*.

In the context of his creative restatement of psychoanalytical thought, Brown writes:

> We quote Freud: "All the instincts, the loving, the grateful, the sensual, the defiant, the self-assertive and independent— all are gratified in the wish to be the father of oneself."
>   The Oedipal project is not, as Freud's earlier formulations suggest, a natural love of mother, but as his later writings

recognize, a product of ambivalence and an attempt to overcome that conflict by narcissistic inflation. The essence of the
Oedipus complex is the project of becoming God—in
Spinoza's formula, *causa sui;* in Sartre's, *être-en-soi-pour-soi.*
By the same token, it plainly exhibits infantile narcissism
perverted by the flight from death.... The fantasy of becoming father of oneself... remains even after the destruction of
the Oedipus complex....

The inevitable legacy of the Oedipal project is the radical
deformation of the human ego and the human body. The
castration complex finally enforces the separation of the
child's body from the mother's body, but traumatically, so
that individuality, a true synthesis of Eros and Death, is never
attained. Human narcissism, still burdened with the *causa sui*
project, still seeks an unreal independence and thus gets mor-
bidly involuted.[10]

4

RIPENESS

You must realize that life-and-death itself is nirvana. We cannot speak of nirvana apart from life-and-death.

—Dōgen

THE SHIGA HERO APPEARS at last to acknowledge himself the master of his own fate when we encounter him in the second part of *An'ya kōro* and a few other mature works which may be considered parallel to it. With a resolution that he has not shown before, he finds himself a wife, fathers children, renews old friendships, and strengthens his ties to his brother. From time to time he is also able to devote full attention to the worlds of art and nature, which become inseparable in his increasingly traditional outlook. But again unhappy events in his domestic life drive him back into himself; and, once within himself, he inevitably returns to old obsessions.

As before, he is initially inclined to attribute his problems to a hostile and wholly external fate. Yet, through his intuitive self-analysis, he comes to discern in himself unusually strong tendencies toward the "morbid involution" which Freud and Brown have demonstrated to be one of civilized man's most distinguishing traits. Instinctively, the hero penetrates to the roots of the matter without turning to others for help. Here, however, he does receive valuable advice from those close to him and finds at least a general inspiration in religious wisdom—most evidently, but not exclusively, in Buddhism.

As we have seen earlier, he specifically rejects the false promises held out by latter-day Zen priests who would claim to provide systematic enlightenment into the ultimate facts of life and death. (We may surmise that he would likewise shun orthodox psychoanalysis: perhaps the closest Western counterpart to the established Zen sect in modern Japan.) But at length he senses profound truth in the words of medieval Buddhist teachers, though he confesses that he scarcely "understands" them. In a purely individual and no doubt imperfect way, the hero at least temporarily achieves something like the state described by Dōgen, the founder of Japanese Zen, when he wrote: "Although we have not yet left birth, we already see death. Although we have not yet left death, we already see life."[1] And at the end of the final stage of the life that Shiga has created for his alter ego, the reader becomes aware of the seeming paradox mentioned in the introduction: having reached the height of his artistic powers, as his hero has found peace of mind and fullness, Shiga virtually ceases to write.

The second part of *An'ya kōro* has perhaps a special appeal for Western readers. Previously encircled by a twilit inner landscape that is only too universal, Kensaku emerges here into the light of the outside world for whole stretches of the narrative, which shares with us his fresh perceptions of the social and natural surroundings. He sees things with something of the foreigner's detachment and wonderment, not merely because he has moved from Tokyo to Kyoto, the seat of the old civilization, but because he manages now and then to escape from himself.

Not long after he has arrived in Kyoto, Kensaku chooses his own bride. This in itself is an indication of his newfound confidence, as arranged marriages are still very much the rule in his society. But once his interest has been aroused by a distant glimpse of the woman, he must depend on the conventional channels to accomplish the intricate negotiations that accompany a traditional Japanese marriage. Kensaku is both amazed and faintly amused, as we may be, by the smooth tactics of snooping friends, solicitous relatives, and well-placed connections which lead to a formal meeting with the woman—Naoko is her name—and eventually to matrimony.

Shortly before his marriage Kensaku returns to Tokyo for a farewell visit with Oei, who is soon to leave for the Japanese colony in Manchuria. She has been asked by a cousin to join in a business venture there, the nature of which is not made clear to Kensaku; but he has his suspicions. He is resigned yet regretful on parting with her: he is "sorry not only for himself but for Oei as well."

On his way back to Kyoto, Kensaku tracks down with customary

tenacity a hazy recollection of the previous night's dream. It begins
with a visit to a friend who is here called simply "T." though he can
clearly be identified with a former classmate of Kensaku who has been
briefly introduced before. (An aeronautical engineer only recently
returned from abroad, Tatsuoka, to give his full name, appears to be
an object of near adulation for Kensaku.) In the dream, they enter
together a cavernous building where a kind of circus sideshow is in
progress. Inside one of the cages that have been set up a number of
small baboons are milling about and jostling each other.

Fascinated, Kensaku stands watching these manlike creatures display their animal instincts, then he is suddenly seized by panic and flees
outside. He takes refuge in another large building—it is the Ueno
Museum, he recognizes—and conceals himself just inside the huge
portals. He knows that he is being pursued. Catching sight of a group
of soldiers drilling on the adjacent plaza, he calls out to a laggard and
persuades him to exchange clothes. No sooner has he put on the
uniform than a band of policemen arrive and arrest him. The uniform
does not fit him in the first place, and he has put it on all wrong. It is
no wonder they have caught him, he comments to himself with a wry
smile.

This dream reveals both elements of wish fulfillment and signs of
anxiety in Kensaku's mind as he approaches marriage and an entirely
new life. Here, as earlier in the narrative, "T." (Tatsuoka) represents
for him a self-controlled, mature figure who, through his pioneering
work on airplanes, contributes to the society in a truly beneficial way.
In his company, then, Kensaku is at first merely intrigued by the
aggressive, instinct-ridden baboons (safely locked up in a cage): a
spectacle symbolic of the archaic underground of human consciousness which he has explored within himself at such length. Through a
vague association with both his recent past and his uncertain future,
perhaps, the sight suddenly becomes painful to him. And so he takes
refuge inside the large, familiar portals of a famous museum—a re-
pository of the distant past in man's collective history, and, according
to one interpretation, "a storehouse of infantile memories" when it
occurs in dreams.[2] Before venturing out from his sanctuary he feels he
must disguise or "transform" himself. But he botches the attempt, and
his lack of surprise on being apprehended suggests that he has not fully
expected to make good his escape in the first place.

Almost like an analyst congratulating his patient, Kensaku remarks
to himself that he has done well to recall the dream: "If he had not
discovered the source of his vaguely unsettled feeling, it would have

been enough to spoil his day" (5:327). And once again we observe how sensitive the hero is to his unconscious life.

After his marriage, Kensaku gradually becomes acquainted with his wife; although he is not so sentimental as to invoke the word love, in time he acknowledges to himself that she has come to be a part of him. He feels especially drawn to her at moments when she seems to betray some small foible, as when he catches her apparently cheating at cards (though he later discovers that he has misconstrued what was only a natural oversight on her part). His growing happiness in the marriage is reflected in the narrative's description of the coming of spring to Kyoto—the blooming of various kinds of cherry trees, the succession of ancient seasonal festivals. In the fall, his wife gives birth to their first child, a son. On the night when the event takes place, Kensaku is in the mountains outside of the city attending a "fire festival" at the village of Kurama. The birth of his son is thus surrounded by an aura of primitive and virile ritual.

The short story *Takibi* (Night Fires, 1920; translated below) also belongs to this idyllic period following the Shiga hero's marriage. As mentioned above, it is made up of a sequence of simple activities and anecdotes which the hero and his wife share with a group of friends while staying at an inn by a mountain lake. It is perhaps the best example of Shiga's ability to make a polished story (in Akutagawa's words, "a story without a story") out of "anything."

Beginning with a game of cards on a rainy day, the lyrical prose sketch progresses through a detailed flashback which recalls the previous evening's pleasures—a tree-climbing contest at twilight—and comes to center on the events that ensue after the game breaks up. They work for a while on a small cottage which the innkeeper, "K-san," is building for the hero and his wife. After dinner, they take a boat ride across the lake and discover a camp fire which a group of herb gatherers have left burning while they sleep inside an abandoned kiln. Following their example, the hero and his friends row over to a nearby beach and build a fire of their own.

They pass the rest of the evening by the blazing fire, telling each other anecdotes of wild animals and seemingly supernatural occurrences on the mountain. K-san does most of the talking, with occasional responses and promptings from the others. The last and longest of his recollections concerns a narrow escape from death that he had one snowy winter night when he attempted to climb the mountain. Having misjudged the depth of the snow, he began to flounder partway up the slope. He almost dropped off into a fatal sleep but managed to drive himself onward until he was close to home. Much to his surprise, he came upon a party of men from the inn whom his mother had sent out to meet him. K-san later learned that she had distinctly "heard him calling," although at that moment, he calculated, he had been lying in the snow far below and had not even considered calling out for help.

Here the narrator-hero interpolates a brief comment on K-san's relations with his family. Long ago, his mother had been deserted by his father, who would come around only in the summer—with his young mistress in tow. K-san despised his father's ways, we are told, and opposed him bitterly on many occasions. And so "he had grown all the closer to his mother, and she to him." Although the hero's rather sentimental remarks on the special relationship between mother and son may strike us as characteristic, they seem somehow out of place in the otherwise spare and objective narrative approach that Shiga has adopted in this story.

For the most part there is no attempt to present individual relationships among the characters. We are instead given an impression of the group as one harmonious whole, enjoying together the sights, sounds and smells that are described in fine detail throughout *Takibi*. From time to time the hero and his wife engage in light bantering, usually at the expense of the wife. But the main emphasis is on the flow of images and the characters' shared perception of them. These culminate in a pyrotechnical display produced by glowing brands which the group hurls out into the lake before returning to the inn.

With its long moments of unspoken participation (Lévy-Bruhl's "participation mystique") in a common experience of the still surroundings, as well as the anecdotes about "supernatural" and extrasensory occurrences, *Takibi* represents the rewards of a healthy unconscious life, in contrast to the potential dangers and disorders often associated with the primary process in other works. And, according to one interpretation, lakes and other bodies of water may be seen as symbols of the mind itself, especially "the limpid depths of the psyche."[3] The standard Freudian view, which links water images to birth and rebirth,[4] would also be appropriate to this phase of the hero's life. Within the context of his inner development, *Takibi* portrays in an unambiguous fashion this most serene period he has experienced so far, unlike the parallel passages in *An'ya kōro*, where the brief idyll abruptly reverts to disenchantment and anxiety.

In the first of two disasters that strike Kensaku and his wife, their newborn child contracts a serious disease and dies an excruciating death shortly thereafter. Kensaku curses the "malevolent twist of fate" which has turned the happy event of his son's birth into "another means of making him suffer" (5:448). In a strange coincidence he even sees proof that it has all been predetermined. On the night after the child's birth, he went to a concert which included a performance of Schubert's setting of Goethe's poem "Der Erlkönig." At the time, he found the piece merely distasteful, with its "cheap and obvious style of expression." Now, as he recalls this song about an infant's abduction by the harbinger of death, he considers it an ill omen that was meant for him. Kensaku retreats into himself again and makes little effort to console his wife. On this bleak note the novel's third section ends.

The fourth and final section begins with another unhappy episode, which sets in motion a last recapitulation of several recurring themes in the Shiga hero's history, if only so that in the end they may be negated or transcended.

Kensaku learns that Oei's venture in Manchuria has failed, leaving her all but destitute. He decides to bring her back to Japan and, reluctantly entrusting Naoko to the company of their witless maid, departs soon after for the continent. On his return, he senses from the moment he is reunited with his wife at the station that something has gone wrong.

The sequence of scenes, dialogue, and narrative backtracking in which Kensaku relentlessly pursues his intuition until the facts of the matter have been laid bare is among the most dramatic in the novel. In the course of these scenes he discovers from Naoko that she has been seduced by a cousin of hers, who arrived on an unexpected visit during his absence. Through a long interrogation of his wife, Kensaku unearths every action leading up to the assault. And, delving further into her past relations with this cousin, he ascertains that they had a distinctly erotic character at one time in her childhood.

There are certain technical details in these chapters that one would want to discuss in a close critical approach to the novel. For example, there is an abrupt shift in point of view that takes us away from Kensaku's field of vision for the first time in the long narrative (5:480–81). More or less from the vantage point of the now omniscient author (though it could be argued that Naoko's long confession has conveyed most of this "background" to Kensaku), the scene in which Naoko is seduced by her cousin and one of her early erotic encounters with him are here revealed in retrospect.

Yasuoka, for one, finds this transition somewhat artificial and adduces the usual sort of biographical evidence to suggest that the whole

episode may have been invented by Shiga out of a trivial incident in his
brother's life, rather than experienced by him in one form or another.[5]
He comments that Naoko's single act of "adultery" and its
foreshadowing in her childhood are deprived of some reality by this
technical "flaw," and that even the hero (equated with the author in
Yasuoka's approach) does not appear to be entirely convinced by these
events.

Leaving technical and biographical questions aside, I would prefer
to digress briefly on the larger thematic significance of this new betrayal which a woman has unwittingly inflicted on the hero. Shiga
himself has written of *An'ya kōro:* "The subject I have treated in this
novel rests on the premise that even when a woman is more or less led
into an indiscretion, for which, indeed, she herself may suffer, in
certain cases there are others who must suffer for it far more than
could be imagined. . . . The way it works out in the novel, the hero is
first made to suffer for his mother's mistake, and no sooner has he
escaped from this curse than the process is begun all over again by his
wife's indiscretion" (7:21).

According to Shiga, then, the main theme of *An'ya kōro* is adultery
and its unhappy consequences, the brunt of which must be borne by
the son or husband rather than the mother or the wife. Yet, whatever
Shiga's conscious intentions may have been, if there is any unifying
"subject" in the novel's first part, it is not adultery and its repercus-
sions but the ancient dream of supplanting the father and, in Brown's
harsh words, its "radical deformation of the human ego." The hero
suffers less from the facts of his origins—even if one supposes them to
be true—than from the fantasies of his childhood. To be sure, these are
the most basic and universal fantasies, but they are unusually prolonged and obsessive in his case.

Similarly, in the second part it is perhaps of little consequence
whether or not his wife's "indiscretion" is portrayed in a wholly
realistic manner on the level of plot. (I find it quite convincing in
comparison to the denouement of the first part.) It is of greater
significance that she too has here been implicated in the web of
incestuous wishes and jealous rivalries which has been spun out within
the Shiga hero's mind. However illusory these entanglements may be,
they are disturbingly real for him.

Thus, as Kensaku's wife, Naoko has been given her own "dream of
harima," although hers assumes a much less convoluted form. It is no
more than a simple memory of a child's normal indulgence in an erotic
game. (And yet, the narrative states, "it is by no means innocent.")

Like *harima,* the game that Naoko recalls having played with her
cousin appears to be a pure invention on Shiga's part—another example of his extraordinary "daemon," as Yasuoka remarks.[6]

The game is called "turtle and terrapin." The cousin starts it off by
hiding an inkstone in the garden. A "child," acted by one of Naoko's
girl friends, is then sent out to find it. Naoko, who has been assigned
the role of "mother," lies waiting with her cousin in the *kotatsu.* When
the "child" finds the inkstone she calls out, "Mother! I have caught a
turtle!" At this point Naoko replies, "That is not a turtle," and her
cousin bellows, "It's a terrapin!"

I cannot claim that I understand the particular terms of this game.
But I would agree with Yasuoka's opinion that the general drift of
"turtle and terrapin" is strongly erotic—though it hardly seems
"obscene," as the omniscient author comments (5:480). Reminiscent
of Kensaku's own childhood experiences of this nature, while lying in
her cousin's embrace Naoko feels "a strange sinking sensation which
she never felt before," and when her brother suddenly finds them at
this game, she is "too ashamed to look him in the eye, though she
could not have said why" (5:481).

Nevertheless, we have been given two outwardly important incidents of adultery in the plot. But let us recall another one of Shiga's
own remarks on *An'ya kōro,* an observation which in this case is
confirmed by the work itself: "Here I have written mainly about the
development that takes place within the hero through his reactions to
incidents in the plot. I have not placed much emphasis on these
external incidents themselves" (5:21–22).

In a dominantly subjective approach, the author always runs the
risk of forfeiting the semblance of reality that is so vital to certain
kinds of dramatic and artistic effects achieved in more traditional
modes of storytelling. Shiga has clearly chosen to assume this risk by
aiming at a different order of reality. Because of the constant interior
focus on *An'ya kōro*'s hero—and especially because of the frequent
probing into his unconscious life, the "mistakes" of his mother and his
wife that are suddenly revealed in the plot may appear to arise largely
from the depths of his mind.

Shiga's own remarks would all but encourage us not to take at face
value the novel's treatment of the "subject" of adultery. Beginning
soon after the discovery of his mother's indiscretion, Kensaku has
speculated at considerable length on the general questions of adultery
and "the sins of women." He has even contemplated writing a novel
about a flagrantly "sinful" woman who has come to his attention

recently—and whom he rather admires for her refusal to submit to conventional morality. Unlike other notorious vamps who have publicly recanted their sins, becoming "professional penitents," as he scornfully observes, this woman has stood her ground.

We have seen elsewhere that the Shiga hero's excursions into speculations of a general nature are often prompted by very specific problems in his own life; his intellectual curiosity, if such it may be called, rarely extends to questions by which he does not feel directly affected. This is clearly the case with his speculative digressions on adultery and "women's sins." It has also been suggested that the reality or unreality of the adulterous act which is attributed on the factual level of plot to his wife, as earlier to his mother, is finally a moot question. To conclude the discussion of what Shiga has called his "main subject," we may resort once again to the reductive viewpoint of psychoanalysis proper, partly on the grounds that Shiga's own approach seems at times almost clinically inward and backward.

On the early attitudes toward sex which develop in the young child, Patrick Mullahy comments: "With knowledge of sexual relations he tends to erotic phantasy, to which he is impelled by the pleasure of picturing the mother, or whoever stimulates the greatest sexual curiosity, as secretly unfaithful and engaging in clandestine love."[7] More or less normal in a child, then, this secret "pleasure" of unfounded or exaggerated jealousy may in adults become a neurotic compulsion and a kind of self-fulfilling prophecy. So the psychoanalysts tell us, and many characters in modern fiction (Proust's would be an outstanding example) bear witness to their gloomy diagnosis. Yet in this respect Shiga is closer to the therapists than to some of the authors of such characters. He does not allow his hero to revel in the secret pleasure, nor his readers to enjoy the spectacle.

In the short story *Amagaeru* (Tree Frog, 1923), written while he was working on the second part of *An'ya kōro,* Shiga did delve, only tentatively and rather facetiously, into the "secret pleasures" of cuckoldry. Sanjiro, a provincial sake brewer and a frustrated writer (or a superannuated *bungaku seinen:* "literary youth," in the common Japanese phrase), is eager for his loving but semiliterate young wife to share in his avocation. Preoccupied with business, he sends his wife by herself to a lecture by a visiting author in a nearby town, arranging for her to stay overnight with friends. When he goes to fetch her back the next day, he learns from the friends that she has spent the night with the visiting author. On the way home, as Sanjiro broods over the incident and tries to coax a confession from his wife, he suddenly finds

himself reconstructing the seduction scene in titillating detail: "He felt
the blood suffusing his cheeks, and heard his heart pounding in his
chest. This author, whom his friend had described as 'bursting with
physical vigor' and his own beautiful, buxom wife—the thought of the
two of them together aroused him in a peculiarly potent way. His
mental picture of them went far beyond any casual imagining about
strangers making love (3:174–75)." The story ends with a vivid
glimpse of two tree frogs enjoying conjugal bliss, or so it strikes
Sanjiro, in their nest inside a telephone pole—an invoking of the
pathetic fallacy which, partly because it is so rare in Shiga's works, as
in those of more traditional Japanese writers in general, seems forced
and maudlin. (A more successful piece on the trials of married life is
the genuine fable—or "fairy tale," as Shiga himself called it—*Tensei*
[Reincarnation, 1924; translated below], in which a long-suffering
wife, after a lifetime of being scolded by her irascible husband, loses
patience and devours her still censorious former spouse when they are
reincarnated as, respectively, a fox and a duck.)

But in *An'ya kōro*, Shiga is not disposed to play, whether in the
forced manner of *Amagaeru* or the deceptively innocent style of his
later "fairy tale," with the themes of conjugal infidelity and deep-
rooted discord. Kensaku is shown to be aware of "a sick tendency," as
it is described, which almost leads him to make Naoko review in detail
the scene of her cousin's attack (5:499). Instead, he is eventually
forced once more to search out the roots of his trouble within himself.

Kensaku tells his wife that he has forgiven her. Yet he is not at all
sure that he can forget the episode. He seems to recognize the decisive
role which his own deep-seated feelings will have in determining its
final effect on their marriage: "To dwell on it will only make matters
much worse," he admits (5:486). But before he comes to realize fully
that the terrible things which "go on happening" to him are largely
self-inflicted, a strong hint from a friend is required—and finally a
grim object lesson from himself.

The friend, named Suematsu, is an old acquaintance with whom
Kensaku has only recently grown intimate, having found more room
for such relationships in his maturity than he appears to have had in
his youth. Shortly after his discovery of his wife's indiscretion, Kensaku meets with Suematsu and, in a very roundabout way, seeks his
advice. Speaking in a general vein, he confesses to his friend that he is
impulsive by nature, and tends to arrive at final moral judgments of
both people and "situations" merely on the evidence of his first,
intuitive impressions. Then he adds in his own defense, "But most of
the time my judgments prove right in the long run."

"Only because you choose to think so," Suematsu responds frankly. He tells Kensaku that he can be quite annoying to others with his "moods" and his "feelings," and that he often strikes people as egotistical and overbearing because of them. Suematsu further comments that in his view it is not Kensaku himself who makes these irksome judgments: "They're made by a tyrant who lives inside you," he says. "And you yourself are probably his prime victim" (5:490).

Kensaku protests that everyone is to some extent ruled by such irrational impulses. But the narrative states: "He could not help admitting to himself that none of his past struggles had been directed against an object in the outside world. All this time he had been grappling with something inside himself." He pursues the sudden insight and ends with a silent cry of anguish: "To spend one's life at war with something inside oneself—it would be better never to have been born!" (5:491).

Seeing that Kensaku has taken his words to heart, Suematsu tries to comfort him. "That's the way you're made," he says, "and you might as well get used to it. So long as you manage to free yourself from anxiety it won't matter."

Kensaku stands gazing up toward the steep hills on the eastern border of the city. Suddenly he catches sight of "a strange black object moving through the clouds—and against the prevailing wind." He later learns that what he has seen here is an airplane that eventually crashes in the mountains just outside of Kyoto. But at the moment he feels "something close to terror"—almost like a primitive man who has been confronted by an unknown and unnatural phenomenon. And indeed, as his talk with Suematsu initiates a gradual change in his self-perception, similarly the low-flying airplane that interrupts their conversation augurs a complete change in his view of the outside world, the world of "men's work" and collective progress.

Kensaku soon proves to himself that, as his friend has gently suggested, he is still unable to control his strong unconscious urges; or, as expressed in the psychoanalytic cliché, that his ego is truly not the master of its own house. Shortly after the birth of their second child, Kensaku and his wife set out on an excursion with the infant. They are accompanied by Oei, who has been living with the couple since her return. At the station Naoko delays over changing the baby's diapers. Much to Kensaku's anger, she barely manages to reach the platform as the train starts to move. He grabs the child from her and climbs aboard. When Naoko steps onto the ladder, he reaches down and strikes her with such force that she is sent hurtling backward onto the concrete platform.

Naoko suffers only a mild concussion from her fall. But she is bewildered and frightened by Kensaku's behavior. He tells his wife that it was a "purely involuntary" reflex which dictated his violence at the station. Yet she suspects that her mistake still rankles deep inside him, for all his tolerant opinions on the transgressions of "weak" womankind.

Oei wonders if her intrusion into the ménage has not caused a rift between Kensaku and his wife. Kensaku strongly rejects this suggestion, adding that his outburst has had nothing to do with Naoko either: it stems wholly from his own "unsatisfactory approach to life." But the reader too may wonder if Oei's quiet presence in the background has not in fact had some subtle influence on Kensaku's relapse into indecisiveness and anxiety. We have earlier been told that, in his depression after discovering his wife's unwitting betrayal, he has wanted to throw himself into Oei's arms "like a child." As this is "naturally out of the question," he has laid his head on his wife's breast instead. But he has "a sudden sensation of striking up against an iron plate" and feels as though he has been rudely "awakened from a dream" (5:500).

We may conjecture, then, that the hero has again been tempted by the dream of his lost childhood idyll, even after he has fathered a second child of his own, and even though he has testified with chilling candor that his earliest recollections reveal at most the memory of a paradise already lost. And once more he abandons this ancient and chimerical dream—if only after lashing out blindly at the woman who, like his mother, has betrayed him and, as in reality his wife, has denied him the chance of reviving the seductive vision in a new form.

Kensaku wisely recognizes that there is something wrong with his "approach to life." When Naoko openly reproaches him with his failure to live up to his promise of forgiveness, he replies: "There is some truth in what you say. But as far as I'm concerned, it's my problem and mine alone. I suppose that it is selfish of me to see things purely from my own point of view. But I can't help it. That is the way I am. If it amounts to not recognizing you, I can't help that either. I have to be content with myself as I am" (5:514).

These words may indeed sound selfish to us. But they are also simply honest. In the course of our review of the hero's life we have seen him most often shut up within himself, emerging only occasionally to engage in dealings with others. Sometimes we have not even been sure whether the reported deeds of these others have taken place in the outside world or whether they too emanate from his own mind.

Clearly, if there is to be any change in his marriage or in his apparently
stagnant career, the change must likewise come from within.

Kensaku decides to go away on another journey. He asks his wife to
think of herself "as a widow" in his absence. Naoko considers this "a
morbid thought." But it will prove to have been in a certain sense
prophetic.

His destination is Hōki Daisen, a mountain temple on the Sea of
Japan coast. This same region serves as the setting for the short story
Kinosaki nite (At Kinosaki, 1917; translated below), which may be
considered parallel to the final phase of the Shiga hero's portrait
presented in *An'ya kōro*.

In the first part, it will be recalled, the hero's sojourn on the Inland
Sea coast has been devoted to a review of his origins which ends in
their drastic revision. During his stay on the Sea of Japan coast, which
is described in the novel's second part and in *Kinosaki nite*, he again
changes his attitude toward life, through learning to face death with
equanimity. He does not teach himself this lesson by means of
philosophical inquiry or religious discipline, though his experience
certainly has philosophical and religious implications. It is rather by
close observation of various creatures in their unpredictable cycle of
life, through encounters with simple, stoic fellow men, and finally
through an unadulterated foretaste of his own death that the hero
comes to embrace the nirvana principle, in which life and death are
united.

With a promise to "rise above" whatever it is that has been bother-
ing him, Kensaku takes leave of his wife and sets out alone one
midsummer day. His first stop is the hot springs at Kinosaki, which he
finds remarkably "pristine" for a resort town. Here it is that the
narrator-hero of *Kinosaki nite* comes to recuperate after a near fatal
accident. He has been hit by a train, we are told, and has some cause to
fear possible complications in his spine. The circumstances surrounding Kensaku's journey are clearly quite different. Yet his despair with
his "approach to life" is not dissimilar to the physical trauma sustained by the narrator of *Kinosaki nite*. And if the latter's unflinching
contemplation of life and death has been suddenly forced upon him by
an external event, Kensaku feels a no less compelling inner need to rid
himself of recurring anxiety and uncontrollable aggressions.

The narrator of *Kinosaki nite* goes straight to the roots of the
general human malaise called anxiety, roots which are partly biological, as well as psychological, and ultimately bound up with death. He
does so by relating three final incidents he has observed in the life-

and-death cycles of nonhuman creatures: a bee, a rat, and a salamander. This sequence of incidents, observed so closely as to be experienced vicariously, brings him more and more immediate impressions of death: its loneliness and tranquillity; its initial violence; its arbitrariness.

Unlike Kensaku on his journey of discovery, the narrator of *Kinosaki nite* has already become half-acquainted with death through his recent narrow escape. "In one way or another," he tells us, "I had become intimate with death" (2:176). The experience has enabled him to accept the prospect of his death in a general fashion. He has even pictured to himself his own corpse, rotting in the grave beside the bones of his grandparents. "It will happen sometime," he reflects. But his sudden accident and the efficient modern medical treatment that followed have scarcely given him the chance to reflect on the precise nature of death. In the course of his stay at the hot springs resort, he has an opportunity to satisfy his no longer merely idle curiosity about death, what it looks like, the way it must feel, and its inseparable connection with living.

One day the narrator finds a dead bee lying on the tile roof below his window. The dead bee gives him very much "the feel of a dead creature"—and both the redundancy here and the minute description of the body leave no doubt that he sees it all with extraordinary clarity. The sight produces an impression of utter tranquillity, he tells us, and a sense of *sabishisa*: usually translated as "loneliness," or else "sadness." But in this context it should perhaps be acknowledged that neither of these words conveys the meaning very precisely. Rather, they too narrowly restrict the connotation of *sabishisa*, which may describe a quite positive, if largely passive, æsthetic-emotional experience—as it does here, I would suggest.

The subsequent spectacle of the drowning rat shows the narrator a very different aspect of death: the violence that accompanies the act of dying, the struggle *in extremis*, which is exacerbated in this instance by the rat's human tormentors. After its neck has been skewered with a long stick, the rat is thrown into a river. Some of the onlookers pelt it with stones as it thrashes about in the water, fighting for its life. Eventually the rat moves downstream, still alive but apparently moribund. The narrator comments: "However sympathetic I had come to feel with the silent nothingness that follows death, these strenuous exertions that precede it filled me with fear" (2:179).

He speculates on what his own reaction would be were he to approach this close to death, whatever the cause. In spite of his new intimacy with the utter stillness that follows death, gained from his observation of the bee, he suspects that he too would "most likely" subject himself to this awful struggle. Of course man has the choice of suicide, he adds—an alternative not open to other creatures, who must fight "to the death." But he seems to deny the possibility of this choice to himself as well. Finally, he cannot be sure what effect his present attitude toward death will have at the crucial moment. He concludes that, in any case, the prospect of the last agony need not vitiate his acceptance of death itself. If he must struggle, he comments to himself, "so be it." And if he can sink quietly into that perfect stillness, so much the better.

The third and final encounter is the most immediate and presents the strongest challenge to a merely passive acceptance of the perfect still-ness. For this time the narrator himself becomes the agent of death, albeit unintentionally. While walking along by a stream one day, he sees a salamander perched upon a rock on the opposite bank. The creature calls to mind a truly morbid vision that he first conjured up some ten years ago. The vision is morbid in the sense that it pertains, not to the fact of imminent death which exists in all forms of life, but to a premature fear of the idea of dying which is peculiar to the human species. The sight of several salamanders clustered around a drainage pipe had prompted him to wonder what it would be like to be reborn as one of them. The mere memory of the morbid thoughts that had crossed his mind then is enough to disturb the serene mood to which he has recently attained. Yet presently he manages to overcome the superstitious associations that these creatures had for him in the past. He no longer feels threatened by the salamander, which lies motionless on the other side of the stream.

Without fear or malice, then, and only because he wants to see the salamander swim, he heaves a stone in its direction, hoping to startle it into the water. By sheer accident, the stone strikes the creature. It leaps into the air and falls back on the rock, dead.

At first the hero experiences "a strong revulsion," as though horrified by another manifestation of his destiny, we may imagine—that "malevolent fate" to which we have seen him attribute various untoward events in the past. After his momentary presentiment, how-ever, he does not begin to lament his fate. He continues to feel the pity of what has happened to the salamander through his agency. But he is now touched by "the pathos of all living things" (ikimono no sabishisa).

The pathos lies in the ineluctable necessity of dying that is part of the organic process itself. Beyond this general necessity, the manner in which a particular creature reaches its death is distinctive and arbitrary. The narrator comments: "As by chance I had not died before, so by accident the salamander now lay dead" (2:182). Yet it is precisely the distinctive experience of death, no matter how arbitrary, which gives each living thing its individuality. On the most basic, biological level, death is the natural result of the tendency toward inertia that exists in all organisms. From a nonmystical religious point of view it is nothing less than the fulfillment of life. In the sublime words of the preacher: "To every thing there is a season . . . a time to be born, and a time to die . . . a time to kill, and a time to heal" (Ecclesiastes 3:1–3). As a former Christian and, increasingly, an admirer of the medieval Zen masters, the Shiga hero has presumably come across such words. Yet, characteristically, he does not grasp their meaning until a concurrence of inner need and direct experience forces recognition.

More than any other creature, man can determine the specific content of his life within the large cycle of his biological existence: birth, self-preservation, reproduction, and senescence. But as the hero comes to realize in *Kinosaki nite* and the last chapters of *An'ya kōro,* men cannot determine their own deaths, with the problematical exception of suicide, which he appears not to countenance. Nor can they avert the quite final end that awaits them, whether individually or collectively. In the conclusion of *An'ya kōro* we shall see him firmly reject mankind's efforts to cheat death with what he now considers to be empty and coercive delusions of "immortal" accomplishments and the whole notion of progress.

The narrator of *Kinosaki nite* stops at lucid and unsentimental reflections on his own situation which are grounded in his contemplation of life and death in the nonhuman world. From our earlier acquaintance with essentially the same figure, we deduce that in the past he has sought to deny death. But the easy sublimations which the society provides in the form of orthodox religious myths and vulgar modern positivism have not been enough for him. His has been the constant flight from death of the so-called neurotic—an escape inward and backward that is both a regression to infantile narcissism and, as Brown states in the passage cited above, a perversion of it.

After his near fatal accident and his close look at the life and death of animals, the narrator is able to affirm his natural being as a particular organism that lives and dies side by side with other creatures, rather than exclusively as a member of a family, a class, a nation, or a race. These pseudospecies owe their identity partly to the self-deceptions which they impose on the individual, their aggressions against rival groups and their depredations on entire nonhuman species, all in the name of immortality. The narrator repudiates such aspects of a shared identity when he accepts the immediate reality of death, with its loneliness, arbitrariness and finality. In the end he declares quite simply: "To be alive and to be dead are not opposite extremes. They are not far apart at all, I felt" (2:200).

To live as one who does not ceaselessly fear and flee from death, whether consciously or unconsciously, and who knows that each moment of life is inextricably bound up with death—this, then, is the mature Shiga hero's alternative to those negative and fantastic measures whereby he has earlier tried to escape from "living as one already dead." The more fully delineated experience of Kensaku, whom we have left on the first stop of his journey at Kinosaki, confirms and enlarges upon the clear insights into life and death which the narrator of this fine story has reached.

Feeling "purified" by his overnight stay at the hot springs, Kensaku visits a nearby temple the following morning. There he admires a painting of a pair of eagles by a famous Chinese artist. He is particularly struck by the frank depiction of the procreative instinct in the male eagle, which perches wings outspread on a rock in the sea and eyes his mate from afar. This is the first of several vivid sights encountered by Kensaku along the way—small details, such as stalks of green rice shining in the sunlight, which remind him of the world's essential things as he is about to begin his retreat on the mountain.

To reach Daisen Kensaku must hike a long distance from the station. He hires a guide, who proves to be an affable companion, and together they set out for the mountain. Auspiciously, they pass by a bamboo pole from which dangle a bunch of gourds, "white and exceedingly long" (5:528). At one time the center of the young hero's life and later described as an emblem of "nature's grand design," the gourds here suggest a ripeness that he finds in this last stage of his journey.

The narrative mentions places of note, local legends, and various flowers growing at the roadside in a manner reminiscent of a medieval travel diary. The approach to the mountain temple begins with a brief but remarkable interlude at a tea hut partway up the slope. Inside, Kensaku and his guide are served by a garrulous woman. In addition to the proprietress, there is an old man who is described as "tall and silent like a withered mountain tree that has long been exposed to wind and rain." He stands motionless at the doorway, gazing out on a scene which, Kensaku comments to himself, he must have watched for countless years. Kensaku cannot imagine that the old man is thinking of the future. Nor is he likely to be dwelling on the present. And by now he has perhaps forgotten his long past as well. "Like an ancient tree or a moss-covered rock," Kensaku concludes, "he is rooted to the mountainside. If he thinks at all, his thoughts are no more than those of trees and rocks" (5:533).

When they arrive at the temple Kensaku is welcomed by the priest's wife and a young daughter who, already married and living elsewhere, has come home to spend the summer on the mountain. He is given lodging in a small annex behind the temple's main building, and soon he is settled in a quiet, contemplative life. He passes several hours each day at a small abandoned shrine in the middle of the woods, watching raptly the varied life of animals and insects. He is soothed by the frolicking of lizards, the perpendicular flight of dragonflies, and savors his emancipation from the burden of human ties: "He thought of all the time in the past that he had wasted on petty dealings with his fellow men. The world that opened up before him now seemed ever so much wider than the one he had left behind" (5:541).

A hawk tracing slow, graceful circles in the air prompts Kensaku to reconsider manmade engines of flight. Airplanes now seem to him very ugly contraptions. Recalling his earlier notions of mankind's restless instincts and the unconscious "common Will" which he once postulated, he finds that his outlook on these questions has changed completely. "Could it be natural and instinctive for men to thrust up into the air and plunge below the surface of the ocean as though they were birds and fish? In one way or another man's unrestrained wanting and striving would at length bring him to grief. Sooner or later the human race would be severely punished for its overweening pride in knowledge" (5:541).

Kensaku renounces his belief in a benevolent unconscious Will as a force for progress, and indeed the whole concept of progress through "men's work." By no means does he reject the notion of unconscious instinct altogether. (And we are reminded that the Shiga hero has always been committed to living by his instincts, in whatever form they present themselves most forcefully to his consciousness.) Rather, he recognizes that the aggressive drive to produce and "progress" beyond one's own basic needs is not a truly vital instinct at all.

We may interpret that this false instinct, which "formerly he imagined to be revealed in everything he saw and heard," corresponds to what Marcuse has called the performance principle: "the prevailing

historical form of the reality principle . . . which is that of an acquisi-
tive and antagonistic society in the process of constant expansion."[8]
Kensaku realizes that what he once supposed to be a natural, innate
urge is in reality imposed externally on the individual by society. And
so he negates the performance principle, wishing now to live a simple
life in harmony with his own best instincts.

Kensaku continues his reflections at the secluded shrine, which is
dedicated to Amida, the Buddha of Infinite Light and Life. At this
point the nirvana principle itself is invoked. "He knew nothing about
Buddhism," we are told, "yet he was strongly drawn to the unfathomable realm that the Buddhists call nirvana or the bliss of perfect
stillness" (5:542). Perhaps we need not be too concerned with what is
to be understood by "nirvana" in this instance, as Kensaku's own
thoughts on the subject are shown to be quite vague. And by using the
Freudian term "nirvana principle" I do not mean to ascribe a
specifically psychoanalytic interpretation to the notion as it occurs
here. But precisely because it has been a very ambiguous phrase ever
since Freud invented it, and because it designates a universal inner urge
rather than a historical religious doctrine, it seems appropriate to the
present context.

We may infer that nirvana does not have for the hero its original
sense of complete extinction—even though the words which follow,
jakumetsu iraku (translated above as "the bliss of perfect stillness"),
might be more faithfully rendered: "the enjoyment of a quiet state
beyond annihilation." The narrative adds that recently Kensaku has
been reading Zen texts, which he has borrowed from his brother (only
the *Rinzairoku* is mentioned by name). Again we are told that he does
not "understand," but his perusal of these texts has somehow "improved his mood" (7:225). We may suppose, then, that his intuitive
image of the unfathomable realm is colored by the Zen masters'
transformation of nirvana into a fully realized existence which unites
life and death in this world.

There is, indeed, a certain resemblance between the passage cited
above in which Kensaku rejects the aggressive "performance principle" and Dōgen's famous exhortation to practice enlightenment in the
here and now: "Fish swim in the ocean's depths without ever reaching
its bounds. Birds fly throughout the sky but do not exhaust its limits.
Never have the fish strayed from the water nor the birds from the air.
They use these elements according to their needs, both great and
small. . . . Clearly, for them life is water, life is sky . . ., and by analogy
we may say that for men, whether their lives be long or short, there is

only the practice of enlightenment in their own proper sphere of existence."9 As Zen places more emphasis on self-reliance than any other Buddhist doctrine, it is natural that Kensaku, with his constant search for self-enlightenment, should find inspiration in the words of its founders. But he is most deeply affected by a simple avowal of faith in Amida's Pure Land (attributed to the Abbot Eshin) which he comes across on one of his books: "'When we have turned away from this defiled world and truly rejoice in the prospect of rebirth in the Pure Land, our salvation is assured.' How simple these words seemed! Kensaku wished that he could join hands with the Abbot Eshin" (5:542). And he continues to resist the established Zen sect, which intrudes itself upon him during his stay in the person of an unctuous monk who comes begging favors. On the pretext of inviting Kensaku to a laymen's retreat, the monk at length asks him to vacate his cabin for the use of a visiting Zen master. Annoyed by the monk's deviousness and his wheedling tone, Kensaku refuses to participate.

His life on the mountain is by no means given over entirely to solitary meditations, although from the outset these lend a distinctly religious aura to his experience there. Partly in spite of himself, Kensaku establishes friendly relations with the priest's daughter, Oyoshi, and with a local carpenter named Take, who often comes up from the village to do chores at the temple. They are good, simple people, and Kensaku is drawn to them instinctively. Yet, while the spare characterization of them is quite realistic, eventually they emerge in an almost saintly light.

Kensaku hears from Oyoshi that Take's wife is considered to be a nymphomaniac. It is common knowledge that she has had many affairs both before and after her marriage. Yet the carpenter has never said a harsh word about his wife to anyone and reputedly prepares the family's meals when his wife is engaged with one of her lovers. Upon reflection Kensaku finds Take's extraordinary forbearance "not inconceivable." He reviews his past attitude toward the unwitting infidelities of his own wife and his mother, who now appear quite innocent by comparison. But still he cannot silence a few qualms, though they soon pass, about the temptations to which his wife might be exposed in his absence. So strong is the compulsion to indulge in the "secret pleasure" of jealousy.

On the eve of a final ordeal which Kensaku undergoes at the close of the novel, he learns that Take's wife has been knifed in a quarrel with her current lover. He is quite shaken by the incident and momentarily regrets that he has once again allowed himself to become involved in emotional ties with his wretched fellowmen. But his heart goes out to Take—this simple man whose example has contributed, no less than his contemplation of nature and perusal of religious texts, to the change which has gradually come over him. While recalling that the Shiga hero has elsewhere reflected on his early experience with Christianity only to repudiate it, we may nevertheless recognize the important role that is filled by a gentle carpenter at the end of his journey. Take is clearly not one of those full-blown "Christ figures" of the sort that abound in the novels and films of the partly Christian and post-Christian West. But there is perhaps some connection.

Oyoshi briefly plays a more openly religious part in the last act of the hero's inner scenario. One night Kensaku dreams of an arcane yet intensely satisfying ritual. It is plainly of a Shinto type, in contrast to the generally Buddhist quality of his "spiritual" reawakening (and the vaguely Christian implications mentioned above). In the dream, Oyoshi appears dressed in the white robes of a Shinto priestess. Kensaku stands midway on a flight of stone steps that lead up to a shrine. Aware that Oyoshi has just been celebrated as "a living goddess," he watches while she glides smoothly down a bed of logs which has been laid over the incline for the occasion. As she draws near, Kensaku is pleased to note that she wears her usual "slightly vacant" but beautiful expression ("well suited to a medium," he remarks) and has not been made conceited by the great honor accorded to her. She sweeps by, very close to him, and the long sleeves of her robe brush across his face. At that moment he experiences "an ecstatic sensation"; then he awakes (5:546–54).

Afterward Kensaku is surprised by the erotic effect which the outwardly sublime events of the dream have produced on him. Recently he has imagined himself to be free of such feelings. Yet of all the dreams recorded for us, both in *An'ya kōro* and in other works, surely this is the purest and most beautiful. If, as Freud tells us, dreams represent fulfillment of our most deep-seated wishes—a fusion of past wants and present hopes for the future—we may conclude that Kensaku has arrived here at a satisfying compromise between old, unrealizable desires and his newly acquired religious outlook. Instinctively he would seem to have recapitulated one of the rituals by which his prehistoric ancestors both sublimated and perpetuated their longing for the First Mother.

This final dream episode also contains an element of self-detached humor that has long been lacking in the hero's view of his inner experience. At the time, he is both awed and amused by the spontane-

ous vision. Later, he cannot resist teasing Oyoshi about her appearance in his dream. He likens her role to that of a well-known modern
"shamaness": Nakayama Miki, the foundress of Tenrikyō. Of course
Oyoshi is much more attractive, he adds. At a loss for a reply, the
young wife and mother simply laughs and shrugs her shoulders.

As if to assure the monastic solitude he hoped for on his departure,
Kensaku has informed his wife that he will not write to her unless
some urgent need arises. But he finds that he misses her very much and
soon breaks his resolution. In a long letter he describes to her his
peaceful routine and writes about the change that has come over him
during his short stay on the mountain:

> I don't recall ever mentioning this to you, but I have been
> plagued for years by a certain kind of arrogance. In the short
> while that I have been here, I think that I have already begun
> to rid myself of these delusions. When I was in Onomichi,
> alone, as I am now, these delusions kept me in a constant state
> of irritation. But now it is quite the contrary. So long as my
> present feelings stay with me I am confident that I will cease
> to be a danger to myself and to others. This new sense of
> humility is a wonderful experience for me (though I should
> add that I don't necessarily mean humility in relation to other
> people).... I am fairly sure of myself right now. But it would
> be foolish to leave the mountain while there is any chance of
> my falling back into the same old ways [moto no Mokuami ni
> naru]. So I shall stay here until I have a firm grip on these
> feelings and have made them a part of me. Then I'll come
> home to you. (5:554–55)

"A certain kind of arrogance" in the past, a new sense of humility
("though not necessarily in relation to others"), and a hope that he
will not "fall back" once again—such perceptions would indicate that
he has in fact achieved a remarkably clear knowledge of himself. There
is no pretense of having adjusted, willy-nilly, to the demands and
conventions of the outside world. The change has taken place "spontaneously," he tells his wife, and wholly within himself, although we
might add: with the aid of nature, the inspiration of several religious
texts, and living examples of simple humanity at its best.

Ever since he first arrived at the temple, Kensaku has been eager to
climb to the top of the mountain. Eventually he is presented with an
opportunity to share a guide with a party of Osaka businessmen who
have come on a holiday. They are to begin the climb early in the
evening in order to reach the summit by sunrise. When he awakes on

the morning of the appointed day, Kensaku is sick with what appears
to be a mild case of food poisoning. Determined to go through with his
plans, he rests during the day. By late in the afternoon he feels well
enough to make the climb.

He finds the group from Osaka in high spirits. In a thick dialect,
they joke among themselves and address friendly remarks to Kensaku.
As they begin the ascent they call out a mountaineer's chant: "rokkon
shōjō oyama wa seiten" ("purifying the six senses—the clear mountain
air"). After a few hours Kensaku begins to feel weak. He falters as the
path grows steeper and finally asks the others to go on without him.
He will rest awhile, he tells them, then he will return to the temple by
himself. After some hesitation, they part with him and resume climbing. Kensaku pulls on a sweater that he has brought along. Then he
leaves the trail:

> He walked through the grass until he found a good spot. He
> sat down and leaned back against the slope. Inhaling deeply
> through his nose, he gave in to a pleasant feeling of fatigue.
> From far above he could hear the men's voices calling out at in-
> tervals: "Rokkon shōjō oyama wa seiten!" Presently it grew
> still again and he found himself alone under the broad sky.
> The grass quivered gently in the chill breeze that blew across
> the mountainside.
>
> From exhaustion he felt himself falling into a light-headed
> stupor. His body and mind began to melt into the vast nature
> around him. He was a blade of grass in comparison to the
> boundless immensity that enveloped him. To evaporate into
> these ethereal surroundings, to return to his original element,
> was a joy beyond words. It felt something like dropping off to
> sleep without a care in the world—and he was already half
> asleep.
>
> This was by no means the first time that he had experienced
> a sense of merging with nature. But never before had there
> been this euphoria. Until now he had always felt a sensation
> of being sucked into the void, rather than of melting into it.
> The intense pleasure had been accompanied by an impulse to
> resist, and the difficulty of resisting had brought on acute
> anxiety. What he felt now was altogether different. He had
> not the slightest will to resist and gave himself over to the
> pleasure of sinking effortlessly into the surroundings.
>
> There were no night birds to break the stillness. A thin
> mantle of fog hung over the earth below, obscuring the lights
> of the villages. All he could see were the stars and, beneath

them, the shadowy mountaintop that crouched over him like a huge animal with its back thrust up. It occurred to him that he might have taken the first step on the path to eternity. And yet he felt no fear of death. If he were to die now there could be nothing to regret in such a death. But in his mind, by eternity he had not meant death. (5:578–79)

Kensaku sleeps awhile. He awakes at dawn to a brightening sky whose color seems to him "imbued with compassion." After watching the sun rise over the bay in the distance—a scene described with lyrical brilliance—he painfully makes his way back down to the temple. Here he falls unconscious, and the narrative point of view shifts temporarily to that of the omniscient author (as it has only once before in the novel). We learn of Kensaku's precarious state, the concern of Oyoshi and her mother, and the arrival of a doctor. Intermittently, there are glimpses of Kensaku's feverish hallucinations. In moments of lucidity, we are told, he is conscious only of having been "purified in mind and body."

His condition grows somewhat worse. It is tentatively diagnosed as cholera by one doctor, but this later proves to be mistaken. The women at the temple are nonetheless alarmed and send at once for Kensaku's wife.

With Naoko's arrival, the narrative adopts her point of view for the first time. It is mainly through her eyes and thoughts that we are shown the brief closing scene in which she and her husband are reunited. Kensaku momentarily regains consciousness as she enters the room. He tells Naoko of "a wonderful feeling" that he has had. Startled by his fervent tone, she assures him that he will soon be well. Then Kensaku closes his eyes and drifts into a peaceful sleep. Naoko watches him intently and wonders if he will in fact recover. At the moment it does not matter to her. She vows to herself that she will stay with him always.

The concluding chapters of *An'ya kōro* raise certain technical questions, of the sort encountered in the sequence where Naoko's indiscretion is revealed. The two shifts in point of view, which take us from the hero's inner voice into the mind of his wife by way of the omniscient author, are undeniably disconcerting. One need not resort to narrow and prescriptive notions of point of view in fiction—the fourth unity, as it has been called—to acknowledge that Shiga's treatment of the technique at the end of his novel is unconventional. But we should recall that the novel also begins unconventionally with a "prologue" narrated in the first person. And there is, after all, nothing inherently satisfying about novels which scrupulously adhere to a single point of view. On the contrary, we enjoy being "disconcerted" occasionally if the formal disruption fits in with our understanding of the work on some other level.

Some readers may nevertheless feel that *An'ya kōro* should end with Kensaku alone on the mountain—not for any technical reasons, but because this would seem a more natural conclusion in the light of all that has gone before.

Shiga once expressed surprise that several well-known critics considered *An'ya kōro* to be "a novel of love." "I am not interested in so-called love stories," he commented, "and have never had the slightest intention of writing one" (8:22). And certainly it seems odd to call this severe and unsentimental work "a novel of love." Aside from the problematical closing scene, there is little attempt to show the kind of mutuality in the hero's relationship with his wife that the critics presumably had in mind when they invoked this catchword.

If *An'ya kōro* is "a novel of love," it is more precisely a novel about self-love: neither "modern egotism," as some of the intellectual historians would have it; nor "petit bourgeois subjectivism," as the postwar Marxist critics would insist; but the painful and dubious project of achieving a mature love of self that is rooted in healthy infantile narcissism and tends toward eventual fulfillment in death.

It is indeed a questionable venture. "Rationalized" modern society is by definition utterly opposed to it. The state finds it intolerable, the more so the more authoritarian the regime. (No doubt for far more innocuous reasons, the wartime publication of a cheap edition of *An'ya kōro* was halted by the government censors.)[10] And literary scholars of various persuasions will find it an unsuitable subject for "serious fiction." Even in Japan, where personal fiction has occupied a special place, the writer is expected to keep his ego within bounds and to concentrate on the surface phenomena of consciousness and humdrum everyday life.

Western readers, as well as some contemporary Japanese readers, may consider themselves justifiably cynical about an author's attempts to tell all in his works, and in the process to recreate his own life rather than some entirely fictional substitute. We suspect that when an author pretends to fix his gaze resolutely inward and backward, ignoring the "real" world of the newspapers, factories, and laboratories, the result is not likely to be another Proust. For if Proust's narrator takes as his point of departure his "wretchedness and agitation" while he waited for his mother's goodnight kiss, and his joy when at last she arrived to bestow it, he soon appears to have put aside such childish things.[11] Everyone has had an "Oedipus complex," we are told; but in an unresolved or imperfectly sublimated form, the experience does not seem a fruitful subject for literary representation—with the exception of myth and a few "visionary" modern works, of which Shiga's is perhaps a partial example.

In a word, we know that self-denial and sublimation is the stuff of which literature is made. The modern West has allowed for a certain amount of Whitmanesque celebration of the self, a strain which is particularly strong in American authors and others influenced by them. The outwardly robust and indestructible egos of characters created by Lawrence, Hemingway, Mailer, etc., have no doubt been welcomed by many readers as consolation for small lives in a world where the possibility of true individuality appears to exist in inverse proportion to the bland encouragements of its popular prophets.

Yet we have seen that in *An'ya kōro* and various other works Shiga has presented us with a "robust ego" only at certain critical junctures. Elsewhere, we are confronted with identity fragments, a distinctly adolescent self which at times appears in danger of dissolution, and even the scrawny figure of the rejected little boy-id forlornly playing in a moonlit garden. One imagines that for many Western readers this would be an embarrassing, if not a frightening, spectacle. And when, toward the end of *An'ya kōro* and in such short works as *Takibi* and *Kinosaki nite*, the Shiga hero seems finally to achieve that much cherished goal of the modern West, "mature selfhood," it is in some respects all but relinquished. At least temporarily, it is sacrificed to a collective *participation mystique* in natural and vaguely supernatural phenomena, which may strike the Western reader as somewhat primitive and childlike; to clear visions of death that, in spite of our intellectual efforts to embrace the "nirvana principle," we may resist as in themselves morbid; and in the end to a religious experience which, from a partly Marxist or Freudian point of view, one is inclined to consider a relic of the childhood of the race or a merely individual regression to infancy.

Lying against the slope of the mountain, which crouches over him "like a huge animal"—that is, much as in the "anaclitic" posture of the infant at its mother's breast, Kensaku gives himself over to the euphoria of dissolving into the surrounding nature. The anaclitic (literally, "leaning up against") stage of early childhood gets its name from the libidinal attitude of the small child, as well as its physical posture. According to the psychoanalysts, during this stage the infant feels itself at one with the surrounding world. As Freud describes it in *Civilization and Its Discontents:* "Originally the ego includes everything; later it detaches itself from the external world. The ego-feeling we are aware of now is thus only a shrunken vestige of a far more extensive feeling—a feeling which embraced the universe and expressed an inseparable connection of the ego with the external world."[12]

But precisely! the fully sublimated modern rationalist will say. Who would want to go back to that? What is the point of it? And how does it benefit society? The cliché-mongers will remind us that man is a social animal. The conscientious ideologues will take the self-deluded poets to task for shirking their responsibility when they do not face up to this hard fact. And the literary critics will strenuously object to preoccupation with these semimystical states—if their bias is historicist, on the grounds that it does not fit into any of the accepted historical categories; from a formalist point of view, because attempts to describe such experience tend to strain the limits of the language and to violate the harmonious æsthetic order with their evocation of Dionysian chaos.

Shiga himself has evidently had some doubts along the way about the maturity of his literary vision. Shortly before completing *An'ya kōro* (when he was slightly over fifty), he wrote: "A certain novelist died at a ripe old age. Just before he took his last breath, he looked back on everything that he had written, and all of it struck him as mere child's play. What an unbearable thought!" (7:27).

Perhaps some of Shiga's works are in various ways "child's play," though this phrase need not be construed in a pejorative sense (and in this connection we may recall Baudelaire's remarks on the role of the artist's childhood in the expression of his genius). In the foregoing discussion it has been suggested that Shiga's style sometimes seems repetitious to the point of a child's "echolalic speech" and that his works are lacking on the whole in large designs and solid structures. In the course of our only partial review of his protean hero's inner development, we have concentrated on a few recurring themes, most of which display what could be called regressive tendencies and in general an almost obsessive concern with the basic issues of coming of age within the human family.

We have not explored here the possibility that the problems which have often absorbed the Shiga hero, and the "child's play" in which he has frequently indulged, are not entirely universal, but partly a reaction against a still strongly patriarchal culture within a society where other traditional values, including sturdy artistic conventions, had been seriously eroded in a short period of time. Nor have we considered the distinct possibility that the more positive, mother-loving aspects of the oedipal situation in which the Shiga hero is so deeply involved are not felt to be a "problem" at all by most Japanese readers. The prominence of mother-lover figures and the motif of "the lost mother" in the most various works of Japanese literature from the *Genji monogatari* to the novels of Tanizaki Jun'ichirō make it clear that this whole area of man's consciousness is far from being taboo or disesteemed.[13]

Yet we have seen in Shiga's works themselves that this psychological involvement is profoundly disturbing to the hero and at certain points threatens to engulf him. It is only after he has freed himself from the specifically oedipal manifestations of his longing for the lost mother that he begins to enjoy all the other instincts—instincts toward love of self and one's "soul mate," unity with nature, religious faith—which are originally fostered during the infant's charmed existence under the mother's complete protection.

If Kensaku regresses once again as he lies half-conscious on the mountainside, it is to the earliest years of life when the child embraces the universe, rather than to the period when he engages in vain strivings to supplant the father. But must this sublime experience, this purification of mind and body, as the hero later recalls it, be reduced to the negative category of regression? Or, as Freud has phrased the question, in his essay on religion entitled *The Future of an Illusion:* "Since men are so little accessible to reasonable arguments and are so entirely governed by their instinctual wishes, why should one set out to deprive them of satisfaction?"[14] Why indeed!

I have stressed here the illusory and fantastic qualities in Shiga's literature both because they stand out in my reading of the works and because the Japanese approach to Shiga, as well as to most other writers, often seems almost perversely intent on robbing the author of his greatest gift: the ability to create dreams in which readers may or may not choose to share. But by describing the works as, at their best, illusions and fantasies, and by emphasizing the Shiga hero's "daemonic" and childlike propensities, I have naturally not intended any sweeping criticism. By the time he reaches the end of his journey, the Shiga hero has very few "illusions" about himself and his world. Whatever illusions remain, if such they must be called, are religious and archetypal in character, purified and enriching.

To the passage quoted above, Freud added that in making his

rationalist critique of religion, he himself may be "chasing an illusion." I believe that Freud was indeed chasing a rather dangerous
illusion when he tried to bring religion, as well as the rest of man's
age-old habits, under the control of the reality principle. Surely few
societies have stood in greater need of the nourishment of certain kinds
of illusions than that of post-Meiji Japan. Beyond the sometimes
stifling confines of the Shiga hero's inner world lies the dreary macrocosm of ever more bureaucratic and industrial modern Japan, with its
totalitarian myth of the sacred state. While there is certainly room for
various criticisms of Shiga's works from many different perspectives, I
fail to see the point of those which object only to his failure to portray
this world. Other writers—most especially Natsume Sōseki—had already done so in a devastating manner. And we are by now all too
familiar with the futility of redundant expressions of alienation in
modern literature.

Among the alternatives open to the modern artist is that of a
narcissistic retreat into the self; or, as the case may be, a retreat behind
a somewhat confused array of identity fragments. This relation to
what is known as the real world may not hold much promise for
whole-some and vigorous creations, and perhaps lends itself more
readily to expression through poetry, drama, and the visual arts.
(Shiga once confessed that if he had another life to live he would prefer
to be a painter; 7:426.) Although it may not be conducive to the
writing of good novels in the traditional sense, "narcissistic with-
drawal," accompanied by a simple, childlike acceptance of one's
natural surroundings and one's neighbors, is nevertheless a good way
for a sensitive man to survive in the modern world.

Apropos of Shimazaku Tōson, several of whose children died from
malnutrition while he dedicated himself to his writing, Shiga once
asked whether the sacrifice of a single life is justified by even the best
works of literature. He clearly did not think so in Tōson's case
(3:462). And it is obvious from the course of his own career, by no
means prolific and prematurely ended, that he did not want to give too
much of himself to his works, although he no doubt gave a great deal.
His restraint was of course made possible in part by his financial
independence.

Modern Japan has exacted a heavy toll from its writers in the form
of suicide and lives filled with more than the ordinary share of human
suffering. Rather callously, one may add that the eagerness with which
many of them have let the world know of their suffering, and even of
their suicidal tendencies on occasion, often mars the works for which

they have sacrificed so much. Shiga has successfully cast some of his alter ego's pains and pleasures within a universal and mythic context that those of us far removed from his world can understand. And where he has failed, one imagines that the failure has been in the interest of his private life, which was certainly very long and, according to most accounts, contented.

TRANSLATIONS

Shiga Naoya, self-portrait, 1912 (courtesy of Iwanami shoten)

FOR GRANDMOTHER
Sōba no tame, 1911

I often get the feeling that all my friends have secretly turned against me. I know very well that it comes only from some unhealthy, passing state of mind of my own, but if I make the mistake of going to see someone in such a mood, I am liable to speak and behave in an unpleasant, threatened manner, and end by parting in a spirit of isolation and anger. At these moments I invariably think of my grandmother. "When you come right down to it," I tell myself, "she is the only one."

My grandfather died exactly five years ago. He was a great man—everyone who knew him has always said so. He was very much the patriarch of our family and, in my grandmother's eyes, something approaching a demigod. He took very good care of himself and remained in excellent health until he was seventy-nine, when he contracted cancer of the stomach. Although most men his age would have died a quick death, the healthy body he had built up over the years put up a strong fight. The agony went on for several months, a terrible sight to see. My grandmother, who had been by his side since the distant time when she was a girl of sixteen, nursed him with a ferocious strength. I looked on incredulous at her tenacity and stamina as the weeks went by. Where did this frail old woman, already seventy herself, get such strength? I respected and loved my grandfather. But at this stage my worries focused on my grandmother, who I feared might not outlive him should the struggle go on.

Having taken to his bed at the end of September, my grandfather finally died early in the New Year. As soon as he stopped breathing, the hushed room began to echo with sobbing voices. My grandfather had been one of many children, and there was a large number of nieces and nephews who had come a long distance to be with him at the end.

After a while I could not stand to hear the weeping anymore and went out toward the parlor. Along the way, just inside the latticework door of the side entrance, stood an albino whom I had seen somewhere before. "The —— Funeral Home," he announced, "at your service!" He told me they were most eager to be of assistance in our time of need.

I was taken aback that he should have come so quickly. My grandfather had only been dead a quarter of an hour. As the funeral home in question was way down around the corner where the streetcar stops, it was not possible that he could have been sent for and arrived within fifteen minutes, however young and swift he might be. It was very odd. I answered that I knew nothing about the arrangements, and passed on.

As it turned out, the funeral, the wake—everything was in fact entrusted to the albino's establishment. (A rival mortician, I later heard, had showed up only fifteen minutes after the albino.)

After burying her husband, my grandmother gave various people the impression of one with no more purpose in life. It made me sad to see her succumb this way. And, indeed, not long after she became a widow, her health began to decline.

She was, however, a woman of strong passions, not the sort to sink into passive indifference toward things around her. We shared the same room, and after my grandfather's death she took to complaining about my habit of sleeping late in the morning. We quarreled about it almost every day, it seemed. In the same irrepressible way, she would meddle in other areas of my life, until I began to lose my temper, speaking to her harshly and at times going out of my way to irritate her.

Once, I don't remember how it began, I entered into a particularly bitter argument with her that left her in tears. When she had been reduced to silence, I hurled a final string of insults at her and went off to take a bath. In a little while she appeared at the bathroom door clutching a cane. So she's going to hit me now, I thought to myself, and hunched over to receive the blow. Without a word she set about whacking me with the cane as hard as she could on my bare back. When I scoffed and told her it didn't hurt a bit, she muttered and aimed a few more blows against the nape of my neck, then left the room, slamming the door behind her. It was not long after this encounter that she lost the strength for such reprisals, no matter what provocation I might offer. And it was then that I began, unaccountably, to brood about the albino.

From time to time I passed him in the street. He would be loping along, arms and legs swinging out from his body, dragging his clogs over the pavement, in an altogether ungainly fashion. His pale, pinkish, translucent skin, beneath which the veins were faintly visible, was mapped with little brown spots. His oval face converged on sunken cheeks; the corners of his mouth turned up, giving him a perpetual grin. As he went along he would dart sly looks at the faces of passers-by with his gleaming gray eyes. Whenever I passed him I would be seized by a sudden rush of reflexive tension. Then I would recall the day of my grandfather's death and picture the albino lurking just outside the large house, waiting eagerly for the final moment. Accompanied by spontaneous rage, the thought occurred that he was now working a fatal spell on my grandmother. This notion would rankle and send me into a ludicrous paroxysm of ineffectual anger. And yet for two years, nothing happened.

Two years later I caused a great furor in the family because of my involvement in a certain affair. My father announced that I had been disinherited and should leave the house at once. I was resolved to exile myself to the country, drawing on the money I had persuaded my grandmother to deposit in my name, and had gone so far as to arrange for a house which I was to occupy in a few days' time. At this juncture my grandmother's nerves, always stretched to the breaking point in any case, went to pieces under the strain of worry. She collapsed, and for a time seemed on the verge of dying. Everyone in the family was resigned to it, and I could not bring myself to leave immediately as planned. When ten days had gone by, it became clear that at least she would not die, but the doctor said she would need three or four months of complete rest before she would be on her feet again. It was during this episode that the prospect of my grandmother's death first took on a frightening reality for me.

"It's all very well for you to up and leave," one of my uncles said to me, "assuming you really don't care about the inheritance. But your grandmother has only a couple of years left at most. There's time enough for you to do whatever you want after she's found some peace and come to the end."

"As long as I can keep her worried," I rejoined, "she won't die. With her it's 'peace' I'm afraid of more than anything."

My uncle chuckled, but I was quite serious. And I secretly despised the doctor for pronouncing so blandly that she had but a couple of years to live.

My grandmother did in fact recover, little by little. But she was no less cantankerous as her health improved than she had been as it declined, and she caused both the nurse and my stepmother a good deal of trouble. When she was out of sorts, I was the only one who could give her a stern scolding.

I had for some time been planning a trip abroad but did not hesitate now to give it up once and for all. Having lost my mother at the age of thirteen, I had been brought up since then almost exclusively by my grandmother. Indeed, such faults of mine as willfulness and weakness under pressure were viewed by the rest of the family as the deplorable result of her blindly indulgent love. During her illness she often cried over this family consensus, which never failed to drive me either to anger or to tears. Whenever my dead mother was brought into the discussion, I would forgo the attempts at angry self-justification and simply cry. At times I tried to imagine what it would be like to be left alone in the world by this old ally and adversary of mine.

My grandmother continued to recuperate and after two months was at last able to leave her bed. Yet she had been visibly weakened by her long illness, and her present condition caused me a more general, and more helpless, kind of anxiety. "You'll just have to live to a ripe old age," I would roughly order her, adding words to the effect that I was, after all, on the point of *doing* something in the world. She would nod, but with a quizzical look in reference to the "something." Then I would lose my temper.

One night I had a dream.

I open my eyes—still dreaming—and see my grandmother leave the room. But the toilet is occupied, I say to myself; my mother has just gone in with Masako (my youngest sister) in her arms. I make no move to get up, however, and presently hear my grandmother washing her hands; then she comes back into the room. When I get up and go over to tuck her in, as is my habit, I discover a pair of tiny hands protruding from the sleeves of her bed jacket—Masako's. Through an immediate intuition I know that as she brushed by my mother in the corridor the baby's hands had somehow got stuck there. A knot of fierce tension forms at the pit of my stomach, while outwardly I remain utterly calm and passive.

Maintaining my cool exterior, I call to my mother in her room, which is the first one down the corridor. She appears with Masako; the baby is sleeping peacefully, her head lolling back in her mother's arms; and her hands are as they should be. I quickly look over at my grandmother's sleeves: in place of the baby's hands a large clump of hair—my hair—now lies spread out there, about three inches of growth still attached to the scalp. I cry out to myself, "There is some thing in the house."

Not daring to touch my head, I simply ask my mother to call my father. Without a word she gets up to leave the room. Then there is total silence. As though sound asleep, neither my mother nor my grandmother speak at all. An invisible malevolent force holds sway over the whole house. I can feel it. And I know that to so much as blink in the face of it would be fatal. I see now that one of my little sister's hands, which dangles down across my mother's sleeve, has turned a dark earthen color. Involuntarily, I leap up out of bed and start toward my mother. Whereupon I feel something slip by me from behind. Not hesitating for a moment, I go after it as, with astonishing speed, it slides ahead, opening partitions and doors in its path without making a single sound. Then it leaves the house through the side entrance.

For a second I think to myself: a foreign woman; but no, I instantly conclude, it is the albino. He is fleeing—flying toward the outer gate, dragging a gray skirt over the ground. Suddenly I take hold of him from behind.

Then I woke up. I lay awake for quite awhile, breathing heavily and

contemplating the circular reflection of the round bedside lamp upon
the ceiling. I noticed with some surprise that my grandmother's eyes
were open, too. When I told her about my dream, she said, "Really? I
just had the exact same one." A shudder went through me. But the
next morning it became apparent that this too had been part of my
dream.

The dream stayed with me for a very long time.

When I was a child, there was a boy in the class below me whom,
for no reason whatsoever, I loathed. One day my deep-seated animos-
ity got the better of me, and I pounded his face with a rubber ball until
he cried. Not long after, however, I had a complete change of heart.
It happened because of a dream in which he appeared, beautifully
dressed, altogether appealing to look at and charming in his attitude
toward me. The next day I felt for him a kind of love.

But to become so obsessed with the albino because of a mere dream
seemed to me at first absurd, even barbaric. Yet, reflecting on what
had happened when my grandfather died, I berated myself: to entertain such scruples and relax my guard was to invite disaster. I often
saw the albino slinking down the street, hands thrust under the lapels
of his robe, the picture, it struck me, of a half-starved carnivore
searching for prey. But how very different, how dynamic he appeared
when he was dashing about alongside a funeral procession, seeing to
one thing and another! And what righteous anger I felt on behalf
of the unsuspecting women mourners, strangers though they were,
dressed all in white, weeping as they followed his lead!

My grandmother appeared to me to have gone into another decline,
though I could not be at all sure, which was disturbing in itself, how
far this view was colored by my own peculiar perceptions of her.
When I came home late of an evening she would ask me where I had
been; she took to asking me for something to nibble on between
meals—I would fetch her a few crackers, the sort of thing strictly
forbidden even to me as a child; and if I went off on a trip for a couple
of days she would be so upset that I would regret my thoughtlessness.
All of these small signs of deterioration led me to the conclusion that I
must do something about the ill-omened albino.

A relative who came to visit one day remarked to my grandmother,
apropos of an old invalid in his own immediate family, "When a sick
man starts to droop from the weight of his bed jacket, he's not long for

this world." It chilled me to hear these words, both because my grandmother passed them on with the comment that indeed her bed jacket weighed heavily on her, and because I was forced again to imagine how it would be when she was gone. We all must die, hardly anyone lives to be a hundred—this sort of thing I of course knew perfectly well. Still, I wanted her to live to at least ninety, when I would be in my forties. I would really have to do something about the albino—something! But my thoughts on the subject went no further than that.

That fall, after a sequence of abnormally warm days it suddenly turned very chilly. My grandmother caught a cold that went by slow degrees from bad to worse. She developed a constant cough and grew alarmingly short of breath. The time I have been dreading has come, I told myself.

I don't know the name of the disease, but the nature of it is such that phlegm collects in the lung and progressively constricts the space for breath, hence the rapid gasping. From time to time the phlegm wells up in the throat, producing a convulsive coughing that is terrible to see.

My grandmother would cough and cough and not begin to expel all the choking phlegm. Rolling her eyes upward, she tried to cough up more, to no avail in her weakened state. I could not help her any further than to support her with my arms from behind. When she had lost the strength to cough anymore at all, she would gasp hard once and stop breathing. Her grip tightened on my arm and she doubled over in anguish. Her entire body, small and emaciated as it was, was concentrated on the effort to take in air. Still the breath would not come. Her face turned red, her upturned eyes seemed to implore. Ineffectually, I sought to lend her my strength; I coughed myself, loudly and rhythmically, as though she could draw on my lungs. She would appear on the brink of going under at any moment. My father and mother came in to look on in helpless consternation.

When these crises occurred I would resolutely fix my gaze on a dark corner of the room and stare for all I was worth. Not that the albino's gray eyes were gleaming there in reality; but I would conjure them up, and when they appeared, glare at them with as much intensity as I could muster. The protracted coughing fits and their painful aftermath, when I could not bear to look at my grandmother, perhaps only *seemed* long; if one were to time them, I suppose they lasted no longer than so many seconds. But while they lasted I had to focus my eyes somewhere else, and would invariably return to my staring match with the dark corner. Finally, the phlegm oozed thickly through her lips and the nurse wiped it away with a piece of gauze. When it was over, my grandmother would be thoroughly exhausted. As I helped her stretch out again, she would silently close her eyes, their sunken sockets brimming with tears. There were several of these crises before she at last began to rally. Inhalents were administered eight times a day, two doses at a time. Lying down, she would breathe in the vaporized medicine, such that too strenuous an application would result in further coughing. But eventually the treatment proved effective and she began to show real progress. With the steam rising constantly from a metal basin on a large hibachi, her breathing grew more slow and regular, though it was still far from strong.

Once again, I reflected, my grandmother had gone to the very brink and yet somehow pulled through. I had a strong feeling that, had I not been in the house, she would not have survived on either occasion. I was no longer so very sure that it had to do with the albino. But whatever it was that had come twice to attack her, I must have some power over it. Of this much I was certain beyond a doubt. At the same time, I was constantly vigilant lest I be lulled into a false sense of security as I watched her condition improve day by day.

My grandmother completed her recovery within only three months, much sooner than I had expected. The doctor nevertheless advised a further convalescence at the seaside, in the vicinity of Kugenuma, until the end of February. On the morning of our departure the baggage was sent ahead to Shimbashi Station and the two of us left the house in rickshas. When we rounded the corner and passed in front of the funeral home I noticed large bouquets of fresh and artificial flowers set up outside the door. White paper lanterns, "dragon's head" bells, and other funeral decorations were propped up below the eaves. Black-clad workmen squatted down on the gutter plank, smoking cigarettes. From what could be glimpsed inside the establishment it was clear they were not preparing this paraphernalia for still another funeral to be held elsewhere; it was not a matter of business as usual.

My heart leapt at the mere possibility, which immediately crossed my mind, that the albino had died. And in fact he was nowhere to be seen. As my ricksha passed on beyond the funeral home I was suddenly filled with the exhilarating sense of a heroic victory. I chafed under the unrealizable impulse to shout out my triumph to my grandmother, whose head poked out forlornly from her kerchief in the ricksha several paces behind mine. She was still wearing that sweetly blank expression when we met at the station, dabbing at her eyes to wipe away the tears brought on by the wind, quite oblivious to what . had happened. "Silly old gramma!" I wanted to tease her and slap her on the back.

The albino was dead. I was somehow thoroughly convinced of this fact.

To rejoice in someone's death, to feel almost pure, unalloyed delight—I would never have imagined this was possible for me.

Like most people, I naturally considered the funeral business a necessary evil. But there are thoughts that those who practice this business should never think. And I suspected the albino of having dwelled incessantly on these very thoughts.

I was opposed to war, of course, and to all killing (nor have my views changed since); the institutional murder of capital punishment I have always found unjustifiable. Nevertheless, I was able then without a qualm to rejoice in the albino's death, of which, I could not help feeling, I had in a certain sense been the cause. And for good or for ill, I was indeed beside myself with happiness at what had happened.

Having grown very strong and healthy at Kugenuma, my grandmother returned at the end of February.

For some time I kept a close watch on the funeral home around the corner. But the albino was no more to be seen.

I expect to be taking my grandmother to the seaside again this winter; her health is even better than it was last year.

SEIBEI AND GOURDS
Seibei to hyōtan, 1912

This is a story about a boy named Seibei and gourds. Since these events took place, Seibei has lost the special affinity he once had with gourds. Soon afterward, however, he found something to take their place: painting. He now paints with the same zeal that he formerly lavished on gourds.

Seibei's parents were not unaware of the fact that on occasion he went out and bought gourds. He had already acquired about ten of them, ranging in price from a few sen up to fifteen sen apiece. He was very adept at preparing them for display, cutting the opening, extracting the seeds, even making the stopper, all on his own. He would begin by curing the gourd with tea dregs then polish it relentlessly with the sake he had stored up from the leavings in his father's cups.

Seibei's passion knew no bounds. One day he was walking along the shore road, meditating as usual on gourds, when something very striking caught his eye. He gasped. It was, as it turned out, the bald head of an old man who had just then sprung out from one of the little roadside stands that were strung out there, facing landward. But Seibei took the baldpate for a gourd, and for the several moments that lapsed before he saw his error he marveled at this truly splendid-looking specimen. When the truth dawned on him, he could not help being astonished at himself. He watched the old man as, his perfectly mottled head bobbing up and down, he disappeared into a side street. Then Seibei burst out laughing—a great peal of laughter for his own ears alone. He went on laughing uncontrollably as he ran along for a tenth of a mile and more, and even then he could not stop.

Such was his passion. Wherever gourds were sold around the town, antique shops, vegetable stands, dry goods stores, even sweetshops, not to mention the odd establishment specializing in these curios, he would stop and gaze transfixed.

Seibei was twelve years old, still in elementary school. Instead of playing with his schoolmates after class, he would go into town by himself and seek out new gourds. At night he retreated to a corner of the parlor, where he sat working on his latest acquisition. When the cutting and cleaning out were done, he poured sake into the gourd, wrapped it up in a towel, and placed it in a metal container, which he then stuck into the charcoal footwarmer for the night. As soon as he got up in the morning he rushed to remove the gourd and inspect the beads of moisture sweated all over the skin. This was a sight he never tired of. Finally, he carefully bound the gourd up with string and hung it from the eaves in a sunny spot. Then he went to school.

The town where Seibei lived (it was officially designated a "city") was a commercial center of sorts and a port; but it was small enough in area that, although it was much longer than it was wide, you could walk the whole length within not much over a hundred paces. In spite of the surprising number of shops dealing in gourds, then, it was likely that in his almost daily rounds he had seen them all.

Seibei was not especially interested in old gourds. He preferred them fresh and uncut, their skins still intact. And he had acquired almost exclusively specimens that were, quite simply, "gourd-shaped." A carpenter friend of his father who came to call one day remarked, as he watched Seibei fervidly polishing a gourd, "I s'pose a child *would* like that plain and simple kind mostly." "But whoever heard of a kid messing around with gourds in the first place," Seibei's father muttered distastefully, with a look in his direction.

"Look here, my boy," said the carpenter, "what's the point of stocking up on gourds like that, so plain and ordinary. Why don't you get yourself some special ones—odd shapes and what have you?"

"These are good enough for me," said Seibei with cool disdain.

Seibei's father and his guest fell to discussing gourds between themselves. "That one they had at the fair last spring as a special exhibit—'Bakin's Gourd'—now there was a beauty!" said Seibei's father.

"It really was huge, wasn't it!"

"Yes, and very long."

Seibei laughed to himself over this exchange. "Bakin's Gourd" had been a great success with the fair-goers, but at a glance he had judged it utterly ridiculous—whoever this Bakin fellow might be—and fled from the exhibit.

"I didn't like it at all," he said aloud, "It was just big and ugly."

His father's eyes popped wide open with anger. "You don't know a thing about it—keep your mouth shut!"

Seibei said nothing more.

One day while Seibei was walking down a back street where he had seldom been before, he came across an old woman selling dried persimmons and tangerines in front of a private house. From the latticework shutters behind her little stand dangled twenty or so gourds. "Please ma'am," he said, crossing over, "may I have a look?" Inspecting them closely one by one, he discovered a gourd no more than six inches long, of a quite ordinary, regular shape—so perfect that he could hardly keep himself from scooping it up then and there. He asked the price.

"For you, dear, I'll let it go for only ten sen."

"All right. Now don't, please . . . you *mustn't* sell it to anyone else," he all but ordered her. "I'll be right back with the money."

Off he ran and in no time at all, breathless and red in the face, he came back, made his purchase, and ran home with it. Afterward he would scarcely let the new gourd out of his hands. He even began taking it to school, going so far as to hold it under his desk and polish it in class. In the end he was caught at this by the teacher, who was particularly indignant that such a thing should happen during the moral training period.

The teacher came from another region and took a very dim view of the natives' interest in gourds and the like. A man much given to lecturing people on the Way of the Warrior, he had attended three of the four performances by Kumoemon, the swashbuckling balladeer, when he came on tour to the little theater in the local Quarter, to which the teacher normally gave as wide a berth as possible; nor was he more than mildly annoyed when his pupils teased him for his martial tastes by mimicking Kumoemon on the playground. But this incident of Seibei and the gourd had sent him into a rage. In a quivering voice he had arrived at the verdict that such a boy could have "no future whatsoever." The offending gourd was confiscated on the spot. Seibei could not even bring himself to cry over it. He simply went pale and, when he was home again, sat at the charcoal-warmer staring off into space.

Presently the teacher appeared at the door, clutching a bundle of books, and asked for his father. The father being still at work, the teacher wasted no time in launching into the matter with Seibei's mother. "This type of behavior," he pronounced, "we really must expect the family to deal with seriously." Seibei's mother was thoroughly intimidated.

Seibei, his lips trembling, shrank into his corner at the man's threatening, outraged tone. Hanging from the wooden pillar directly behind the teacher were a considerable number of finished gourds. Seibei was filled with trepidation lest they be detected.

But the teacher wound up his tirade and took his leave without discovering the collection. Seibei sighed audibly. His mother burst into tears, then commenced a rambling, querulous sort of scolding.

When, not long after, Seibei's father came home, as soon as he heard what had happened he grabbed the boy and thrashed him with abandon. Again the assertion that Seibei had no future. "I can't stand having a worthless punk like you in the house," his father concluded. Whereupon the gourds hanging from the pillar caught his eye. He fetched a sledge hammer and smashed them to pieces, each and every one. Seibei looked on, pale and silent as before.

The confiscated gourd was given by the teacher for immediate disposal, as of a particularly offensive piece of refuse, to the school janitor, who took it home and hung it from the pillar in his small, sooty room. Two months later, hard pressed for a small sum of money, he quickly decided to sell the gourd for whatever paltry price it might command. He took it to a curio shop in the neighborhood. The proprietor held it up and studied it from various angles. A hard look came over his face as he thrust the gourd in front of the janitor and said, "I'll take it off your hands for five yen."

The janitor could hardly believe his ears. But, cunning man that he was, he said with a straight face, "I really couldn't part with it for that." When the dealer went up to ten yen, he refused again. In the end, they struck a bargain at fifty yen. The janitor exulted to himself over having got from the teacher for nothing an article that fetched the equivalent of four months' wages. He naturally said nothing about it, not to Seibei, much less to the teacher, and so no one had an inkling of what had become of the gourd. But neither could the janitor ever have imagined that eventually the curio dealer sold the gourd to a local rich man for six hundred yen.

Seibei now throws himself into painting with a vengeance. By the time this new passion swept him away, he had already lost all feelings of resentment against the teacher, and against his father as well, the dozen or so shattered gourds notwithstanding. And yet his father has been after him again of late, for wasting so much time on painting.

MANAZURU
1920

It was late December on the Izu Peninsula. The sun had gone down, leaving the world in bluish shadows. A boy of twelve or thirteen years was walking down the high road that overlooked the deep sea, leading his younger brother by the hand. The boy's look was pensive. His brother's small features were creased with fatigue and impatience; he followed along wearily as though begrudging each step. But the older boy was too absorbed in his own thoughts to notice. He was thinking very hard about (though he would not have thought to use the word) love.

Not that he had never heard the word. Once he was aimlessly trailing after an instructor at his school, who had at his side a new female teacher—she was still quite young. The instructor turned around abruptly and spoke to him.

"Here's a poem for you," he said.

> My love is like a skiff
> Cast adrift on fathomless seas;
> No safe harbor bids me rest;
> I am at the mercy of the waves.

Does that make any sense to you?"

The instructor was laughing and peering sideways into the woman's face. She looked down and said nothing, but her face flushed to the borders of her ears.

The boy too felt awkward and shy somehow. For a moment he was not sure whether these words had been addressed to him or whether he himself might not have spoken them.

"Well? Did you understand it?" asked the instructor once again.

Instead of answering, the boy looked down at the ground as the woman had done. Effortlessly he pictured to himself a small boat tossing gently on a vast expanse of water far out to sea. But what was this about love? The poem had not made much sense to him.

He was the son of a Manazuru fisherman. His skin was dark and his head was large. On this large head he wore a sailor's hat which looked rather too small by comparison, even though he had it pulled down over his crown like a mountain priest's skullcap. His head and throat were trussed up with the elastic cord that held the hat on. The effect was hardly in keeping with the pangs of love he was suffering just then; it gave him a clownish air, in fact. Yet no matter how outlandish and comical it might appear, for him the sailor's hat was not to be dismissed so lightly.

Having received a New Year's present of a small sum of money from their father that day, he and his brother had set out for Odawara to buy themselves some geta. But before they reached the geta shop the boy spotted the sailor's hat on display in the window of a fancy dry goods store. He wanted it as soon as he saw it. And so, with scarcely any thought of the consequences, he had bought it, spending all his money in one swoop.

The boy had an uncle who, having started out as an ordinary stonecutter at Nebukawa, was now a chief warrant officer in the navy. This uncle often told him stories of the seafaring life, and he had made up his mind that he too would be a sailor some day. He was particularly impressed once when, pointing out a round, ovenlike contraption that bulged atop the smokestack of a locomotive bound for Atami, his uncle laughed and said, "Would you look at that boiler! It's as small as a kitchen stove!" As this was all the boy knew of steam engines, his uncle's scorn was enough to fill him with admiration. He became more eager than ever to go to sea when he grew up.

The boy had been overjoyed, then, at discovering the sailor's hat. But already he had some regrets. He could not help feeling sorry for his little brother, who had been so excited along the way about the new geta he was to have. And with a sinking feeling he wondered what his short-tempered father would say to him when he found out that the money meant for both his sons had been used up by the oldest. He was sure to be very angry.

Yet he forgot those cares soon enough as he wandered through the streets of the busy town, with its gates and shops trimmed with festive pine branches in preparation for the New Year. He was on his way to pay his respects at the shrine dedicated to Ninomiya Sontoku—he had heard a great deal about this sage during his childhood—when he encountered a troupe of roving minstrels who came clattering into an intersection as he was about to cross.

The troupe was made up of three players of the sort known as hokai minstrels for their constant refrain of "ho-kai! ho-kai!" The boy looked them over one by one. Strumming on a small koto, there was a man of forty or so who seemed to be part blind. Then a woman— perhaps his wife—white with paint and powder from forehead to fingertips, straining her shrill voice for higher and louder notes as she plucked on a moon-shaped lute. The third was a young girl about his own age. She too was heavily made up, though the powder clung to her thin, drawn face only in splotches. She played a small set of clappers and sang as if wailing out her sorrows for the whole world to hear.

The boy was most taken with the older woman, the one with the lute. Her eyes were drawn upward by a bandana bound tightly across her brow and were made to look the more narrow and slanted by rouge daubed at the corners. Around her waist she had a soiled white crepe sash, of the kind usually worn by men, which was tied in the back with a slender cord so that it drooped down in loose folds.

When the troupe moved on, he followed after; everywhere they went, he trailed behind. Passing through the back streets, the minstrels came to a small restaurant and went inside. The boy stood waiting out in front, still holding his brother by the hand like a faithful shaggy dog on a leash.

From the high road that led back to Manazuru the Miura Peninsula could be seen in the distance; floating up above the murky twilight against the horizon still bright with the sun's last rays, it stretched out thinly into the open ocean. The water in the foreground was already covered over with dark shadows. Only a small fishing boat emerged clearly, illuminated by red flares set up around the bow. The boat was secured by a thirty- or forty-foot length of rope and bobbed up and down gently on the waves close to shore.

In the sound of the waves washing over the rocks below, the boy was sure he heard the rustle of the koto and the soft notes of the lute which had filled his ears just a while ago. With a special effort he could hear it simply as waves. But as in moments of weariness we soon sink into reverie no matter how we might struggle to rouse ourselves, the waves would change back into koto and lute in his ears. Then, through this flowing accompaniment, he heard the woman's thick voice singing. He could even make out some of the words: "the flowering plums . . . my handsome soldier . . ."

And here he recalled how, with arms hanging down, she had touched her hands together; then, sinking almost to her haunches, she spread and closed her legs, tilted her head this way and that. He pictured her kicking out with her feet two or three times in succession, or (in "the foundling's sword dance") throwing up her glistening white arms as if to weep and carressing a chipped and faded doll with her cheek. He felt strangely troubled by it all.

The Odawara coast loomed dimly behind him in the evening haze. Suddenly the woman seemed very far away. What was she doing now?

How he envied the young girl with the piercing wail her life with the troupe! But he did not care for her at all. While he was waiting patiently outside the restaurant, she had looked at him sharply from time to time with obvious ill will. Eventually she went up to the woman, who was busily exchanging cups of wine with the man, and tattled on him. Or so the boy gathered from the glances she kept throwing in his direction at that point, which made him break out in a cold sweat. But the woman showed no interest. She barely looked out at him once and resumed talking with the man. He had breathed a sigh of relief.

It was quite dark now. Fishermen's flares began to glow here and there in the offing. The half moon hanging high in the sky shone more brightly than before. And it was still about two miles to Manazuru.

Just then the small local train for Atami chugged into sight; spewing out red cinders from its smokestack, it soon overtook the two boys as they hurried along, a little out of breath. The weak light cast by the

lamps of the two passenger coaches momentarily lit up their profiles
before the train passed on into the darkness. After a while the younger
brother, who lagged a pace behind though his hand was still clutched
firmly in the boy's, spoke up and said, "The minstrels were on that
train. I saw them." The boy's heart beat so hard he could hear it. Yes,
he thought, maybe he had seen them, too, for a brief second. The train
had already rounded a promontory up ahead and could no longer even
be heard.

The boy noticed at last that his brother was exhausted.

"Are you tired?" he asked, feeling sorry for him. His brother did not
answer. "How about a ride?" he said softly.

There was still no reply. Instead, the brother turned his head away
and looked out across the black sea. If he tried to speak he would start
to cry; the more gently he was treated the more he felt like crying.

"Okay," said the older boy, letting go of his brother's hand and
bending over in front of him. "Hop on."

Without a word he toppled over onto the boy's back. Struggling to
hold back the tears that were welling in his eyes, the brother pressed
his cheek against the nape of the boy's neck and shut his eyes tightly.

"Cold?" the boy asked.

He shook his head almost imperceptibly.

The boy began to think about the woman again. The likelihood of
her having passed by just now made his fantasies more vivid than
before.

The train goes off the track as it rounds the bend across the promontory and hurtles down over the precipice. The woman strikes her
head on a rock and lies there at the base of the cliff. Then, over and
over again, she suddenly appears out of the darkness at the side of the
road.

All this he saw as happening before his eyes. He even had a strong
premonition that she was already waiting for him up ahead.

His brother had gone to sleep on his back. Feeling the full weight of
his load for the first time, the boy jogged the leaden body up and down
as he walked along, which only made his burden worse. His arms hurt
until he thought they were about to break off, and still he pushed on.
It seemed quite necessary to him that he carry this load the rest of the
way, though he could not have said why. Thrusting his head out like a
turtle, he inched his way forward step by step.

148   *Manazuru*

At length he came to the promontory. Nothing had happened here. When he reached the other side of the bend in the road, all of a sudden there was a woman coming toward him, holding a lantern up before her. His heart leapt. He heard the woman calling to him.

It was his mother. Worried because they were so late, she had come out to meet them.

The brother was by this time fast asleep, but when the boy hoisted him off onto his mother's back he woke up. As soon as he saw his mother, all his dammed-up impatience and sorrow burst forth in a stream of tears and confused complaints. The more his mother scolded him, the louder he raged. Both the mother and her older son were nearly at their wit's end when the boy thought of something. He took off the sailor's hat and put it on his brother's head.

"Hush up," he said. "You can have it for keeps."

At that moment, he did not particularly mind parting with his new hat.

THE RAZOR
Kamisori, 1910

Yoshisaburo of the Tatsu Barbershop in Roppongi had taken to his bed with a cold. Of all times to be sick, and he hardly ever was, it was the eve of the ceremonies for the imperial ancestors, the peak season for the military trade. On his sickbed he now regretted having dismissed, only recently, his two assistants, Gen and Jita.

Yoshisaburo was only slightly older than they, and had himself been apprenticed at the Tatsu until the former master, much impressed with his skillful wielding of the razor, had given him his only daughter's hand in marriage and, at the same time, passed on the management of the shop. The assistant Gen, who had quietly had his eyes on the daughter himself, resigned not long after. Jita, a much more mild-mannered fellow, had soon learned to call his former colleague "boss," and stayed on. Within half a year the former proprietor died, and his wife but a few months later.

Yoshisaburo truly was a master with the razor. And fastidious to a fault. Should a customer's face be ever so slightly rough to the touch after a shave, he would finish by all but plucking out each remaining whisker one by one. He gave such close shaves that the customers would say he had spared them a day's growth; yet they never com-

149

plained of any irritation to the skin, nor had he in ten years on the job so much as nicked a man's face. His record was spotless.

Two years after Yoshisaburo took over, his onetime fellow apprentice Gen reappeared. In view of their long association, he could only accept the man's apologies and take him back into the shop. In the meantime, however, Gen had changed a good deal, and for the worse. He tended to shirk his duties, and began to entice Jita along on his frequent visits to the ladies of doubtful virtue over at Kasumi-cho, where the soldiers went. When it came to Jita's taking money from the shop for these escapades, at Gen's instigation, Yoshisaburo spoke up and repeatedly warned the more gentle and impressionable of his assistants. But it was too late. Jita had acquired the habit of putting his hand in the till and, a month or so ago, had been dismissed along with Gen.

Yoshisaburo was now making do with a very pale young man of about twenty, named Kanejiro, who was singularly lacking in energy, and a thirteen-year-old boy named Kin, whose abnormally elongated head likewise failed to inspire confidence. As he lay tossing feverishly on his bed, he worried to himself that now, at this busy season before the holiday, the likes of these two could scarcely be expected to fill in for him.

Toward noon, customers crowded into the shop. The rattle of the glass door opening and closing and the scuffing of Kin's worn clogs as he shuffled to and fro grated on Yoshisaburo's frayed nerves. Again the shop door opened, and a woman was heard announcing herself as a servant from the Yamada household in Ryudomachi. "The master is off on a journey tomorrow evening," she said. "Please sharpen this by tonight. I'll come back for it." To Kanejiro's reply that they were very busy and would do it by next morning, if that were agreeable, she reluctantly assented: "Very well, if you're quite sure."

No sooner had she closed the door behind her than she opened it again and called in to Kanejiro, "I don't like to bother him, but could you ask the boss to do it?"

"I'm afraid that the boss..."

"Kane! I'll do it," Yoshisaburo shouted from his bed in a hard, hoarse voice.

"Yes ma'am! We'll see to it," said the assistant. Again the door closed behind her.

Yoshisaburo cursed softly to himself. He stretched out his pale, grimy forearm against the silk lining of the coverlet and contemplated it awhile. He was aware of his fever-leeched body as of a dead weight apart from himself. His eyes focused intently on the soot-stained paper dog hanging from the ceiling. It was encrusted with flies.

He half-listened to the conversation going on in the shop out front. A few soldiers were weighing the various merits of local restaurants and bemoaning the rotten army rations—though since the weather had grown chilly, one of them allowed, you could just manage to get the stuff down. Somewhat soothed by this talk, Yoshisaburo lazily rolled over

He savored his new tranquillity and watched his wife, Oume, bathed in the milky twilight that filtered through the doorway of the adjoining small kitchen, as she went about preparing dinner, the baby still strapped on her back. "I'd better get it over with," he said to himself. But the effort of raising his leaden body to a sitting position made him dizzy, and he flopped back against the pillow.

Oume came in from the kitchen, dangling her wet hands before her, and gently asked if he needed help to the toilet. Yoshisaburo tried to say no, but he could barely hear his own voice. When his wife had removed the covers and pushed aside the basin and the medicine bottles by his bed, he said again, "No, it's not that." But again his hoarse voice seemed not to reach her. His brief spell of tranquillity was shattered.

"Let me pull you up from behind," Oume said in a cajoling tone. With what little force he could muster, Yoshisaburo hurled back at her, "Bring me the leather strap and Mr. Yamada's razor. Now."

After a moment's silence, Oume ventured, "But are you up to it?"

"Never mind! Bring them *now*."

"Well, if you're going to get up you'll really have to put on a bed jacket..."

"Didn't you hear what I told you?" This in a hushed voice taut with anger and frustration.

Undaunted, Oume wrapped the bed jacket over his shoulders from behind as he sat up and prepared himself for the chore. Yoshisaburo stiffly hoisted one hand to the collar of the jacket and tossed the garment off.

Without a word, Oume slid open the dividing partition and went down into the shop, returned with the leather strap, and, as there was clearly nowhere to hang it, set about nailing a small hook into the wooden supporting post next to the bed.

Even when he was well, Yoshisaburo found this particular task irksome if he was not in the right mood; now, with his hands trembling feverishly, he made no progress at all. Painfully aware of his mounting irritation, Oume repeatedly urged him to leave the task to the assistant Kane. Her husband made no reply. But after fifteen minutes or so his strength gave out. With a look of utter exhaustion, he sank back onto his bed and dozed off.

Yamada's maid, on the pretext that she happened to be passing by, came to fetch the razor early in the evening.

Oume boiled some rice gruel for her sick husband but could not bring herself to wake him from his much needed sleep—and, almost certainly, risk incurring his wrath again. And so she put the meal aside and left him alone, until about eight o'clock, when she began to worry about the medicine he was supposed to take. Woken from a sound sleep by his wife's persistent shaking, Yoshisaburo was unexpectedly docile. As soon as he had eaten he lay down and went back to sleep.

A little before ten he was roused again and given more medicine. Idle thoughts drifted through his mind. There was an unpleasant sensation of his own warm breath trapped around his face by the coverlet, which he had pulled up to just below his eyes. He cast a listless gaze around him. The black leather strap was still there, hanging from the post, solid, motionless. The lamp gave off a murky, cloying orange light that shone on his wife's back as she sat in a corner nursing the baby. The whole room seemed smothered in fever.

From the narrow earthen passageway between the house and the shop the apprentice Kin called out in a quavering voice. Yoshisaburo's response, hoarse and muffled by the coverlet, could not be heard at first and had to be repeated.

"What is it!" he managed at length to say in a sharp, distinct tone.

"Mr. Yamada's razor is back again."

"Another one?"

"No, the same. He said he tried it right away and it wouldn't shave very well. He doesn't need it till tomorrow noon, so he'd like you to have another look at it."

Having ascertained that the Yamada maid had already gone home, he said, "All right, let's have a look." He stretched his arms out over the covers to take the razor case from the boy, who was crouched down on hands and knees at the foot of the bed.

"But your hands aren't steady," said Oume, doing up her robe as she came over to his side. "Wouldn't it be better to ask Mr. Yoshikawa at Kasumi-cho to do it?"

Yoshisaburo ignored her and reached out to turn up the wick of the gas lamp. He took the razor from the case and turned it this way and that under the light. Oume sat down by his pillow and placed a hand on his forehead. With his free hand he brushed hers away in a show of annoyance. He ordered Kin, still in attendance at the foot of the bed, to bring him a whetstone at once.

When the whetstone had been set out, Yoshisaburo got up; resting one knee on the tatami, he began to sharpen the razor. The clock struck ten in slow even measure. Oume sat looking on in silence. She knew it was pointless to say anything more.

After applying the razor to the whetstone awhile, he went back to the leather strap. The slapping sound of the razor against the strap seemed to revive the stagnant atmosphere of the room. In vain Yoshisaburo strained to steady his trembling hand, to adjust himself to the rhythm of the task. Then, suddenly, the hook that Oume had attached to the post came loose; the strap flew off and wrapped itself around the razor.

"Look out!" cried Oume. Afterward she glanced fearfully at her husband. His brow contracted into a scowl full of tension.

Yoshisaburo extricated the razor from the strap and, wearing only the thin bed jacket, started toward the shop.

"But you *mustn't*," Oume half-sobbed.

Yoshisaburo paid no attention. He went down across the narrow passage into the shop, Oume following behind. Not a single customer remained. The apprentice Kin sat lackadaisically in one of the barber chairs, facing the mirror.

When Oume asked where Kane was, young Kin replied, almost solemnly, "He's gone courting Tokiko."

"He told you that himself?"

Oume chuckled. Her husband maintained his tense expression.

"Tokiko" was a woman of uncertain background—said to have once been a proper little schoolgirl—whose ménage now ran, a few doors away, what purported to be a military provisions shop. She invariably had a couple of young men sitting around in the shop: soldiers, students, working men from the neighborhood.

"Well, go tell him to come back and close up," Oume directed.

"No. It's too early."

At this automatic negative response from her husband, Oume fell silent.

Yoshisaburo resumed his sharpening, which went somewhat better now that he was seated in the shop. His wife produced a padded cotton jacket and contrived at some length, as with an unruly child, to slip his arms into the sleeves. With a look of relief she sat down on the raised threshold, from where she could keep a watchful eye on the sick man's face as he threw himself into his task.

Curled up on the customer's bench next to the window, Kin exposed one leg, on which he practiced shaving, drawing his razor slowly up and down over the smooth, hairless skin.

Presently the shop door rattled briskly open and in walked a short, stocky workingman who looked to be in his early twenties. Wearing a thickly woven unpadded robe tied with an ordinary sash of cheap fabric, he balanced his feet precariously on clogs whose thongs were shrunken beyond repair.

"S'pose you could take a minute or two for a once-over-lightly?" The man stood in front of the mirror thrusting his chin out and rubbing it insistently with his fingertips. Below the facade of city mannerisms his accent revealed he was nothing but a peasant; his bony knuckles and coarse, dark complexion spoke of heavy day labor.

"Best fetch Kane right away." Oume entreated as much with her eyes as her words.

"I'll do it myself."

"Now please, you're not yourself today."

"I said I'll do it."

Cut off sharply, Oume muttered to herself. When Yoshisaburo ordered her to bring his white jacket, she temporized, "But he said he only wanted a quick shave—you won't need it for that," She hoped at least to keep him in the quilted garment.

The young man watched this exchange with an odd, quizzical expression; blinking his small, sunken eyes in a display of solicitude, he asked if the chief barber were sick.

"Oh, just a touch of a cold," said Yoshisaburo.

"They say there's a mean one going around, that's what they say, so you'd better take care of yourself!"

"I appreciate your concern," Yoshisaburo answered in a chilly tone.

As he was putting on his white jacket, the young man gave him a suggestive smirk and reiterated that he was in a great hurry; a quick going over would do.

Yoshisaburo said nothing and put the finishing touches on the blade, rubbing it against the flat of his arm.

"Let's see," the young man maundered on, "if I get out by ten-thirty I can still make it by eleven-thirty..."

Yoshisaburo would have liked to tell his customer a thing or two.

The figure of an ugly woman inside a small hovel of a whorehouse flashed before his mind's eye. She spoke in an unpleasantly androgynous voice. In his fever-wracked imagination the presentiment that she would shortly be joined by this vulgar little wretch conjured up a sequence of revolting scenes. He plunged a cake of soap into water that was by now stone cold, and proceeded with abandon to smear lather over the man's face from under the chin up to the cheeks. Even now the fellow was straining to peek at his face in the mirror. Yoshisaburo could hardly keep from spewing out his disgust.

With a few more slaps of the razor against the strap, he began to shave the man's throat. The blade did not cut well. His hand trembled. And, as he bent over the chair, mucus began to drip from his nostrils, as it had not when he was lying down. He paused now and then to wipe it away, but as soon as he picked up the razor again he could feel new drops forming at the nostrils.

At the sound of the baby crying, Oume went back into the house. Yoshisaburo was overcome by a fresh wave of loathing. The man showed not the slightest awareness that he was being shaved with a dull blade, no sign of pain or irritation appeared on his face. As though his nerve endings were dead. There were other, sharper razors Yoshisaburo could use. But why bother; what did it matter? And so he went on with this blunt instrument. But he began to wield it with some caution, almost in spite of himself. For he sensed that the smallest nick on the man's face would rankle within himself, and would end by inciting him to still further hatred. He felt new fatigue in body and spirit, and his fever seemed to have returned.

After several vain attempts at conversation, the young man had at last been chastened by the barber's unfriendly demeanor and ceased his chatter. By the time the shaving reached the upper part of his face, he had succumbed to his exhaustion from the heavy work of the day and drifted off. Kin had meanwhile stretched out by the window and fallen asleep. Back inside the house the murmurings of Oume comforting the baby had died away. The stillness of the night spread through the shop and house and all around outside. Only the scraping of the razor was to be heard.

As this new fatigue enveloped him, Yoshisaburo's anger and irritation gave way to a feeling of being on the verge of tears. His eyes misted over and seemed about to melt away from the inside with fever.

Having shaved most of the throat, the chin, cheeks and brow, he contemplated the patch of soft flesh on the throat which he had left to the end. It was a very stubborn spot. Possessed by his task and its loathsome object, he had an impulse to slice the little patch off, skin and all, an impulse powerfully reinforced by a glance at the face below him, full of coarse pores brimming with oil. By this point the young man had fallen into a deep sleep. His head lolled back against the chair and his mouth was agape, giving him an air of childlike vulnerability. His teeth were stained and crooked.

Yoshisaburo was bone tired and at his wits' end. He felt as if poison had been injected into all his joints. He could have thrown everything aside that very second and sunk to the floor. Enough! On the point of calling a halt any number of times, he persisted out of a combination of inertia and obsession.

A soft nicking sound and a sensation of the razor catching against the skin. The young man's throat twitched. A mercurial shudder surged through Yoshisaburo's body from head to toe. At that moment all his physical fatigue, and his paralysis of will as well, were swept away.

The cut was barely half an inch long. Yoshisaburo stood motionless and examined it. The tiny slit in the skin at first turned a milky white; then a little splurt of pale crimson and the blood began to ooze up. He continued to scrutinize. The color of the blood deepened and a distinct drop formed at the slit. The drop swelled until it burst, and the blood streamed down in a single thin strand. At this sight he was shaken by a violent emotion.

The force of this inner onslaught was doubled by his never having experienced such a sight. His breathing quickened. His whole being came to focus on the bleeding cut. He could hold out no longer.

He changed his grip so that the tip pointed downward and in one swift thrust plunged the razor into the young man's throat. It penetrated the length of the blade up to the handle. The man did not move a muscle.

Presently the blood came gushing out from the deep wound. The man's face rapidly turned an ashen hue.

Yoshisaburo sank into the adjacent chair as though in a faint. All the tension drained out of him. At the same time, the fatigue he had felt before returned with a vengeance. With his eyes tightly shut, his body limp and motionless, he too looked dead. Even the night grew still as death. Nothing moved. The world had fallen into a deep slumber. Only the mirrors looking down from three sides of the room reflected this scene in their cold, impassive gaze.

THE KIDNAPING
Ko o nusumu hanashi, 1914

One morning my father spoke to me with open contempt. "Where do you think that's going to get you?" he said, referring to my work. "What did we ever do to deserve a lazy punk like you in the family!"

He went on to tell me that he could not stand the sight of me; my presence in the house was a bad influence on my growing brothers and sisters; in me alone were summed up all the evils of the modern world. It was no wonder that society had no use for me and my kind, he added, as if to give me one more slap across the face.

I began by answering him with some tough talk of my own and ended in tears—the first time I'd cried since I could remember.

I left home the next day after sundown, though not necessarily because I had been hurt all that much by my father's words. In the middle of a torrential rain I had my baggage loaded onto a wagon. As I went out, the oldest of my little sisters, who was used to depending on me at home, was in tears.

I stayed for a few weeks at a small inn near Kyōbashi. But I wanted to spend some time alone, away from everyone I knew, so toward the end of September I journeyed some five hundred miles to a small city on the Inland Sea coast. I did not know a soul there.

After lodging in an inn for a while I decided to settle down to my solitary life in a small vacant house that had caught my fancy. It was halfway up a mountain and had a sweeping view of the whole town, the sea, and the islands. Though I had come for solitude, I went so far as to inquire once about a maid, at an employment agency I happened upon while out walking. Inside, a fat old woman sat alone doing patchwork. When she heard that I was single she asked me pointedly if I had any preference as to age. I told her the younger the better. She gave me a withering look and said, "Well, then, we haven't anyone available." I gave up the idea of hiring a maid.

After receiving the key from the landlord I went to the house and opened up the outside shutters. Peering inside, I noticed a filthy-looking cricket, its back curved like a shrimp's, crouching motionless on the half-rotten tatami. As I entered cautiously, a dozen or so more of these creatures began bounding about the room and presently hopped up on to the mildewed wall, where they became still again.

I had men come up from the shops in town to mend the tatami and the sliding doors. Then I called an electrician; but he couldn't come that day, so I borrowed a lamp from the landlord. Finally, I arranged for a gas outlet to be installed.

On going to bed that night in the now clean, six-mat room, my mood was relaxed and tranquil. There was a pleasant, expectant sense of freedom in starting out alone on a new life. Fatigue from the day's activities stole over me as I lay reading a book, and soon I began to doze off with the light still burning. Suddenly something startled me and my eyes opened wide. I started to get up out of bed, then froze when I saw a dark blue centipede about three inches long crawling out from under the pillow. I watched it undulate its many legs as it proceeded deliberately from the bedding down to the mats. I slammed my book down at it, missing by a few inches. The centipede began to move much faster and crawled off into a tiny crack between the mats and the bare wooden step at the threshold. Unable to sleep, I began to read again. After a while the bell at the nearby mountain temple struck twelve.

For as long as I could remember, I had never spent more than three days away from Tokyo. Once, just three years ago this fall, I had suddenly grown very sick of things at home and decided to go to Kyoto for a few months. I packed my bags for a prolonged stay and left Tokyo on a night train. When I arrived the next morning, I checked my bags at the station and spent the day walking around in search of lodgings. All I saw were filthy rooms. Soon I became disgusted with Kyoto too. Lugging my bulky bags, I went back to Tokyo on an early evening train without staying a single night.

My attitude now was quite different from what it had been then; in fact, everything had changed. But because of this experience I wanted to avoid as much as possible the petty annoyances of an uncomfortable living situation. I acquired all the basic furnishings: desk, serving trays and dishes, shelves, an assortment of knives, and a few cooking utensils. I pasted my card by the front doorway and below it nailed up a wooden chocolate box refashioned into a mailbox. I went out and bought some pieces of handsome cotton print to cover up the cracks and smudges on the wall. Over the spots I'd missed I pinned up a few leaf-shaped cutouts of satin cloth.

My house had a fine view, unobstructed in front. I could lie down on the mats and look straight out at the varied scene. In the foreground there was an island, and on the island a shipyard from which the clinking of hammers began to resound early in the morning. A little to the left on the same island there was a hillside quarry. The voices of the stonecutters, singing all day as they hacked away at the rock in the middle of a pine grove, carried high above the town, straight across to the slope where I lived. Late in the afternoon I would sit on the front veranda and look out at this scenery, completely at ease. I could see the tiny figures of children far below on the rooftop platforms of merchants' houses, facing the setting sun as they swung Indian clubs up and down. Above them a few doves fluttered in agitated motion.

The bronze bell of the temple on the mountain struck the hour of six. The deep, resonant tones were answered directly by an echo, and then re-echoed faintly from farther away. On quiet days, each stroke was repeated four or five times. At about this hour the triangular tip of the lighthouse on Hyakkan Island, barely visible between the slopes of the island in the foreground, began to flicker on and off at intervals of half a minute or so. The smelting fires at the shipyard (for bronze, perhaps) were reflected in the water.

Around ten o'clock, with a blast on the horn the steamship that connected the town with Tadotsu on Shikoku came back into port. As the boat moved ahead, the red and green lights on the bow and the yellowish lamps along the deck were reflected on the surface like a beautiful rope dangled out over the water. Now that the commotion of the town's busy streets had died down, the loud voices of the crew and passengers sounded very close.

I was happy with my new life, so different from my life in Tokyo. In a relaxed frame of mind, I resumed work on a long novel I had begun some time ago. I worked between midnight and dawn. In the still hours of the night a faint ringing in my ears would grow to a low roar as I became more and more engrossed in my work. I felt completely alone with my thoughts: it was as though I could see them clearly before my eyes.

After two weeks of such nights, fatigue set in. I had a heavy, dull sensation in my head, my shoulders stiffened, and I felt generally out of sorts. I slept poorly and began to have nightmares as soon as I dozed off at dawn.

A girl of twelve years or so, her face splotched like a gourd skin before it has been touched up, sits on the porch of a small shrine in the shadow of a leafy tree. She is staring at me with an eerie smile. I know that I am dreaming and that in dreams one has only to think of something that might happen, and immediately it happens. Nevertheless I comment to myself: she's going to come my way. And sure enough she comes directly toward me. As she draws closer she grows larger and larger until she seems about to bump into my nose. All of a sudden I am overcome with horror. I twist and turn. But it's no use. When she's close enough to touch me, abruptly she looks down at the ground. Her short hair, coarse and stiff like a straw bag, flops over as she bends her neck. I cannot see her face, but through the mass of tangled hair I catch a glimpse of an unnaturally red underlip drooping down as though she had her tongue out. She is no longer a girl but an aging hag of fifty or so. Without seeing, I know that she's grinning at me underneath the hair.

Although I was conscious of dreaming all the while, this did nothing to lessen the oppressive sense of being threatened. I struggled to open my eyes. When at last I awoke I had an uncanny sensation of psychic fatigue. I lay staring blankly at the ceiling and continued to breathe deeply for a while. Still sleepy, I switched on the light by my pillow and gave myself a massage around the temples and over the forehead. Having kept this up for some time, I began to doze off but was still unable to fall fast asleep. A large, pinkish shape appeared blurrily before my eyes—almost the size of a small mountain, it seemed. But no, I thought, it couldn't be that big. Another nightmare, perhaps. I struggled to ward it off. Then I realized it must be my own nose (I was in the habit of sleeping with my eyes slightly open). I examined the disconcerting shape with more care: it was indeed my nose. With a painful effort I managed to wake myself up again. How could one be frightened of one's own nose? But I knew that if I were to fall asleep again I would only have another nightmare. Finally I decided to get up.

Night after night it was the same. The strain began to tell on me. I was about halfway along with my novel and hoped to finish it at all costs, in spite of my run-down condition. But I became increasingly dissatisfied with the way it was turning out and would flop down on the floor and stare at the walls for hours on end. I began to miss Tokyo and would go down to the station or the post office and hang about aimlessly.

The stiffness in my shoulders grew so severe that I was unable to keep at my work for longer than fifteen minutes at a time, after which I would have to stretch out flat on my back. When I grasped the back of my neck in pain there would be a nasty cracking noise. My moments of euphoria disappeared, my work stagnated, and I came to feel completely on edge. I couldn't sit still for any length of time. I was startled by the slightest noise. One night I threw aside a ball of tissue paper I had used to blow my nose. After a few moments it began to unroll itself with a crisp, rustling sound. There was nothing remarkable in this—a stiff piece of Japanese paper will naturally tend to return to its original shape when it has been rolled up—but it gave me quite a start. It was around this time that the knives in the kitchen started preying on my nerves. I had to wrap them up in newspaper and put them away in my suitcase.

Eventually I gave up working altogether and began to live idly from day to day. With no schedule to keep to, one ceases to distinguish one day from another. I made a four-month calendar out of square-ruled manuscript paper, stuck it on the wall, and crossed out each passing day with my pen.

Two weeks after I had given up working there was still no improvement in my physical health, or in my state of mind. My head felt heavier, my shoulders stiffer than ever. Sleep, exercises, massages, salves, liquor—I tried everything, but the stiffness did not let up. I must have looked like a half-wit, going around with my collar pulled down in the back, geisha-style, and thrusting my neck way out to ease the pain. I had reached a dead end.

I made up my mind to take a trip. I was used to gazing on clear days at the mountains of Shikoku, and decided to go over for a closer look. I took the steamer for Tadotsu one morning and went first to Kompira. I enjoyed the art treasures in the temple there; but the rough bark of a centuries-old tree at the side of the path leading to another shrine attacked my already frayed nerves. After the initial impression, the more I studied the bark, the more frightening it became.

The next day I went on to Takamatsu. I found nothing there to cheer me and felt depressed at the prospect of staying overnight in the town. Hearing that Yajima was not far, I decided to spend the night there. When I went to buy my ticket, I noticed that the local newspaper, whose office was there in the terminal, had sponsored a "treasure hunt and geisha costume show" in Yajima that very day. And sure enough, as I walked along the road toward the mountains I passed throngs of sightseers on their way back. Where the road began to ascend into the mountains it became almost deserted. Surrounded by twilight stillness I climbed up the slope, stopping now and then for breath. Below, the saltworks along the shore came into view. Steam from the brine vats rose in thick white columns over the roofs of the small huts into the serene sky, dotting the horizon for a stretch of several miles. Even in my present state, I could not help being soothed by the sight.

When I arrived at the inn (it was really more of a restaurant than an inn) I became depressed again. I was the only overnight guest and was shown to a wretched cottage which, despite its pretensions to elegance, still smelled of pitch. It did, at least, have a fine view. Across the water Shodojima lay enveloped in evening mist, and here and there other islands bobbed up gently on the surface of the sea. Gondola-shaped cargo boats with lights on their masts rested at anchor far below. Above the pine grove in back of the inn, the moon had come out. Beautiful as it was, though, I could not enjoy this scene. I had thought of spending the next night at Tomonotsu to view the moon over Sensui Island, but gave it up and went straight home. My journey had done me no good.

Some time after my return, I came to hear of a blind masseur who lived at the foot of the stone steps leading up to a nearby temple, the Kongoji. It seemed that he was an arrogant sort and refused to go out on call. And so one evening I set out for his house. The masseur was a large man of about fifty and lived up to his reputation. He scarcely greeted me when I arrived, and responded with only an occasional grunt as I told him my troubles, like a doctor questioning a patient about his condition. When I had finished my explanation, without a word he began to grope around for his pipe. Having found it, he stood hunched protectively over a large metal brazier and started to smoke placidly.

The only light came from a small electric lamp that shone with dim determination over the wide, smoke-filled room. Soiled children's clothing hung in a heap over a bamboo hook above the doorway. A steep staircase, painted shiny black, led from a rear corner to the second story, and at the foot of the stairs there was a small pit hollowed out in the floor for burning charcoal. On some bedding spread out in the opposite corner a woman, who had escaped my notice when I came in, lay sleeping face up. She looked over forty and had rather refined features—the kind of face one might see on a prosperous merchant's wife.

After five or ten minutes the masseur finally set down his pipe with great care next to the brazier and slid along the mats on his knees to the charcoal pit. He arranged a cushion and told me to sit down. When I had removed my jacket and sat down, he took hold of my shoulders and started to massage them slowly.

"Pretty stiff, aren't they!" he said with an unsympathetic chuckle, and then added something in dialect to the effect that they were more than merely stiff. "It must make your head ache," he said, gradually putting more force into his hands.

I have long suffered from a stiffening of the shoulders and, as a rule, prefer a vigorous massage. But I had all I could do to control my temper with the manhandling I received from him. I steeled myself in the pit of my stomach, but sometimes the pain became almost unbearable. "Yoh!" he would shout, and make unpleasant noises by pinching the muscle tissue on my arms and shoulders. I was about to protest. And yet, I thought, resigning myself, perhaps nothing less than these dire measures would work.

"Feel a little looser now?" he asked. I was still holding my breath and couldn't answer for a while.

"Daddy, Daddy," called a wheedling, little girl's voice from outside.

"What is it?" the masseur shouted back over my head. The child went on chattering volubly, but all I could make out was, "Where's Mommy?"

"Come in then, and shut the door tight behind you," he said.

Obediently the girl came in. She was a sweet little thing, about five years old and dark-complexioned. She was puffed out with layer upon layer of clothing and looked as if she would keel over if someone were to give her a nudge. Keeping up a steady nasal patter, she came up behind the masseur and hung on his back as he was rubbing my arms. Stealthily she slipped her chilblained hands inside her father's collar.

"Shall I give you a penny?" he said. She stopped her chatter and nodded assent. While continuing to rub me with one hand he fumbled in his sleeve with the other. "Here you go," he said, tossing a coin halfway across the room onto the floor. The little girl climbed down off her father's back and quietly went over to pick it up. She came back and resumed her jabbering. "Go away now," he scolded her. Presently she went out again.

I went back to my work, but after a day I realized I couldn't go on and abandoned it again. The monotonous days became harder than ever for me. More than the monotony, it was the loneliness that overwhelmed me. I longed for Tokyo and occasionally thought of calling some friends long-distance to invite them for a visit. It occurred to me that day in, day out, week after week, the same gloomy expression had been frozen on my face. My cheek muscles had grown slack and I could scarcely keep my eyes open. Neither a look of anger nor a smile crossed my face. Worst of all, I was no longer breathing deeply and naturally.

I felt like going to a deserted place somewhere and shouting at the top of my lungs to test my voice. One evening when a strong north wind was blowing I went along the coast to the outskirts of town. I stopped near some tile-baking kilns glowing fiercely in the early evening dusk. The pinewood fire, fanned by the strong gusts, crackled with the sound of burning oil. I turned and faced the sea. I thought for a moment of singing, but there was no song to suit my mood. I tried shouting, but my voice seemed small and pitiful. I could muster nothing better. The more I strained my voice the more pathetic it sounded. The cold north wind blew over me from behind. The black smoke from the kilns was caught up in the wind and scattered low out over the heavy sea. I began to feel sad, the way children must feel when they begin to sob uncontrollably for no apparent reason.

A few days later, a gentle, sunny day, I set out from my house in the general direction of town. To reach the town from my house I had to cross over a railroad track. When I came to the grade crossing, a dove was strutting along between the tracks, wagging its head to and fro. I stood and watched it absent-mindedly. "It would be dangerous if a train came," I found myself thinking. I wasn't quite sure if by this I meant dangerous for the dove or dangerous for myself. But naturally the dove was in no danger, I realized. Nor was I, so long as I stood away from the track. Then I crossed and went on toward town. "Suicide is out," I thought to myself.

My life had ceased to have any purpose. The days passed uneventfully and unproductively. Still I did not seriously consider returning to Tokyo; at home there would only be the same monotony.

One night I went to see a troupe of traveling storytellers who were performing at the town's small playhouse. Among the troupe was one genuine Tokyo type. It was a delight to hear some urban patter after nothing but the local dialect for so long. I went back several times after the first night, mainly to listen to him. At one of these performances there was a lovely little girl of six years or so who had been brought along by two ladies, presumably her mother and grandmother. The girl sat on her mother's lap and toyed with her white feather boa, taking it off and draping it around her own neck. Though she could not possibly have understood the jokes, when the audience laughed she laughed, too, very loudly. Her skin was pale and there was something irresistible about the look in her eyes and the shape of her mouth. Scarcely listening to the storytellers on the stage, I continued to gaze over in her direction throughout the performance.

There had not been much of a turnout that night and the front rows were all but empty. Then, in the middle of a story, the little girl stood up and wandered off across the hall toward the stage, sucking on an orange as she went. When she reached the foot of the stage she stood still and gazed directly up at the performer. Whenever he came to the end of a joke she would laugh loudly and unaffectedly, as if it had been told exclusively for her benefit. After the laughter subsided she would turn around to look at her mother, who kept beckoning her to come back to her seat. She shook her head and stayed where she was.

What a sweet child! Indeed, she was truly beautiful. And she called up for me an association from my childhood. She looked very much like a young playmate of mine who had lived in the neighborhood until I was fifteen, when her family moved away. As I walked home that night my thoughts were full of the little girl I had just discovered.

The next night I went to the playhouse again, though I doubted very much that I would find her. Yet there she was, in the same spot, with a man who was probably her father on one side, her grandmother and a maid on the other. I was overjoyed. But I realized that I could not keep staring at her, oblivious to the surroundings, as I had the night before. How I envied her father! Even if I were to marry, I could not imagine myself having such a child; but then, if ever I did have children, I could not be satisfied with anything less. I thought of following them after the performance to find out where she lived—it would be an easy matter if one had a mind to do it. The next moment, though, it struck me as a risky undertaking. It was, after all, a small town.

After these encounters my mood changed completely. I was filled with the feelings of a man in the first stages of love, pleasant feelings that seemed pure and transparent. Yet I was not quite sure what sort of emotions these were. I half understood them but could not have explained them in words. In any case, it was clear enough that I wanted the girl for my own.

When I came to the point where I recognized that I wanted her, my thoughts wandered into fantasy. It was unlikely that I would be able to adopt her. I could easily imagine how much her parents and her grandmother doted on her. No doubt she was their only daughter, I thought to myself.

My fantasies extended to kidnaping. Here my train of thought was momentarily checked by the picture of the little girl weeping forlornly after she had been kidnaped—but she would get over it soon enough, I concluded. I would do everything humanly possible to fulfill my obligations in regard to her future. I would indeed pride myself on providing more thoroughly than her parents would have done for her education, her material well-being, even for her marriage.

I began to speculate day and night on the possibility of kidnaping the girl, and on exactly how I should go about it. Within the confines of my solitary life these fantasies came to have a reality of their own.

In the hopes of catching another glimpse of the little girl, I went back to the playhouse several times and strolled frequently around the town. I had no success. She was not to be found. My vivid fantasies of abduction began to fade. But to what purpose, I asked myself indignantly, should strong desires and genuine love be denied? Walking off with other people's children was not, perhaps, a commendable deed on the whole; but neither was it necessarily wrong in an absolute sense. For example, take the case of a man truly in love who, in spite of the woman's indifference to him and her parents' refusal of his proposals, perseveres and forces a marriage. In many such cases the man's willful behavior is eventually justified by a happy outcome in the marriage. How different was my present position with respect to the girl at the playhouse?

A kind of year-end clearance sale, locally called "the Bazaar of Atonement," opened up in the town, and for about a week the streets were thronged with people. Early in the afternoon of the second day of the bazaar I made another visit to the masseur's house below the temple. The dark-skinned five-year-old I had seen on my first visit was sound asleep, her legs dangling over the charcoal pit. Beside her a girl of twelve or thirteen, no doubt her sister, sat mending dust cloths. While I was being massaged I studied the sleeping little girl and daydreamed about kidnaping her instead. She could not be compared to the girl at the playhouse, but she had a kind of untamed charm that appealed to me.

That night I mulled over various plans for abducting the masseur's child—not that I had reached any firm decision to act yet, but I was growing dissatisfied with merely repeating the same fantasies over and over. As a preliminary step I began cautiously to buy toys and candy. I still suffered from stiffness in my shoulders, but I was bolstered now by a new and pleasant feeling of tense anxiety. Still hoping to come across the other little girl, the one I had seen at the playhouse, I went down to the bazaar every night, although, in the unlikely event I should meet her, I still had no definite course of action in mind.

It was the last night of the bazaar. As I walked along I caught sight of the masseur's wife leading her daughter by the hand about a dozen paces ahead of me. For several minutes I threaded my way slowly through the crowd after them. The mother stopped to buy something, and in the moment her attention was diverted I led the child away. I would not go so far as to call it a skillful performance; but I do congratulate myself on having brought it off without attracting the mother's notice. I was also very fortunate that the girl remembered my face and came along without a fuss. I am sure that no one looking on could have seen anything strange in it at all.

We went directly from the bazaar to a back street, where I bought her some candy. "Your mommy's gone home; you can come with me," I told her, taking her from the back street to a still darker street that ran alongside the railroad tracks toward my house. It was only then that I was sure I had kidnaped her. Up to this moment, had someone who knew her spoken to us, without a doubt I would have delivered her promptly to her parents, as if this had been my intention all along.

Suddenly very agitated, I picked the girl up and started to carry her on my back. She smelled like a country brat. For a few moments I felt already weary of her, as though weighed down by an unmanageable burden. Then I turned to look at her over my shoulder and kissed her on the forehead. I knew, though, that if I was going to show her affection it would have to be in an easygoing, natural manner. Not only in displays of tenderness but in everything I did I would have to treat her in a way to which she was accustomed and which she could accept easily. Otherwise I would only succeed in frightening her. It would be dangerous to arouse feelings in her that were too different from those she had felt in her limited experience of life until now.

Presently we reached my house.

"I'll send the people next door to call for your mother," I said when we were inside. "You'll wait here like a good girl till Mommy comes for you, won't you?"

I made a show of going across to the neighbors, standing outside my door for a few minutes. When I returned I explained to the girl that they were a little busy next door now, and she would have to stay with me awhile. Then I sat down at my desk.

I felt quite unsettled, which was only to be expected, I suppose. My nerves were taut as they had not been for a long time. With no clear purpose in mind I picked up my pen and started to write.

I've done it at last. I have done this terrible thing and I am pleased with myself for having gone through with it. It can't be undone now. I must carry on with it. At the moment I don't know what to do next.

But whatever I do, so far, at least, I have accomplished something I
wanted to do before but could not. I have been too indecisive and
introspective. But for once I have overcome this weakness.

The girl began to sneeze. "Goodness!" I said. "You must have
caught cold riding piggyback. I was so warm I didn't pay any attention." I lit the gas heater in the rear of the room. It ignited with a pop,
startling the little girl. "I'll heat up some water for you," I said, putting
a medicine tin full of water on top of the heater. The girl stared with
wonder into the purple gas flame. I picked up my pen again.

On the face of it, what I've done seems rash and reprehensible.
Whether or not I've acted merely on a whim will be decided by what I
do from now on. I mustn't try to rationalize it for the sake of other
people. And I probably couldn't if I had to. The girl was saying
something and pointing at some toys on top of the wicker suitcase—
the ones I had recently bought for just this occasion, which I had
taken out a little while ago and placed casually in view.

"What do you want?" I asked her.

"That one, if you'd be so kind," she said in a very grownup way.

"Sure. Bring it over here," I told her. "You know how it works?"

"No, I don't know," she answered, and went to fetch it. It was a
celluloid Western-style doll that walked when you wound it up. The
girl looked on gravely as I leaned back against the desk and turned
the key.

"Ready? Watch now!" I cleared off the desk and set the doll down.
With a jerk of its body the doll began to move, walked across the desk
top to the edge and tumbled over, head first. The girl stood watching,
slack-jawed, her eyes glued to the doll until it fell off. She burst into
peals of delight. As its spring finished unwinding, the doll lay whirring
loudly where it had fallen under the desk. "Shall we do it again?" I
asked, winding it up once more. This time I started it off from the
opposite corner of the desk and aimed it so that it would go diagonally
toward the corner where the girl was watching. But the doll did not
walk in a straight line. Tilting its torso left and right, it gradually
described an arc on the desk-top. When it reached the edge I put out
my hand to catch it. Abruptly the girl swept my hand away. The doll
fell off head first again and the girl laughed as merrily as before.

"Goddamn it!" I said, grasping her head in one hand and shaking it
gently. The girl nearly choked with laughter. "This time you do it

yourself." She picked up the whirring doll and thrust it toward me without a word.

"What's the matter?" I said. "Can't you do it yourself? It's nothing to be afraid of."

I told her to wait and went into the next room. I took a glass down from the shelf and poured her some hot water out of the medicine tin.

I set the glass aside, as it was still too hot. "Better wait a minute," I said to the girl. I gave her some chocolate-covered nuts, picking them out of a canister, then handed her the glass of water as soon as it had cooled a bit.

I noticed her hands were filthy. Underneath the dirt they were red and swollen, as if they had been frostbitten. I've got to give her a good wash, I thought. But then it occurred to me that I couldn't very well take her to the local bathhouse. Of course I would have to leave town in any case, and if we were to go away, the big city of Tokyo would be the safest, I decided.

After a while the girl began to talk of home and started to cry. I hushed her by telling her that her mother would be coming in the morning. Thoroughly downcast, she soon fell asleep in her seat. I woke her up and managed barely to keep her awake with games and tricks until close to dawn, when I finally put her to bed.

I was tired, too, but when I got into bed I could not go to sleep. I kept closing and opening my eyes. The figure of the small girl with her smelly hair, stretched out not far away on the same mats and snoring lightly in her sleep, even the disarray of my room, brought home to me that something new and strange had come into my life, something that did not fit in at all with things as they had been before. I felt myself slipping weakly into the conventional view of what I had done. Here it became all too clear that, despite the enormity of what I had already done, I was far from being as single-minded and resolute in my actions as I had thought. I was disgusted with myself. Still, I was not about to give in completely to the spineless conventional view. I could not justify what I had done to others, but at least I could satisfy myself. Considering my previous state of mind there was no telling what might have happened had I not done it. The stiffness was as severe as ever; yet with the resurgence of my natural vitality it had ceased to bother me. My sole source of real worry was the vaguely ominous feeling that the girl and I were at odds with one another.

Listening to the rain which had begun to fall outside, I finally fell asleep around eight o'clock. I had a painful dream.

I am being chased by the intransigent old masseur. As I run along I hold a little blind girl in my arms. (In the dream it is the girl rather than the masseur who is blind.) I am sure that he will kill me if he catches me, as he mistakenly believes that I have defiled the girl. I want to explain things to him, but he gives me no chance. I flee down a narrow, corridor-like passageway, emerging on top of a cliff (it looks like the site of the shrine to Kannon in Tomonotsu). Escape is blocked in all directions. White foam bubbles gently on the surface of the water far below. For a moment I am terror-stricken; then, realizing it is only a dream, I jump off without hesitation and wake up.

It was one in the afternoon and the girl was still sleeping soundly.

I got up and opened the shutters, as quietly as possible. It was still raining lightly. Crouched down on the veranda, I looked out at the misty island directly opposite and to the sea beyond. Then I noticed four or five men climbing up toward me from below, carrying large crates and cloth-wrapped bundles. For a moment I was worried, until I realized that they were on their way to the cottage up behind my house. The cottage belonged to a successful draper, who was perhaps holding a celebration to mark the end of the bazaar. Sure enough, around three o'clock people dressed for a party began filing up the hill, then a group of geisha passed by. Men who looked like caterers kept coming and going. Presently there was a twang of the samisen and I heard singing.

The rain stopped and a large rainbow appeared in the sky, arching over the promontory to the east. The girl awoke at last and looked around her in amazement.

"Come on, let's wash up," I said as cheerfully as I could manage, leading her over to the sink.

As I was scrubbing her face, she began to cry. "I want to go home," she wailed.

"Stop crying, now. When you've had something to eat I'll take you," I said to hush her. I opened up a can of sausages. She refused them with a shake of her head. She devoured some seasoned seaweed and soy-sauce pickles I gave her, then washed it down with a can of condensed milk.

When she was finished, I had no choice but to take her out. It was well after nightfall. Now that the bazaar was over, the town was deathly still at this hour. We walked through the darkened streets bordering on the harbor and started home. When the girl saw that she was being led back to the same house, she went into a tantrum. Self-recrimination swept over me again with sudden force. By an almost physical effort I brought myself under control. But I sensed uneasily that both my mental attitude and my unarticulated feelings toward the girl were on the verge of shifting in some new direction. Since she had begun to distrust me, I too was infected by doubt.

"They're having fun up at the Sasen (the name of the cottage). Shall we have a look?" At last I managed to coax her up the hill. "Then we can take you home. Did you hear them playing the samisen a while ago?"

At the cottage the whole party was clapping time as, one by one, each guest boisterously sang out another verse of some ballad. Holding the girl up, I opened the kitchen window and pointed out the gaily flickering cottage, which seemed to appear and disappear in the darkness.

Come what may, I thought, I must leave this town immediately. I no longer saw anything in the little girl. But I knew that from now on I would have to act forcefully and resolutely in order to cope with the difficulties that were bound to arise. Now, when it was too late, it occurred to me that from the start I had not been so fond of the girl. Still, had it been the lovely child I discovered at the playhouse, at this juncture things would no doubt have been even more complicated and unpleasant than they were with the masseur's daughter.

Toward ten o'clock the party at the cottage began to break up. "I want to go home," the girl said, starting to cry again. An hour or so later the sound of the shutters being drawn announced the departure of the last few guests. As if to catch their attention the girl raised her voice in a loud wail. For the first time I gave her a terrifying look and scolded her in a hushed but biting tone. Thoroughly cowed, she sucked in her breath. The group was just then making their way down the narrow, steep path. "Come on, it's this way!" called the lilting voice of a tipsy geisha. "Hey, don't fall down!" answered a husky man's voice.

With a gentle face I tried to appease the girl. But she had seen through me now and was determined to keep her distance. She was showing a nasty stubborn streak. Though I tried to reason with myself that she was only a child, after all, I found myself growing mean and stubborn, too.

I could not fail to see that the present state of affairs was only the natural outcome of my own actions. Why, then, had I not taken steps to avert this natural and foreseeable result? Even granted that my plight was unavoidable from the start, I should have done everything in my power to prepare myself for it, in the hope of overcoming these difficulties when they arose. Here again I recalled that I had not wanted this particular girl in the first place.

The girl remained grimly silent. She clenched her jaws together and trained her tear-filled eyes on one spot. Now and then she would convulsively snort out through her nose the grief that welled up inside her. Seeing her like this, I came to the conclusion that what I had done was an all but unpardonable act of egotism. Yet I did not consider taking her home. There must be some other way to make her happy, I told myself.

My will weakened steadily. I took out of the desk drawer the sheets of paper on which I had written after bringing the girl in the previous night, and tore them into small pieces. I began to feel like crying.

"Aren't you sleepy?" I asked. The girl did not answer. She would not even look at me. She let herself be lifted into my arms without resistance. My eyes clouded over as I pressed her to me and kissed her on the cheek. We seemed so pitiful, she and I. When I began to cry aloud she raised her voice and cried with me. For a while I could say nothing. Then I said to her, "Let's get some sleep." She assented without looking at me.

With emotions completely different from the previous night's, I lay down to sleep with the girl clasped to my chest. The night before, although I had of course been anxious, I had also felt somehow light and cheerful. Tonight this feeling had vanished. We said nothing. The girl remained rigid as I held her; she showed no sign of being sleepy.

"How about some candy?" There was no answer. I brought her some of the chocolate-covered nuts she had eaten with such relish the night before. She obediently clutched them in her hand where I'd placed them but made no move to put them in her mouth. Still holding the candy, she soon fell asleep.

Despite my fatigue from last night's lack of rest I could not let myself sleep. I was afraid that while I slept the girl would run away.

Whenever I dozed off briefly, I dreamed that she was stealing out from under the covers and slipping away, only to awake and find her still beside me.

The next morning I stood gazing vacantly out at the scenery through the glass panes in the sliding door. Below, a small group of people came climbing the incline, constantly looking up in my direction. There were two policemen, a man with the air of a detective, and, bringing up the rear, a dusky-complexioned middle-aged woman of firm, stocky build: clearly the girl's mother. Her disquiet showed in a fierce scowl. I felt my own face flushing bright red.

I was a little confused. I will give them the best fight I can, I thought. If I were to hand the girl over meekly now, I might as well never have begun with it. I rushed over to the wicker suitcase and took out a heavy chopping knife. Holding it point down, I stood in the middle of the room and waited.

When the time came, I was quite unable to lunge about, swinging the knife. I didn't have the stomach for it. In fact, from the moment I took out the knife I lacked the necessary passion to use it. Instead, I must have presented a terribly commonplace figure, standing there in the middle of the room with a kitchen knife in my hand.

The mother shrieked hysterically as she picked up the girl, who had been sleeping peacefully in the tiny adjoining room. Weeping, the mother began to revile me. I remained silent. With the girl in her arms she came up behind me and struck me square on the back. She paid no attention to the men who were trying to calm her down. Presently I was led off to the police station.

AN ACCIDENT

Dekigoto, 1913

It was a hot, late July afternoon, without a breath of wind. The streetcar hummed monotonously along the track that stretched out like a thin ribbon of mercury down the middle of the broad street. There was scarcely a pedestrian to be seen, only, by a roadside ice cream stand in front of a high concrete wall, two customers crouching down, fans in hand. Above their heads a fig tree dangled its branches languidly over the wall; the leaves curled inward, listless, dusty and dry, uncannily still.

I was seated at the front of the car, leaning up against the window and staring out vacantly. In my sweaty hands I continued to clutch a magazine, half rolled up, that I had given up reading. This way I caught at least a faint, hot breeze as the streetcar traveled forward.

We came to a stop. No one got off, no one got on; and so we moved on wearily to the next stop, where a fat, fortyish woman got on. In one hand she held a small satinet parasol, in the other a damp towel with which she busily mopped herself around the throat as she climbed aboard. Her face was red and drenched in sweat. One or two of the passengers cast a lackadaisical glance in her direction, but most of them just sat limply in their seats as before, their eyes only half open.

There were no more than ten passengers in all. Across the aisle from me sat a young man wearing a thin cotton jacket and a large black cap which bore the insignia of the municipal electric department. With a peevish look frozen on his face, he had half dozed off. Beside him a pair of students, both sound asleep, maintained identical postures of boyish toughness, the visors of their straw caps pulled down over their eyes, their legs sprawled wide apart. A sense of the oppressive heat, and of pervasive dirt, was conveyed by their bare feet stained with sweaty grime tapering off into whitish shins. Beyond them was a large man in Western clothes, somewhat over fifty, with the appearance of a petty bureaucrat. With a soiled imitation Panama hat tilted down against the back of his head, he was leaning forward and resting his chin on top of a walking stick that he held planted on the floor between his feet. His studiously empty expression suggested someone sunken into quite random thoughts, eyes open but not at all in focus. And yet he seemed aware of my gaze, for he straightened up and opened his eyes slightly wider, before lapsing back into his vacant look. Then he began impulsively to dab at his forehead, broad below a receding hairline, with a fuzzy cotton handkerchief rolled into a ball.

I was myself beginning to succumb to the blazing sunlight; even to peer out through half closed eyes was painful. The relentless crush of this malevolent heat assumed in my mind the character of a particularly cruel and undeserved punishment. But what feckless creatures we are, I thought, to submit so readily to frontal attack from the elements in the form of heat, when we pride ourselves on our ingenuity in the face of rain, cold, and everything else.

Suddenly, a white butterfly flew in through a window. It fluttered all around the car, carefree and gay yet somehow very purposeful, like a child alone, intently bouncing a little ball hither and yon.

The streetcar hummed along in the same dreary monotone. The passengers slumped back in dull anguish: no one appeared to care any longer where he was going or why. Oblivious to the distance it had already been carried, the butterfly amused itself, soaring here, dipping there. The dizzying feats of this light-hearted creature helped to ease the pressure that I felt inside my head from the heat, as of being enveloped in a heavy cotton hood.

Abruptly the butterfly flapped up against the ceiling two or three times in succession. Unable to alight there, it dropped down onto a

theater poster: a woodblock print with heavy black lettering announcing a special performance of *Genyadana*. The lustrous wings of
the butterfly, richly powdered, white as snow, were beautiful against
the thick characters carved in the *kantei* style. The butterfly was now
completely still, as if catching its breath after its mad frolic. The
streetcar moved on lethargically. The passengers slumped back in their
seats, everyone by now half asleep. Eventually my mind went blank,
too.

There was a lull of several dreary minutes. Suddenly the motorman
was shouting in a strained voice and my head jerked up. Looking out
over the motorman's raised platform, I saw a little boy about to cut
across the streetcar's path. Without so much as a glance in our direction, he was running pell-mell straight ahead. From our vantage point,
however, his pace seemed all too slow and relaxed—he had yet to
reach the tracks. Still shouting out the window, the motorman was
pulling hard on the brake level. The car began at once to slow down.
But as the boy continued his headlong rush on a course perpendicular
to ours, this only produced the effect of an imminent collision in slow
motion. It was now inevitable. The boy disappeared beneath a kind of
railing out in front of the motorman's seat, and at that instant there
was a loud clang. The streetcar moved forward another six feet or so.
Having at some point retreated to the rear, next to the conductor, on
an involuntary impulse to flee from the disaster, I stood staring at the
backs of the passengers and steeling myself against the shudder that
went through me at that moment. Presently a child's voice was heard
crying loudly. I sighed with relief (a relief that was, I realize, essentially self-centered; but even with this realization, in retrospect I saw
the reaction of that moment as nevertheless good and right).

I joined the other passengers, now clustered at the front of the car,
and looked out the motorman's window. People emerged from the
nearby houses and gathered to watch. The young man from the
electrical department who had been seated across from me was holding the wailing child in his arms. The man was clearly very upset,
speaking in a loud angry voice and darting fierce looks in all directions. The child's terry cloth robe was caught up around his chest in
the electrician's firm grasp, exposing plump buttocks and small,
stunted legs made to look still smaller by the boy's contortions. He
was sobbing uncontrollably. With his large head and his sweat-
soaked, ugly face, the boy was altogether comical.

"It's all right now, it's all right." The electrician patted the boy on the buttocks. Reverting to his irascible tone, he said to the conductor, "Look, you'd better examine him closely." He turned the boy over, thrusting the buttocks up in the air.

"Yes, it would be an error not to," added the large bureaucratic-looking passenger, who had come up beside him and stood nervously peering over his shoulder.

After a fairly thorough examination, the conductor pronounced, "He's all right. Not even a scratch."

The motorman stood apart at some distance dangling the controller handle in his hand. Without a trace of emotion on his face, he said in a cool, matter-of-fact manner, "The catcher in front seems to work pretty well."

"Yes indeed! I should say so!" the bureaucrat chimed in, turning toward the motorman.

Still holding the boy in his arms, the electrician began to shout again. "Listen here," he demanded, "where are the kid's parents?"

One of the onlookers told him that someone had just gone to fetch them.

The boy, whose energies had until now been absorbed in crying, turned himself around in the electrician's arms and tried to squirm out of the tight embrace. At his captor's anger he redoubled his efforts and, when these proved unsuccessful, began to aim his fists directly at the man's face.

"Goddamn it!" Glaring furiously at the boy, the electrician maintained his tight grip and held him out at arms' length.

The bureaucrat, still wearing his panama on the back of his head, wandered about distractedly, muttering to himself, "Yes indeed, it really worked." Then he went back to the boy; stroking the face besmirched with a mixture of tears, sweat, and dust as thick as stage make-up, he spoke soothingly to him: "No need to cry anymore."

Enraged though he was, the boy made no attempt to strike the kindly bureaucrat. He even kept still as the man stooped over to inspect him once more from the waist down.

"My, my. What's this?" His words attracted immediate attention from the small crowd that had begun to disperse. "Seems like the young lad had to take a little leak." Everyone burst out laughing.

Except for the electrician, whose face was still frozen in a fierce scowl. Silently he looked down at his shirt; it was soaked through from just below the chest on down. Again, everyone laughed. Nestled between the boy's slim thighs, his well-formed little penis, no larger than a half-inch gourd, was still moist at the tip.

"You little beggar, you." The electrician gave the boy a hug and knocked him gently on the head with his chin. At this the boy began to wail again.

"A little pee never hurt anyone," the bureaucrat consoled.

A murmur went through the cluster of bystanders as a woman of about forty, dark-skinned and ugly, came rushing across the street. She was very wrought up. No sooner had she retrieved her child from the arms of the electrician than she fixed the boy in a ferocious look and began to scold him. Then she slapped him on the head several times over. The boy cried even louder than before and thrashed his legs about wildly. To restrain him, the woman squeezed him tightly in her arms and shook him as hard as she could, calling him a fool and an idiot.

Having stood aside and watched this scene with the same fierce countenance, the electrician assumed a bellicose stance and shouted at her, "You're the one to blame, you know." A quarrel ensued.

The bureaucrat remained oblivious to this altercation and continued to wander about exclaiming to himself with a peculiar sort of fervor. Seeing that the motorman had returned to his seat, he went up to him and reiterated, "Well, it certainly did work!" Rather superfluously, he tapped with his stick on the wire mesh catcher attached to the front of the car. "Why, it couldn't have worked any better," he said. "It must be the first time this has happened since these things were installed."

His words finally failed to convey the full force of the euphoria that he felt. He wanted to say more but somehow could not produce phrases strong enough to satisfy himself. Nor was he given much encouragement by the motorman's distinctly cool, aloof look.

The crowd of spectators had dwindled, most of them having drifted back to their houses, where they stood under the eaves watching from afar. The woman was apologizing profusely to the conductor. The boy was quiet now, his mouth and nose buried in his mother's large, grossly drooping breasts.

The electrician and the bureaucrat got back on the streetcar. The woman picked up the boy's geta and went home. The car began to move.

The electrician resolutely stripped off his jacket and his urine-soaked shirt. His torso was lean and hard, his skin fair. With the dry portion of his shirt he wiped his body from the solar plexus to below the waist. His biceps and pectoral muscles rippled agreeably. Raising his head slightly, he met my gaze and smiled. "Some shower I got," he said. Without a trace of his former ferocity, his face now radiated kindness, and a wonderful vitality.

Across the aisle, the fat woman and the bureaucrat sat talking together. The bureaucrat spoke ardently and with much gesticulation.

The two students had likewise struck up a conversation.

Indeed, all the previously heat-worn, somnolent passengers showed a new life on their faces.

And I savored within myself a warm and pleasant excitement.

The light-hearted butterfly, I noticed all of a sudden, had left its perch on the theater poster and flown away.

UNDER AN ASHEN MOON
Haiiro no tsuki, 1945

Even with no wind, it was chilly on the platform at Tokyo Station (the roof had yet to be rebuilt), enough so to make me grateful for my unlined overcoat. My companions of the evening had departed on the Ueno-bound loop train. Alone now, I waited for the Shinagawa-Shibuya train.

An ashen moon shone down through thin clouds on the charred ruins over toward Nihonbashi. Somewhat fuller than a half-moon, it hung low in the sky, and appeared unusually close. Though it was not much past eight-thirty, there were only a few other people waiting, scattered sparsely over the broad platform.

A headlight appeared far down the track; after a surprisingly short interval, the train drew up at the platform. I boarded a car that was not at all crowded and managed to find a seat near the door on the opposite side. On my right was seated a woman of about fifty, wearing baggy trousers. On the other side was a young conscript worker, judging from his appearance, no more than eighteen years old at the most. He was sitting sideways next to the door with his back at right angles to the rest of us and his legs dangling over the edge of the bench, where the armrest was missing. I had caught a glimpse of his face as I got on, his eyes shut tight, his mouth hanging wide open. With the motion of the train his torso swung freely to and fro: rather, he would appear to fall forward almost to the floor then bob back into an upright position. It was hard to believe he could be going through these gyrations in his sleep, and so I warily moved over as far as I could without attracting attention.

A good many passengers got on at Yurakucho and Shinbashi, quite a few of them apparently on their way home from foraging expeditions. A ruddy, round-faced man in his mid-twenties came along with an exceedingly large knapsack; he set it down for a moment on the floor beside the sleeping boy, then pushed it up against the seat and stood leaning over it. Behind him, jostled by the press of standing passengers, another, considerably older man with a knapsack peered over his shoulder and asked if he could rest his burden on top of the young man's. Without waiting for a reply, he went to set the knapsack down. "Just a moment, please," said the young man. "I'm afraid I've got something fragile inside." The older man apologized, cast a doubtful look at the thin mesh of the overhead parcel rack, and maneuvered awkwardly for space as he put the knapsack on his back again.

Casting about for some remedy, the young man offered to wedge the other's bundle into the space between the boy and myself. Nodding in appreciation, the older man said, "No no. That's okay. It's not that heavy—I just thought I'd set it down for a minute, but it's not worth the trouble really." I took pleasure in this exchange: people seemed indeed more eager to please nowadays than they had before.

Hamamatsu-cho, Shinagawa—a few passengers got off but many more got on. In the midst of all the commotion, the boy continued to swing precariously forward and back, forward and back.

"Just look at the face on him," commented one of a small group of businessman types who were clustered nearby. His cohorts all joined in his laughter. Although I could not at this point see the boy's face, it probably was quite comical; the businessman's style of speech certainly was; and a faintly warm and mirthful air wafted through the car.

But then the round-faced young man turned to the older man behind him and, jabbing at his own belly with his finger, said softly, "He hasn't got far to go."

Startled, the man silently sized the boy up and murmured incredulously. The businessmen too appeared dubious. "Well, he might be sick or something"—"Isn't he just drunk?"—"No, I don't think it's that..." All at once they stopped their aimless speculation and fell silent.

The cheap fabric of the boy's uniform was torn at the shoulder and had been patched with a piece of towel sewn on from the inside. As he sat with his head bowed forward, his regulation cap worn backward, there was something touching about the grimy, slender neck revealed below the visor. His strenuous gyrations had ceased. Instead, he was rubbing his cheek insistently against the short strip of wooden panelling between the window and the door. He now appeared truly a child, making up to some loved one whom, in his muddled daydream, he had conjured up from the sensation of the soft wood.

The closest of the businessmen, a large man, put his hand on the boy's shoulder and asked him how far he was going. When there was no answer, the man repeated his question; this time the boy replied in a melancholy voice, "I'm going to Ueno."

"Why then you've taken the wrong train—this one goes the other way 'round to Shibuya."

As the boy sat up to look out the window he lost his balance and abruptly keeled over against me. I was taken unawares, to be sure, but even so I later wondered about the reason for my swift reaction at that moment: almost by reflex I rebuffed the boy's body with my shoulder. My action was a direct contradiction of my feelings toward the boy, and afterward I was quite at a loss to account for it. It made me feel a good deal worse that I had encountered virtually no resistance from the boy's body as it collided with my shoulder. My weight was then down to something slightly over a hundred and six pounds. The boy's must have been well below that.

"You were already here when I got on at Tokyo," I said, speaking to him over his shoulder, "so you must have just slept through at Ueno. But where did you get on?"

"I got on at—Shibuya."

Someone observed that he had, then, nearly made the complete circuit.

The boy pressed his forehead against the window in an attempt to make out where we were but quickly gave it up. In a voice that could barely be heard he said, "What the hell, it doesn't really matter."

These words reverberated within me for some time.

The other passengers paid the boy no further heed, nor did I. Clearly, they thought there was nothing they could do. For my part, that is the way I felt, too. Had I been carrying a lunch with me, I could have let him have it, as a salve to my conscience. But what was the point of giving him money? Even in the daytime, not to mention now, at nine in the evening, he would have had a hard time of it finding any food for sale.

I got off at Shibuya, in a bleak frame of mind.

This incident occurred on the sixteenth of October, 1945.

NIGHT FIRES
Takibi, 1920

It started to rain early that morning. Around noontime we gathered in
my room on the second floor for a game of cards. Besides myself and
my wife, there was S-san, who is a painter, and K-san, the innkeeper.
The room filled up with smoke, the game grew tedious, we ate too
many snacks. By the middle of the afternoon we were all a little weary.

Someone stood up and slid open a window. The rain had stopped.
The smell of fresh green leaves wafted through the room as the crisp
mountain air flooded in and dispersed the stale smoke. Revived, we
looked at each other in a new light.

K-san was already halfway to his feet.

"I'm going up to work on the cottage," he said, flexing his hands
eagerly inside his pockets.

"I guess I'll go along and do some painting," said S-san. And so the
two of them went out together.

I sat on the windowsill and watched the mass of white clouds drift
rapidly apart, opening up wide gaps of celadon sky.

S-san and K-san appeared, the one with a box of paints on his
shoulder, the other with a longish jacket thrown loosely around him.
They climbed up the slope toward the cottage, chatting as they went.

They paused awhile in front of the small structure; then they separated, and S-san went on into the woods by himself.

I stretched out and began to read. My wife sat beside me sewing. Just as I was becoming bored with my book, she suggested that we go up and have a look at the cottage.

What we called "the cottage" was a small cabin we hoped to move into soon, which the young innkeeper, K-san, and an old charcoal burner named Haru were building for us.

Today they were working on the privy.

"It's turning out rather nicely," said K-san as we approached. I joined in, and even my wife lent a hand from time to time.

A half hour or so later, S-san came out of the woods, walking over a wet bed of last year's fallen leaves.

"Well done!" he said, admiring the privy. "It projects just enough to give the house a proper shape."

K-san looked pleased and agreed that what he'd expected to be at best a necessary eyesore had become something of an asset.

We had left the whole job up to him. K-san likes making things. But besides the actual building of the cabin, he had also done the original design and selected the materials, all with painstaking care, to give us the most pleasant mountain dwelling possible.

A nighthawk set up its cry: a sharp, hollow sound as of hard wood being struck. It was too dark to work any longer so we quit for the day.

Old Haru-san was pressing tobacco into his pipe with the palm of his hand.

"I've seen some horses and cows wandering around up here," he said. "We'd better put up a fence soon."

K-san laughed and said, "You're quite right. We'd look pretty silly if our masterpiece got eaten up before we've even finished it."

Here on the mountain there was no plaster to be had. Even the sides of the inn itself were but thin wooden boards. The cabin's outer walls consisted of two layers of coarsely woven material, of the sort used to make charcoal bags, with straw matting stuffed in between.

"It would be a real feast for horses and cows," said Haru-san. We all laughed at the spectacle he had conjured up.

Sundown on the mountain was always delightful, especially after a rainfall. As we stood resting by the cottage that evening we shared in the gentle pleasure of reviewing the work we had done together during the day. A vital joy surged among us.

It had rained yesterday as well; then, as today, the skies had cleared in time for a beautiful sunset, made all the more beautiful by a large rainbow that arched from the Torii Pass to the peak of Mount Kurobi. We had stayed outside to enjoy it until the last rays of the sun were gone. Partly to get a better look at the rainbow, we climbed into the tall oak trees that stood around the cottage. Even my wife was persuaded to try it when she heard what a fine view we had. K-san and I helped her up to a spot some twenty feet off the ground. The three of us sat in our tree, S-san in the next one over. Then he and K-san began to compete with each other to see who could climb the highest. Both of them reached close to forty feet up in the trees. Cradled on a lofty limb that branched off at a comfortable angle, K-san called down to us.

"It's like an easy chair," he said as he lay there smoking, and to prove this he started to rock the bough, causing it to tremble like a great leafy wave.

Then Ichiya, as everyone called him, appeared—a feeble-minded boy, whose features were disconcertingly large for his age. Carrying K-san's youngest son strapped to his back, he had come up from the inn to tell us that dinner was ready. By the time we all climbed down from the trees, it was so dark that we needed a light to look for a comb that my wife had dropped from our perch.

Recalling the fun we'd had the previous evening, I suggested that we take a boat out on the lake tonight. Everyone agreed.

Having gone our separate ways for dinner, the four of us gathered again afterward around the broad, sunken hearth on the ground floor. K-san was mixing some condensed milk for the baby with hot water from a large metal teapot on the hearth. Then he went around to the ice house and fetched back a thick oaken plank.

We set out through the dark precincts of an adjacent shrine that nestled hidden beneath towering fir trees. As we passed by the Kagura Hall, K-san called out to the man selling amulets.

"Go ahead and use the bath," he said.

Between the stout trunks of the firs the lake's silvery water shimmered before us.

The small boat was beached on a sandy strip at the shore. We stood waiting on the wet, black sand while K-san scooped out the water that had collected in the bottom of the boat from this morning's rain. Then he laid the oaken plank across the middle of the boat, adjusted it slightly, and invited us aboard. My wife got in first, S-san and I took our places, and we pushed off onto the lake.

It was a calm evening. A glimmer of twilight still lingered on the horizon to the west. Yet the surrounding mountains now appeared almost black against the sky, like so many lizards' backs.

S-san spoke up from the bow, addressing himself to K-san. "Mount Kurobi looks awfully flat tonight," he said.

"Mountains always look lower in the dark," K-san answered from the stern where he sat smoothly working the short scull.

"Look!" exclaimed my wife. "There's a camp fire over on the shore."

We had just started around toward the other side of a small island called Odorijima. The fire was glowing on the opposite shore—or rather the fires, one of them a reflection in the still water.

"Who could it be at this hour?" K-san wondered aloud. "Possibly a group of *warabi* pickers camping out for the night. There's an old charcoal kiln over there that no one uses anymore. They might be sleeping inside it. Shall we go over and have a look?"

K-san pushed hard on the scull to change our course; then the boat was gliding smoothly through the water again. He told us of a surprise encounter he had once had near here with a water snake, while swimming back from the island to the shrine. Talking of such things, we soon drew near to the other shore.

It appeared to be as K-san had suggested: the fire was burning by the kiln door.

"Do you suppose there really are people inside?" S-san inquired.

"I'm quite sure of it," said K-san. "But maybe we should take a closer look. If nobody's there, we ought to put the fire out."

"I'd like to explore a bit anyway," said my wife.

As the boat touched the shore S-san jumped out, painter in hand, and pulled the bow up between two rocks.

K-san crouched down in front of the kiln door and peered intently inside.

"I was right," he announced. "They're fast asleep."

The air felt chilly and we were all grateful for the fire.

S-san poked an ember out to one side with a small stick and used it to light a cigarette.

There was a soft rustling noise inside the kiln; then someone groaned in his sleep.

"They must be pretty warm in there with this blaze going," said S-san.

"It will die out soon enough, though," said K-san, throwing a few stray sticks on the fire.

"And it can get very cold here at dawn, especially if you've just wakened from a deep sleep."

My wife was worried about the sleepers. With the fire so close, wasn't there some danger of asphyxiation?

K-san assured her it was all right, so long as the fire was kept on the outside. "But when kilns get old," he added, "they sometimes collapse all of a sudden. It's especially risky when it's been raining."

"Dear me! You really should warn them, don't you think?"

"Yes," S-san agreed, "maybe you should."

K-san laughed heartily. "I doubt if they need any warning now. We've been talking so loud I'm sure they heard every word."

Again there was the sound of dead leaves rustling inside the kiln. We all laughed.

"Shall we go along?" my wife suggested, in an unsettled tone of voice.

When we reached the boat, S-san climbed in first and sat in the stern. "I'll do the sculling this time," he said.

The lake was utterly still between the shore and the island. Looking straight down over the edge of the boat into the water, one could see the clear, star-filled sky.

"Why not build a fire ourselves," said K-san.

As he worked the scull S-san was whistling "Die Donauwellen" (a constant refrain with him) and seemed not to hear at first. Then he asked, "Where shall I land?"

"Straight ahead will be fine," said K-san, looking out over his shoulder from the bow.

We all fell silent for awhile. The boat slipped quietly through the water.

"What do you think?" I said to my wife, breaking the silence. "Could you swim from here to the shore?"

"Well—I suppose I could."

K-san expressed some surprise that she could swim at all.

"How early can one swim in these parts?" I asked him.

"Right about now, if it's a warm day. I was already swimming last year at this time."

"It's still a little cold," I said, with my hand in the water. "Though come to think of it, I've had morning dips in other mountain lakes after the leaves have turned color in the fall, and it wasn't as bad as I expected. I've even swum in Ashinoko early in April."

"Those were the good old days," my wife teased, knowing how susceptible to cold I really am.

At this point K-san said we should land. With a few strong sweeps of the scull, S-san sent the bow scraping over the sandy shore.

"Isn't it a bit wet to start a fire?" my wife asked as we got out on the beach.

"We'll use birchbark for kindling," said K-san. "It burns well even when it's wet, because it's so oily."

After asking us to gather a few handfuls of the bark, he himself went off to pick up firewood in the dark forest overgrown with ferns and leafy plants. The glowing red tips of the cigarettes that he and S-san were smoking served as tiny beacons for us after we split up to do our work.

The old birchbark was scored and tattered. We took hold of the shreds that curled out from the trunk and peeled it off in strips. From time to time the sharp report of breaking deadwood rang out through the silent forest from the direction where K-san had gone.

When we had gathered all we could carry, we brought the kindling down to the beach. It amounted to quite a heap. Suddenly K-san came bounding out of the woods, plainly startled.

"I saw some of those worms," he gasped, "the ones with the tails that glow in the dark. They're disgusting! The way they wiggle their tails at you—like this." K-san loathed inchworms and the like—any kind of larvae.

We walked to the edge of the woods to have a look, with S-san leading the way.

"Was it around here?" he asked, turning toward K-san, who was following a few steps behind.

"They're right there, aren't they? Don't you see something shining?"

"Ah yes. Here they are," said S-san, striking a match for closer inspection.

Each worm's main segment was about an inch long; to this was attached an outsized tail that wriggled languidly up in the air. Their tails were glowing dimly at the tips, a dull blue.

"What's so scary about them?" said S-san.

"All I know is I'm not about to walk around up here now that I've spotted them . . . Let's go back and build our fire!"

We all went down to the beach again.

Though still wet, the birchbark caught fire right away, sending up a column of thick black smoke as from a kerosene lamp. K-san fed the flames with sticks of wood, starting from the smallest and gradually building up. In no time at all we had a blazing fire. Around us the shore and forest were suddenly illuminated; even the trees on the island across the water emerged out of the darkness.

K-san brought the oaken plank over from the boat and set up a bench for us to sit on.

"You're a real mountain boy in every way," S-san said to him. "That is, except for the thing you seem to have about those worms."

"Yes, it's true. It's not so bad when I have some warning, but I do get pretty scared when I just stumble on them."

"There must be something more frightening than glowworms on the mountain," said my wife.

"No, besides them there's nothing I'd call really frightening."

"Aren't there any large snakes?"

"None."

"How about vipers?" I asked.

"Sometimes you see them down around Minowa, but I've never seen one up here."

"I suppose there were wolves roaming about at one time," S-san suggested.

"Yes—and not so long ago at that," said K-san. "When I was a child I would listen to them howling in the distance at night. I can remember the terrible lonely feeling it gave me."

He told us how his late father, who liked to fish after dark, was surrounded by wolves one night; he had to make his way back through the water, grabbing onto the rocks along the shore. K-san then recalled having seen the carcass of a half-devoured horse in the meadow, shortly after they first opened up the grazing land on the mountain-side.

"That same year," K-san added, "they set traps of meat filled with dynamite. The wolves were killed off within a week."

I mentioned that I had come across the skull of some small animal down in the ravine a few days ago, in the place known as "the valley of hell."

"It must have been a badger," K-san concluded. "It could have been killed by an eagle. Badgers are almost defenseless you know."

Just to make sure, my wife (who is something of a coward) asked him once more if there was, then, nothing out of the ordinary on the mountain.

"Well, to tell the whole truth," said K-san with a chuckle, "I did see a phantom monk once."

"Oh, I know what you mean, you saw your own reflection in that thick fog," my wife said with a knowing air, having had such an experience herself one morning, while viewing the "sea of clouds" from the Torii Pass.

"No, it wasn't that. It was something else."

He had seen it as a child. On his way home from Maebashi, at a point some five miles past Kogure, it suddenly appeared in the middle of a large pine grove. A dim light kept flickering and fading about a hundred yards ahead of him, and in this light a tall, dark figure would rear up to a height of at least ten feet.

Eventually he passed by a man resting on the roadside, with a huge load strapped to his back. What he had seen, he then realized, were the matches that this man had been striking while walking under his load, in an attempt to light up a cigarette.

When K-san had finished telling this story, S-san commented, "That's the way things usually turn out with these so-called phantoms and supernatural happenings."

"And yet there are times," said my wife, "when things can't be explained so easily. I don't know about phantoms and the like . . . but I do believe, for instance, that our dreams contain omens."

"Yes. That is a different matter," S-san agreed. Then as though suddenly remembering something, he turned to K-san and said, "But didn't you have such an experience yourself once? I mean the time you were stranded in the snow."

When we said we had never heard about this episode, S-san urged him to tell us.

"I guess you would have to call it a little uncanny," K-san began.

Last winter, when the snow already lay two or three feet deep on the mountain, he had had to make an unexpected trip to visit a sick sister in Tokyo. Although her condition had been reported as grave, it turned out not to be so serious after all. He stayed with his sister only three days.

Having arrived back in the middle of the afternoon at Mizunuma—the train stop nearest the mountain—he at first intended to wait until the next morning to make the climb home. But it seemed a waste of time to delay his homecoming almost a whole day, when it was only a matter of six or seven miles. If at close range the mountain looked difficult to climb, he speculated, he could always stay with someone at the base of the slope. And so he changed his mind and left Mizunuma that afternoon.

By sundown he had come as far as the second of the several torii that mark the ascent to the mountain shrine. There was a bright moon in the sky, which combined with his undiminished energy and eagerness to make him overconfident. He decided to go on the rest of the way.

The snow grew deeper and deeper the higher he climbed. There was twice as much as there had been when he left for Tokyo just a few days ago. The depth alone makes little difference, of course, so long as there is a well-trodden path; but it was as if not a soul had passed here since the blizzard, and he sank up to his waist in the soft, fresh snow. Everything had been obliterated under the even white covering. He soon became unsure of the path, and, although he had traveled this route countless times since his childhood on the mountain, he began to feel lost.

Up above, the torii at the entrance to the pass stood out clearly in the moonlight. In the summer, the dense grove that surrounds this place would have obstructed his view; but the pass now looked very close, with no leafy branches in between—nothing but snow, which always alters one's sense of distance. In any case, he could hardly turn back at this point. And so he crawled on antlike up the steep slope.

It proved to be much further than it had looked. He seemed to be making very little progress. Perhaps he really should turn back, he began to think. But if he lost his way down there he would be in an even worse predicament; here, at least, he could almost see his destination up ahead.

Breathing heavily with each small step, he continued to climb. He no longer felt any definite fear, nor even a vague anxiety. A kind of numbness had come over him, a certain drowsiness.

"Later on," K-san commented here, "I realized what a close call I'd had when I remembered that feeling. That's how the snow kills people. It puts them to sleep. And then they never wake up."

We marveled that he had been able to go on without panicking, once "that feeling" had begun to creep over him. But he had, of course, steeled himself then. His body has always been strong, and he has had more experience than most men with treacherous snows.

After two hours he had at last reached the crest of the slope where the pass opens up. Although the snow was still deeper here, he had only to go down a little way through the pass and he would be on flat terrain, close to home. He looked at his watch; it was already past one o'clock.

Then two specks of light appeared in the distance down below. Lanterns! Amazed that someone was out at this hour, and on such a night, K-san rejoiced at the prospect of even a brief meeting with these unknown human figures after his lonely struggle. With a burst of new energy, he descended through the pass.

He met the lantern bearers by the place where the river forms a deep pool called Kakumanbuchi. As he approached them he recognized his brother-in-law, U-san, and then three workmen from the crew of ice cutters who were staying at the inn this season.

"Welcome home!" said U-san. "You've had a rough time of it, I imagine."

"Where on earth are you going at this time of night?" asked K-san.

"Why, your mother woke us up and told us to come out to meet you," he answered, as though it had been a perfectly natural arrangement.

K-san felt a shudder of astonishment.

"Naturally, I had not told anyone I would be home that day," K-san explained to us. "As I heard it after I was back in the house, my mother had been lying down with Miichan (K-san's oldest child)—she was not really asleep, it seems—but in any case, she suddenly got up and went to wake U-san. She told him I was close to home now, and asked him to go out and meet me along the way. Then she apparently added, 'I heard him calling.'

"She was so definite about it that U-san saw nothing strange in what she'd said to him. He woke up the workmen, got dressed, and went out.

"I asked a few questions to pinpoint just when all of this had happened. It was right around the time when I was in the worst way down below, after I'd started feeling drowsy. Everybody goes to bed early on the mountain—usually between seven and eight o'clock, so they must have all been fast asleep by that time. It's obvious my mother was very sure that she'd heard something; otherwise she would never have woken everyone up and sent them off in the middle of the night."

"Had you been calling out?" asked my wife.

"No. I was way down on the other side of the pass. It was pointless to call for help."

My wife nodded, with a few tears in her eyes.

"It must have been more than just a vague feeling," K-san continued, "to make her even think of asking anyone to go out in such deep snow at that hour. Up here you have to be very careful how you're dressed before you go outdoors in the winter. If one of the gaiters that we wrap around our legs comes undone, it freezes stiff as a board and can't be put on again. So it takes at least twenty minutes to get ready. All the while, my mother was busy lighting the fire, fixing a snack for them to take along—and apparently without a single doubt about what she was doing."

This episode was especially moving for those of us who knew something about K-san's relationship with his mother. I am only slightly familiar with the circumstances, but it seems that K-san's father, now dead, was to the end a rather poor husband, though by no means a bad sort on the whole. (His friends called him "Ibsen," because of a certain resemblance to the playwright.) During the year, he lived with his mistress somewhere around Maebashi. Summers he would come to stay awhile on the mountain with the woman in tow—long enough to pick up the proceeds of the business, at least.

K-san was thoroughly disgusted by his father's ways. He opposed him openly on many occasions, though to no avail. And so he had grown all the closer to his mother, and she to him.

While we were talking, an owl had begun to hoot from the island out on the lake. "Goro—suké!" it would say, then after an interval, "Ho—ko!"

The fire had burned down low. K-san took out his pocket watch. "What time is it?"

"It's after eleven."

"Shall we go back?" said my wife.

Picking out glowing brands from the fire, K-san began to fling them out into the water one after another. Red sparks scattered here and there as the sticks flew through the air. This was reflected in the water by a second bright red streak that traced the same curve as the shower of sparks. Where the two arcs intersected from above and below, they were both extinguished with a soft hiss, swallowed up in the darkness. Delighted, we all joined in. Then K-san took the oar and with excellent aim splashed water over the embers remaining upon the beach.

We got back into the boat. Over by the kiln the pickers' fire had died down. The boat rounded the island and glided silently forward toward the shrine grove on the shore. The owl's hoot faded into the distance.

AT KINOSAKI
Kinosaki nite, 1917

I went by myself to the hot springs of Tajima-Kinosaki to convalesce after my accident. I had been hit by a train on the Tokyo loop line, and was told by the doctor that there was some slight risk of my developing meningitis where I had been injured on my back. Such a development would surely prove fatal but was, he said, highly unlikely. I would not be wholly out of danger, however, for two or three years; in the meantime, rest and caution were imperative. And so I went on this journey intending to stay for something over three weeks, which would bring me to well over a month since the time of the accident.

My mind was still not quite clear. I had become terribly forgetful. And yet a tranquillity such as I had not known in recent years came over me, and I felt at peace. The rice harvest was about to begin; the weather was favorable.

As I had come alone, there was neither the need nor the opportunity to talk with anyone. I spent my days reading and writing or sitting back in a chair set just outside my room looking up at the mountains and down at the people passing by; and I went out for walks. One pleasant walk was to take the road that leads gradually upward from town alongside a small stream. Where the stream cuts down around the flank of the mountain, it creates a small pool that is full of brook trout. If you look closely you can also see large river crabs, hairy, resting motionless like stones on the bottom. I would often take this walk before dinner. The thoughts that came to mind in the chill evening air, by the thin blue stream traversing solitary autumn ravines, naturally tended toward the melancholy. Yet, for all my gloomy thoughts, I felt quiet and contented. Many times I thought of the accident, of how close I had come to finding myself under the sod of Aoyama: my face cold and blue and stiff, the wounds I had suffered still there and on my back, untreated; the bodies of my grandfather and my mother lying beside me, nothing passing between us. Such were my thoughts. Melancholy though they were, they did not fill me with dread. It would happen some day. When? In the past, whenever I wondered about the "when," I had unconsciously thrust it far into the future. Now I had come to know it could be anytime. I was meant to die right then but did not. Something had not let me die. There was work for me as yet undone. According to a life of Lord Clive that was read at my school, he had been much encouraged by such notions in his later undertakings, and I would have liked to view my own narrow escape in this light. Indeed, I did, in a certain sense. And yet my spirit had grown so unaccountably tranquil. In one way or another, I had become intimate with death.

My room was off by itself on the second floor and so unusually restful by day. When I was tired of reading and writing I would relax in a chair on the balcony. To one side of my room the roof of the inn's entranceway was joined to the building with wooden panels. Beneath the paneling there was apparently a beehive; for there was always, when the weather was clear, a quantity of plump, tiger-striped bees busy at work from morning until close to sundown. Once they had squeezed themselves out through the cracks between the panels, they would drop down onto the roof of the entranceway. There they would use their front legs to make fine adjustments on wings and antennae; then, except for a few that continued to walk about awhile, they would thrust their wings tautly forward and take off with a low buzzing sound. They gathered speed as soon as they were in the air, swarming toward the potted *yatsude* shrubs that had just come into bloom. I idled away much time at the railing of my balcony, entertained by the comings and goings of these bees.

It happens one morning that I discover a dead bee on the roof. Its legs are folded tightly under its belly, its antennae droop lackadaisically over its face. The other bees appear coldly indifferent. They continue to pass close by as they purposefully fly to and from the nest but show no sign of alarm at this spectacle. The bees busily going about their work now seem especially alive. And the one that lies collapsed in their path, rooted to the same spot, I note at intervals, all day long, seems especially dead. The bee remains there for about three days. It is a very tranquil sight to see. It is, to be sure, lonely to look at this solitary corpse on the cold rooftiles after the other bees have returned to the hive at twilight. But it is also thoroughly tranquil.

One night it rained very hard. By morning it was clear; the ground, the foliage, the roof had been washed clean. The bee's body was gone. The others went on buzzing industriously around the hive while the dead one, most likely swept down the rainspout, would now be encased in the mud somewhere below, legs bent, antennae drooping as before. It would remain frozen there until the outside world wrought some new change in its situation. For that matter, it was possible that ants had already come to drag it away. But even that prospect conveyed a sense of great tranquillity, in that this bee, which had toiled so furiously, was now utterly still. I felt a kinship with that stillness.

Not long ago I had written a short story entitled "Han's Crime," in which the principal character kills his wife in a jealous rage, intensified by a strong, almost biological impulse, upon discovering an affair she once engaged in with a friend of his before their marriage. The story I had written centers on Han's motives and reactions; now I wished to rewrite it from the viewpoint of his wife, ending with the tranquillity of her lying in the grave after the violence is over. Although I did not, finally, carry through with my resolve to write "The Murdered Wife of Han," the urge to recast the piece into her point of view was very strong—and very unsettling, since it was quite opposite to the outlook on such matters maintained by the hero of a novel I was working on.

One morning after the dead bee had been swept out of sight forever, I left my inn on an excursion to a park at Higashiyama that affords a view of the Maruyama river, where it flows out into the Sea of Japan. Along the way, in front of the spa at Ichinoyu, a small stream flows serenely down the middle of the road toward its confluence with the Maruyama. As I walked down this road, I came across a small crowd of people gathered on a bridge and the adjacent banks. They were peering down into the stream and making quite a commotion, the cause of which, I soon saw, was a large rat that had been thrown into the water.

The rat is swimming frantically in a desperate effort to reach safety. Its neck has been pierced through with a broiling skewer over half a foot long, which protrudes a few inches above the head and below the neck. The rat keeps trying to crawl up onto the stone embankment. Several children and a rickshaman who looks to be about forty begin to hurl rocks in its direction but fail to hit the mark. As the rocks ricochet off the embankment, the crowd roars with laughter. The rat at last manages to gain a foothold in a crack between the stones of the embankment, only to be blocked in its upward progress by the protruding skewer and fall back into the water. The creature resumes its struggle to escape, by whatever means, with a vengeance: this much is clear from its movements, even if one cannot read the expression on its face. In the apparent conviction that, regardless of the piercing skewer, if only it can get away it will be saved, the rat swims back into midstream. The children and the rickshaman throw more rocks, rising warmly to this new challenge. Startled by the rocks, a few ducks that have been foraging by a laundry station at the water's edge extend their necks and stare suspiciously. As the rocks land here and there with a loud splash, the ducks' look of suspicion turns to consternation; necks outstretched, with much quacking they start to work their webbed feet as fast as they will go, and paddle away upstream. I finally lack the stomach to watch the rat's inevitable end.

Afterward, I retained in my mind's eye, with amazing clarity, the image of this creature struggling for all it was worth against its fate of certain death. Once again I felt sad and lonely, but this time I was upset as well. This was surely what dying was like. The suffering that comes before that tranquillity I aspired to was frightening. However sympathetic I had come to feel with the silent nothingness that follows death, these strenuous exertions that precede it filled me with fear. Animals have no choice, lacking the recourse of suicide, other than to struggle that way to the bitter end. What would I do, I wondered, if I found myself in a plight similar to the rat's? Would I not behave in the same way? I could not help reflecting that indeed I had approached that state after my accident. I had chosen the hospital myself and supplied directions to those who were helping me; I had insisted that they call ahead lest the proper doctor be unavailable when I arrived and my treatment delayed. I was myself astonished later on to recall how lucidly my mind had focused on a few vital matters when I was in fact partly unconscious—and even though, for all I knew, I was facing a crisis of life and death. Not that I was unaware of the gravity of my situation, but I had gone along inexplicably unscathed by any strong fear of death. I did at length turn to a friend at the hospital and ask him what the doctor had said—would I pull through? And when he replied that my injury was apparently not fatal, I felt a sudden surge of strength. All my tension had given way to elation. But how would I have reacted had I been told it was fatal? I could not be sure. It was quite possible that I would have despaired. And yet, it struck me, at that moment I might well not have been overwhelmed by the fear of death, as one expects the case to be in the abstract. I now imagined that, confronted with the most pessimistic diagnosis, I would nevertheless have persisted in my will to survive and done everything in my power to that end. I would not then have acted so very differently from the rat. And if it were to happen to me again . . . I put it to myself, and decided that even now I was likely to react in more or less the same fashion as the rat had. And so it seemed that my impulse to accept death whenever, however it might come had not had any immediate effect in reality; yet it was just as real to me as the will to survive; and I could only conclude that if, when the time came, my spirit of acceptance were to prevail, well and good, if not, so be it.

One evening some time after this encounter I was leisurely walking up the hill that follows the little stream out of town. Where the road crosses the Sanin Line tracks (just before the tunnel) it suddenly grows steep and narrow, the stream turns into rapids, and the houses disappear. When I reached that point I really meant to turn back but allowed myself to be led on by one prospect after another "just up the road," until I had rounded quite a few bends. The surroundings were cloaked in a pale blue aura, the air was cool enough to produce a slight chill on the skin, the enveloping stillness not so much soothing as vaguely unsettling. There were tall mulberry trees growing along the roadside. On a branch that stretched out over the road from one of the trees on the opposite side, I noticed a single leaf that fluttered constantly in an even, steady rhythm. Without a breath of wind, in the

stillness only faintly interrupted by the murmur of the stream, there
was this leaf unmistakably flapping back and forth, back and forth. I
could scarcely believe my eyes, and was even a little frightened. But my
curiosity got the better of me. Just as I went over to investigate from
underneath the tree, a breeze came up. Whereupon the leaf ceased to
move. It was, I realized, a quite ordinary phenomenon. And I had
thought I knew a good deal about such matters!

It was becoming noticeably dark. There was no end to this business
of going on "just up the road," I told myself, and firmly decided to
turn back. My gaze wandered for a moment toward the stream. On
the far bank was a large rock, at least three feet across, that slanted
down into the water, and on the rock there was a small black
creature—a salamander. It was still wet, its color particularly lustrous.
It lay against the sloping rock with its eyes fixed downward on the
flowing stream. A trickle of water from its body etched a dark,
inch-long mark on the dry surface of the rock. I crouched down to
have a clearer look, out of nothing more than idle curiosity. I was no
longer disgusted at the sight of salamanders, as I had been at one time.
(Among such creatures, the ordinary lizard, of the sort one sees in
stone walls and the like, I am rather fond of; geckos I loathe above all
things that crawl; and salamanders I don't feel very strongly about one
way or the other. Ten years or so ago, it is true, when I was at
Ashinoko, I used to see salamanders clustered around the drainpipe of
my hotel and think to myself how horrid it would be if I were one of
them. I would conjure up the possibility of being reborn as one, until it
became a kind of automatic association. But I had long since got over
this strange notion.)

Simply out of curiosity, then, I take it into my head to startle the
salamander and make it move. I can already picture it wriggling down
the rock in its ungainly way. I pick up a stone the size of a small ball
which lies at hand and, still in a crouching position, toss it across the
stream. It can hardly be said that I have aimed at the salamander, and
even if I did, I am much too poor a shot to entertain the possibility of
hitting it. I hear the stone knock against the rock then plop down into
the stream. Simultaneous with the first sound the salamander appears
to hop a few inches to one side. Then its tail arches up in the air. I
cannot make out what has happened, it does not at first occur to me
that I could have hit it. Slowly and effortlessly the arch of the sala-

mander's tail collapses. At the end of its rigid forelegs braced against the incline of the rock, the toes curl inward, and its whole body flops forward listlessly. Its tail now glued flat against the rock, the salamander does not move a muscle. It is dead.

What a foolish thing I have done, I thought to myself. I kill insects all the time, to be sure, but this was different: to have killed without the slightest intention of doing so was somehow utterly repugnant. I was undeniably the agent, but this had come about through sheer random chance. The salamander's death was in a real sense quite accidental. As I crouched there lost in thought, the world narrowed down to myself and the salamander. From the point of view of this particular creature, I could see the pity of it. At the same time, I felt with equal force the gentle pathos of all living things. By chance I had not died and by chance the salamander had. Moved by the pathos that lay in these realities, I made my way back to the inn along the dark road now barely visible at my feet. When I came within sight of the lights at the edge of town, my thoughts turned to the dead bee. By now it would have been soaked into the ground with the rains we had since had. And the rat—it was not unlikely that its water-logged corpse had been carried downriver with other pieces of refuse and been washed up on the seashore. And here am I, I noted to myself, walking down the road. I knew I ought to be grateful for this fact. And yet I could not bring myself honestly to exult in it. To be alive and to be dead were not opposite extremes. They were not far apart at all, I felt. It was now quite dark. My eyes could make out nothing but the distant lights. Unaided by sight, my feet moved very haltingly. Only my thoughts moved swiftly, oblivious to the surroundings, confirming me in that sense of my recent experience at which I had already arrived.

I left Kinosaki when my three weeks were up. I have in the end been spared the serious complications which could have developed out of my injury. Or, at least, that of meningitis.

REINCARNATION

Tensei, 1924

1

Once there was a man who had a foolish wife. The man loved his wife, but her foolishness often caused him to lose his temper and launch into lengthy tirades full of harsh words. At such times the wife could only lament the foibles she had been born with and murmur weak protests.

"Deep down, you really regret that you married a fool like me, don't you? I know you do."

"Yes. I do."

"But do you *really*?"

"Yes, I really do. But it's too late to do anything about it. I've accepted it."

And the wife would protest and cry.

2

One day, to vent his anger, the husband explained to himself, "The female animal is not susceptible to reason." Later, in a somewhat improved frame of mind, he added, "But if one must keep an animal, better a domesticated than a wild one. There are an awful lot of men with wild animals on their hands—some of them downright dangerous. I should be grateful I've only got this sow to worry about, when I think of all the men who have to live like lion tamers."

Thus he succeeded in consoling himself. (His notion of women's liberation went no further than to allow them the same emancipation from outright slavery as that which had at length been granted to Negroes.)

3

Like the proverbial birds of a feather, all the maids his wife hired were fools. Nothing in the conduct of the household was done the way he thought it ought to be. In his better moods, he was able to ignore all this. But when he was out of sorts, he found himself overwhelmed by the countless number of bones he had to pick. Indeed, he could not help marveling, somewhat sheepishly, at the force of his own righteous indignation.

"Foolishness, foolishness! Everywhere I look that's all I see. It blankets the house like a great cloud of dust . . . Don't dare open your mouth or your eyes." So he would loudly declare, but as a statement of fact, with no histrionics or theatrical gesticulations.

"Will you be off on one of your little retreats, then?" his wife would rejoin.

"Yes. I really have to get out of this house. Get my things ready right away."

"Same old story."

"Just pack the bags, will you?"

"But what makes you so angry? There's no earthly reason for it, you know. What have I done?"

"I couldn't begin to tell you. It would take all day—all night too, for that matter."

Such scenes would most often take place at the breakfast table, for the husband had always had trouble getting out of bed in the morning. And he was at his worst on an empty stomach.

4

One morning, when he was in rare good spirits, his wife said with a smile, "The trouble is, you're really *too* bright."

"No," he said, "you are too foolish."

"Well, if that is what's wrong, next time around I'll take care to be reborn as a very bright person. And you might try to come back just a little bit dumber. That way things might even out."

"It's no use. If we both come back as human beings, it's bound to be the same thing all over. Women have always been foolish, and they always will be. It's a known fact."

"Well, what would you suggest instead of a human being?"

"How about a sow?"

"If you'll be a pig too and keep me company . . ." His wife laughed.

"No thank you. Let's forget about pigs."

"Which animals get along best with their mates?"

"Let's see. They say that foxes make pretty good spouses. I read it in an article on fox farming in Karafuto. What's more, they're supposed to be totally monogamous."

"That sounds very promising! I like the idea."

The husband, privately wondering which species might be resolutely polygamous, said to his wife only, "No. On second thoughts, I don't like foxes."

"All right, then. What else?"

"Maybe ducks. Mandarin ducks. They've always been famous for fidelity."

"And they're pretty, besides."

"Only the male is. Wouldn't that bother you?"

"No, not in the slightest. Let's settle it right now. We'll make a vow. And you'd better not forget!"

"If anyone forgets, it's sure to be you. I can just see you having yourself reborn as a regular old farmyard duck. And if you do, you'll be stuck that way, you know."

"I never would!"

"Never? Only too likely, I'm afraid."

5

Now here is where the fairy tale begins. Several decades later, having spent the better part of a lifetime losing his temper and berating his wife on every possible occasion, the husband died a peaceful death.

His wife felt a certain relief, it is true, but she could not help from time to time missing his tirades. She grew increasingly senile, until it appeared that, along with everything else, she had also forgotten to die. For quite a long while she lived on, and rather happily at that.

The husband kept his promise and was reincarnated as a mandarin duck. Waiting impatiently for his wife to die and join him, he thought how very like her it was to carry on with life so nonchalantly. He recalled all the times when, on their way out somewhere, she had kept him waiting interminably by the gate.

6

Several years later, the wife at long last died. When in due course it came time for her to be reborn, she could not remember into which species she was to have been reincarnated. Was it a fox? Some sort of duck? Or was it a pig? She could not remember. But she had an intuition it had been a mandarin duck. Then she recalled something her husband had told her time and time again: "Whenever you have two alternatives to choose between," he would say, "one of them right, the other wrong, without fail you *always* choose the wrong one. One might suppose that once in a great while you'd hit on the right one, if only out of sheer dumb luck. But you never do. You have an almost supernatural knack for making the wrong choice."

This recollection served only to deepen her dilemma. On further reflection she decided that her intuition about the duck would almost surely play her false, in keeping with her husband's analysis of her fatal pattern in such situations. And so she opted for the fox.

7

Up hill and down dale the vixen wandered in search of her mate. To no avail. At length she arrived in a mountain fastness where, exhausted from her fruitless search, faint with hunger after three days without food, she stood listening to the murmur of a stream far below, and resolved to take at least a drink of water. Slowly and painfully, she made her way down the slope.

The mandarin duck that was once her husband lived his solitary little life paddling about in the bluish rapids of this mountain stream. Just then he was half dozing, resting one foot on a rock that jutted up slightly above the surface of a small pool in the stream. Suddenly he sensed the approach of some creature. Just as he was about to scurry off in consternation, he felt the greater shock of recognition: this was the wife he had been waiting for these long years. With an involuntary quack, he flew to her side.

The vixen was equally astonished. In an excess of joy, however, and weak with hunger, she could do nothing but crouch down in the spot to which she had managed to crawl.

Then they looked at one another and in horror realized the mistake that had been made.

Overcoming his visceral repugnance at the odor that clung to the vixen, the transformed husband spontaneously fell into one of his old rages.

"As much a fool as ever, I see!"

8

The vixen wailed out her sorrow and self-recrimination for her mistake. But neither her apologies nor the husband's forgiveness, had he granted it, could have set matters right at this stage. It was too late.

The duck-husband ruffled the downy feathers on his head and flapped his wings in anger. The vixen-wife went on with her apologies until, half unconscious from hunger and fatigue, she could no longer express herself coherently. The enraged fowl before her eyes was still, she recognized, her husband; but, as her remaining strength began to ebb away, he took on more and more the aura of a very tempting quarry. Especially tempting in that he was right in front of her, unlike the various rabbits and field mice which had easily eluded her as yet inexperienced chase. Although a small voice inside her continued to say, over and over again, "but this is your beloved husband," the creature's vituperation wore down her lingering resistance.

She could hold out no longer. Lapsing into a proper fox's howl, she swiftly pounced on the duck and ate him up in a few gulps. So goes the fairy tale.

It is a kind of cautionary tale that could be called "The Perils of Wife-Scolding."

"But tell me, is it intended as a warning to tyrannical husbands?"
"Yes."
"But couldn't it as well be taken as a warning to foolish wives?"
"Do you really think so?"
"Well, at least to those wives who go on loving their husbands in spite of it all."
"Yes, I see what you mean."
"And another thing I would like to know: Is this based on your own experience?"

"Certainly not. My wife is an exceptionally intelligent woman. And I am an exceptionally gentle husband. Hardly a cross word to be heard in our household. Why, you'll even find my name touted in a recent issue of *Bungei Shunju* as one who can teach women the secrets of matrimonial bliss."

NOTES

INTRODUCTION

1. Shiga Naoya, *A Dark Night's Passing,* translated by Edwin McClellan (Tokyo, New York, San Francisco, 1976).

2. *Kobayashi Hideo zenshū* (Shinchōsha, 1956), 3: 94–96. (In citations of Japanese works, all of which were published in Tokyo, only the publisher has been given.)

3. *Akutagawa Ryūnosuke zenshū* (Chikuma shobō, 1958), 5: 134.

4. *Dazai Osamu zenshū* (Chikuma shobō, 1956), 10: 315, 321.

5. William Gass, *Fiction and the Figures of Life* (New York, 1968), p. 213.

6. *Shiga Naoya zenshū* (Iwanami shoten, 1973), 7: 35. (Hereafter all references to this edition of Shiga's complete works will be made parenthetically in the text by volume and page only.)

7. Henri Peyre, *Literature and Sincerity* (New Haven, 1963), chap. 6.

8. Leon Edel, *The Modern Psychological Novel* (New York, 1964), p. vii.

9. Ian Watt, *The Rise of the Novel* (Berkeley, 1957), pp. 176, 207.

10. Jean-Paul Sartre, *Saint Genet, comédien et martyr* (Paris, 1952), p. 501.

11. Sigmund Freud, *Delusion and Dream* (Boston, 1968), p. 133.

12. *Masamune Hakuchō zenshū* (Shinchōsha, 1965), 6: 61.

13. Edward Seidensticker, *Nihon sakka ron* (Shinchōsha, 1964), p. 104.

14. For example, see Edward Seidensticker's essay "The Unshapen Ones" in *Japan Quarterly* 11, no. 1 (1964): 64–69.

15. Guy de Maupassant, *The Odd Number,* with an Introduction by Henry James (New York, 1917), pp. vii–viii.

16. Freud, *Delusion and Dream*, p. 122.

17. Ibid., p. 65.

18. C. G. Jung, *Modern Man in Search of a Soul* (1933; reprinted New York: Harcourt, Brace and World, n.d.), pp. 160, 157.

19. Ibid., pp. 156–57.

20. Nakamura Mitsuo, *Shiga Naoya ron* (Chikuma shobō, 1966) and Yasuoka Shōtarō, *Shiga Naoya shiron* (Bungei Shunjū, 1968).

21. Yasuoka, p. 207.

22. Francis Mathy, *Shiga Naoya* (New York, 1974).

23. Yasuoka, p. 17.

24. Seki Ryōichi, in *Shiga Naoya*, edited by Nihon bungaku kenkyū shiryōkai (Yūseidō, 1970), p. 257.

25. Ibid., p. 261.

26. Mathy, p. 21.

27. Honda Shūgo, *Shirakaba-ha no bungaku* (Shinchōsha, 1960), p. 66; and Yasuoka, p. 222.

28. *Shiga Naoya taiwa shū* (Daiwa shobō, 1969), p. 21.

29. Nakamura, p. 73.

30. For a mercifully brief summary of the "thought" of Mushakōji, see Honda, pp. 37–50.

31. Kuno Osamu and Tsurumi Shunsuke, *Gendai Nihon no shisō* (Iwanami shoten, 1956), p. 28.

CHAPTER ONE

1. Kamei Katsu'ichirō, *Chishikijin no shōzō* (Kadokawa shoten, 1955), p. 69.

2. Erik H. Erikson, *Childhood and Society*, 2d ed. (New York, 1950), p. 95.

3. Jean-Paul Sartre, *L'Etre et le néant* (Paris, 1943), p. 637.

4. Jung, p. 121.

5. Yasuoka, p. 91.

6. See Otto Rank, *The Myth of the Birth of the Hero* (New York, 1941).

7. Kobayashi, 1: 120.

8. Erikson, *Childhood and Society*, p. 406.

9. Sigmund Freud, *Character and Culture* (New York, 1963), p. 265.

10. Freud, *Delusion and Dream*, p. 143.

CHAPTER TWO

1. Hakuchō, 4: 180.

2. Cf. Freud: "The psychological novel in general probably owes its peculiarities to the tendency of modern writers to split up their ego by self-observation into many component egos, and in this way to personify the conflicting trends in their own mental life in many heroes" (*Character and Culture*, p. 41). This is one of the few vaguely psychoanalytic notions to have been taken over by modern Japanese criticism, in which it is known as *bunshin*

and is usually applied in a rather simplified and schematic manner (e.g., author A = characters B and C).

3. Jung, p. 157.

4. Erikson, *Childhood and Society,* pp. 87–88.

5. Cf. "The Great Mother" and "The Terrible Mother," about which the Jungian scholar Erich Neumann has written at considerable length. See, for example, his *Origins of Consciousness* (Bollingen Series; Princeton, 1970), pp. 63–101.

6. *Teihon Saikaku zenshū* (Chūo kōronsha, 1955), 3: 59–60.

7. Akutagawa (Chikuma shobō ed.), 5: 136–37; Yasuoka, p. 208.

CHAPTER THREE

1. Carl G. Jung, ed., *Man and His Symbols* (Garden City, 1964), p. 196.

2. Mathy, p. 121, note 2.

3. Hakuchō, 6: 62.

4. Jung, *Modern Man in Search of a Soul,* p. 12.

5. Freud, *Delusion and Dream,* pp. 25–27.

6. Yasuoka, pp. 84–85, 250. Yasuoka tells us that, in reply to a question as to "how *harima* is done," Shiga laughed and said only, "It's something I thought up."

7. There is a striking parallel here with Baudelaire's view of his own origins, which Sartre cites as follows: "I'm ill, ill, I've got an execrable temperament through the fault of my parents. Because of them I'm falling to pieces. A disproportionate, pathological, senile union. Think of it—forty-five years' difference between them. . . . And what of the chancy fruit of such a coupling?" Jean-Paul Sartre, *Baudelaire* (New York, 1950), p. 159. Sartre naturally takes Baudelaire to task, seeing in this lament another vain attempt "to relieve himself of his freedom." In the case of Shiga's hero, however, the subjective truth of his misbegotten beginnings leads to a new recognition of his freedom as an individual.

8. Claude Lévi-Strauss, *The Scope of Anthropology* (London, 1967), p. 37.

9. Sigmund Freud, *Civilization and Its Discontents* (London, 1930), p. 121.

10. Norman O. Brown, *Life against Death: The Psychoanalytical Meaning of History* (Wesleyan Paperback ed.; Middletown, Conn., 1970), pp. 118, 129.

CHAPTER FOUR

1. *Dōgen Zenshi zenshū* (Shunjūsha, 1930), p. 235.

2. Wilhelm Stekel, *The Interpretation of Dreams* (New York, 1967), p. 95.

3. Stekel, pp. 84–86.

4. Sigmund Freud, *The Interpretation of Dreams* (Modern Library ed.; New York, 1950), p. 272.

5. Yasuoka, pp. 247–63.

6. Ibid., p. 250.

7. Patrick Mullahy, *Oedipus Myth and Complex* (New York, 1948), p. 94.

8. Herbert Marcuse, *Eros and Civilization* (New York, 1962), pp. 32, 41.

9. *Shōbō genzō, Nihon koten bungaku taikei,* 81 (Iwanami shoten, 1965), 104.

10. See *Shiga Naoya taiwa shū,* p. 15.

11. Proust's lifelong ambivalence toward his mother is perhaps the leitmotif in George Painter's masterful biography. See for example, *Proust: The later Years* (Boston, 1965), pp. 50, 55, 309. Yet Painter is careful to keep his accounts separate and does not assign a central role to mother fixation in his discussion of Proust's novel.

12. Sigmund Freud, *Civilization and Its Discontents* (London, 1930), p. 13.

13. In a work entitled *Seijuku to sōshitsu* and subtitled *Haha no hōkai* (Kawade shobō, 1967), Eto Jun has explored the continuing significance of this theme in postwar Japanese fiction.

14. Sigmund Freud, *The Future of an Illusion* (Anchor Books ed.; Garden City, 1964), p. 77.

PRINCIPAL WORKS CITED

In citations of Japanese works, all of which were published in Tokyo, only the publisher has been given.

Shiga Naoya. *Zenshū.* 14 vols. Iwanami shoten, 1973.
——. *A Dark Night's Passing.* Translated by Edwin McClellan. Tokyo, New York, and San Francisco, 1976.
——. *Shiga Naoya taiwa shū.* Daiwa shoten, 1969.
Agawa Hiroyuki. *Shiga Naoya no hito to sakuhin.* Gakushū kenkyūsha, 1964.
Akutagawa Ryūnosuke. *Zenshū.* Vols. 5, 8. Chikuma shobō, 1958.
Arishima Takeo. *Zenshū.* Vols. 2, 3. Sōbunkaku, 1924.
Booth, Wayne C. *The Rhetoric of Fiction.* Chicago, 1961.
Brown, Norman O. *Life against Death: The Psychoanalytical Meaning of History.* Middletown, Conn., 1959.
Dazai Osamu. *Zenshū.* Vol. 10. Chikuma shobō, 1956.
Dōgen. "Bendōwa" and "Genjō kōan." In *Shōbō genzō. Nihon koten bungaku taikei,* vol. 81. Iwanami shoten, 1965.
——. "Shinshin gakudō." In *Dōgen Zenshi zenshū.* Shunjūsha, 1930.
Edel, Leon. *The Modern Psychological Novel.* New York, 1964.
Erikson, Erik H. *Childhood and Society.* 2d ed. New York, 1963.
Eto Jun. *Seijuku to sōshitsu: Haha no hōkai.* Kawade shobō, 1967.
Fiedler, Leslie. *Love and Death in the American Novel.* Rev. ed. New York, 1960.
Freud, Sigmund. *Character and Culture.* Edited by Phillip Rieff. New York, 1963.
——. *Civilization and Its Discontents.* London, 1930.
——. *Delusion and Dream.* Edited by Phillip Rieff. Boston, 1956.

————. *The Future of an Illusion.* Rev. ed. Anchor Books. Garden City, N.Y., 1964.

————. *The Interpretation of Dreams.* New York, 1950.

Honda Shūgo. *Shirakaba-ha no bungaku.* Shinchōsha, 1960.

Ishii Shoji. *Shiga Naoya nōto.* Saitō shoten, 1948.

Jung, Carl G. *Modern Man in Search of a Soul.* New York, 1933.

————, ed. *Man and His Symbols.* Garden City, N.Y., 1964.

Kamei Katsu'ichiro. *Chishikijin no shōzō.* Kadokawa shoten, 1955.

Keene, Donald, ed. *Modern Japanese Literature.* New York, 1956.

Kobayashi Hideo. *Zenshū.* Vols. 1, 2. Shinchōsha, 1956.

Kris, Ernst. *Psychoanalytic Explorations in Art.* New York, 1964.

Kuno Osamu and Tsurumi Shunsuke. *Gendai Nihon no shisō.* Iwanami shoten, 1956.

Marcuse, Herbert. *Eros and Civilization.* New York, 1962.

Masamune Hakuchō. *Zenshū.* Vols. 6, 9. Shinchōsha, 1964.

Mathy, Francis. *Shiga Naoya.* New York, 1974.

Mullahy, Patrick. *Oedipus Myth and Complex.* New York, 1948.

Nakamura Mitsuo. *Shiga Naoya ron.* Chikuma shobō, 1966.

————. *Sakka ron.* Vol. 1. Kōdansha, 1968.

Nihon bungaku kenkyū shiryō kankōkai. *Shiga Naoya.* Yuseido, 1970.

Peyre, Henri. *Literature and Sincerity.* New Haven, 1963.

Piaget, Jean. *The Language and Thought of the Child.* Cleveland and New York, 1955.

Sartre, Jean-Paul. *Baudelaire.* Translated by Martin Turnell. New York, 1950.

————. *Saint Genet, comédien et martyr.* Paris, 1952.

Seidensticker, Edward G. *Nihon sakka ron.* Shinchōsha, 1964.

Shindō Junkō. *Shiga Naoya ron.* Shinchōsha, 1971.

Stekel, Wilhelm. *The Interpretation of Dreams.* New York, 1967.

Sudo Matsuo, ed. *Shiga Naoya.* Kindai bungaku kanshō kōza, Vol. 10. Kadokawa shoten, 1967.

Tanizaki Jun'ichiro. *Zenshū.* Vol. 21. Chūo kōron sha, 1958.

Trilling, Lionel. *The Liberal Imagination.* New York, 1950.

Watt, Ian. *The Rise of the Novel.* Berkeley, 1957.

Wilson, Edmund. *The Wound and the Bow.* New York, 1947.

Yasuoka Shōtaro. *Shiga Naoya shiron.* Bungei shunju, 1968.

Yoshida Seiichi. *Meiji Taishō bungaku shi.* Shubunkan, 1956.

INDEX

Adultery: in *Amagaeru*, 105–6; in *An'ya kōro*, 90, 102–6; in *Han no hanzai*, 64

Aircraft, 77, 83, 99, 107, 114

Akutagawa Ryunosuke, 2, 36, 57, 64, 69, 100

Amagaeru (Shiga) [Tree Frog], 105–6

Amida Buddhism, 115–16

Anima resolution, 72–73

An'ya kōro (Shiga) [A Dark Night's Passing], vii–viii, 1; contrasted with *Wakai* and *Aru otoko*, 69–73; early draft of, 32; "great common will" in, 82–84, 114; journey/voluntary exile in, 87–88; Kamei Katsu'ichiro on, 35–36; Masamune Hakuchō's reading of, 6; point of view in, 120–21; prologue of, 37–41, 78–79; religion in, 29, 88–89, 92–93, 97–98, 109–10, 115–16; Seki Ryoichi on, 19–21. *See also names of specific*

characters and character/types in the novel

Araginu (Shiga), 57–59

Arishima, 29

Aru asa (Shiga) [One Morning], 21, 37, 48–50

Aru otoko, sono ane no shi (Shiga) [A Man and the Death of his Sister], 43, 69–77

Asahi shimbun, 32

Autotherapy, 36, 75–76, 78, 87, 92. *See also* Intuitive psychoanalysis

Baudelaire, Charles P., 35, 41, 213 n. 7 (ch. 3)

Birth, 100, 107–8

Brown, Norman O., 95–96, 103, 112

Buddhism: Amidism, 115–16; in *An'ya kōro*, 29, 88–89, 92–93, 97–98, 109–10, 115–16; concept of karma in, 88–89, 92–93; Zen, 76, 92, 97–98, 115–16

217